TEACHING OF COMPUTERS

TEACHING OF COMPUTERS

Modified Syllabus of B.T.C./B.Ed./B.C.A./M.C.A./M.Sc./ Information Technology/M.Ed. of Indian and Foreign Universities/Training and Technical Institute and Education Colleges Recognized by National Council of Teacher Education/National Council of Technical Education, New Delhi

Dr. Y.K. Singh
Lecturer (Edu.) and *In-Charge*, Computer Centre
Mahatma Gandhi Chitrakoot Rural University Chitrakoot (Satna),
Madhya Pradesh

Edited by
Ms. Ruchika Nath
Corporate Trainer
New Horizon Computer Training Institute Lodhi Road, New-Delhi

A P H PUBLISHING CORPORATION
ANSARI ROAD, DARYA GANJ
NEW DELHI-110 002

Published by
S.B. Nangia
A.P.H. Publishing Corporation
4435–36/7, Ansari Road, Darya Ganj,
New Delhi-110002
Phone: 011–23274050
e-mail: aphbooks@gmail.com

2027

Typeset by
Ideal Publishing Solutions
C-90, J.D. Cambridge School,
West Vinod Nagar, Delhi-110092

Printed at
RD DIGITAL PRINTERS
Ansari road Daryaganj Delhi-110002

PREFACE

Information is defined as recorded or communicated knowledge, which men have been acquiring since the evolution of his mental faculties. Information is a vital resource and plays a crucial role in achieving progress in all human endeavours industrialised counties like the USA, Japan and Germany have long before recognized the value and importance of information. To-day information has become the key factor of progress of any country. And here come the computer, which is the most powerful tool in human hands for storing data and retrieving information till now.

Computer has proved its importance. Due to its enormous capabilities, computer is playing a major role in every field such as in space research, in defence, industries and many more. Computer is a popular machine now a day. Popularity of computers gave rise to its different types, such as analog, digital and hybrid computers based on their working or home computers, PCs' based on their size and speed and super computers.

Generally, the word "Computer" is used in place of computer system. Actually there is a difference between these two terms, computer system and computer technology. Computer only is not very much useful to a user and a user cannot communicate directly without computer. When a user is using computer for communication at that time the computer technology comes in the light. To allow communication between user and computer, various input/output devices are used with computer. These I/O devices with computer form a computer system.

Computers not only store data, it can also efficiently perform various types of mathematical and logical operations. A small chip called, "Microprocessor", does all the processing operations. Companies like Intel and Motorola are involved in producing microprocessor chip on a large scale. All types of operation on a computer system are controlled by a set of instructions. This *set* of instructions gives rise to the term, "Software." In general, software can be defined as all kinds of instructions and programmes that instruct the hardware to perform the desired operations.

Software are of various types: some are used to control the activities of computer system, some are used to develop another software to solve the desired tasks, and some are used to translate the instructions into binary code, because computers can understand only binary code not the English like text or picture. The various types of conversions are described in chapter, "Number System."

The readers of education field will decide its utility, if this volume may give any benefit to them, it will be his success. Almost every aspect of computer-education and training program is covered in this book. The book is carrying twelve chapters and each chapter is developed with suitable pictures, tables and sufficient exercise questions. The author will be highly thankful if you will send your valuable suggestion to up-grade the chapters of this book.

November 2004

Dr. Y.K. Singh

Lecturer (Edu.) & In charge
Computer Centre, Mahatma Gandhi
Chitrakoot Rural University
Chitrakoot (Satna), Madhya Pradesh
E-mail: yksingh1@rediffmail.com

CONTENTS

CHAPTER 1

COMPUTER TECHNOLOGY IN EDUCATION

- Introduction
- Definition and Nature of Technology
- Forms of Infomercial Technology
- Scope of Infomercial Technology
- Aspects of Infomercial Technology
- Objectives of Infomercial Technology
- Exercise Questions

INTRODUCTION

Today we are living in the world of information revolution where the mass media plays a vital role in creating an atmosphere of awareness among masses. Here media means different communicated channels or ways through which information is transmitted to the receiver. Education has thus adopted these technologies to see the better results in teaching and learning and we see a sort of revolution in the field of education.

Eric Ashby (1967) has identified four revolutions in education:

1. The first revolution occurred when societies began to differentiate adult roles, and the task of educating the young was shifted, in part, from parents to teachers and from the home to the school.
2. The second, which in some places antedated the first, 'was the adoption of the written word as a tool of education'. Prior

to that time, oral Instruction prevailed, and it was only with reluctance that writing was permitted to coexist with the spoken word in the classroom.

3. The third revolution came with the invention of printing and the subsequent wide availability of books.
4. The fourth revolution, in Ashby's view, is portended by developments in electronics, notably those involving the radio, television, tape recorder and computer.

The implications of the fourth revolution can be summarized in Ashby's own words. He says: "Any technology, which increases the rate of learning, would enable (as Comenius put it centuries ago) the teacher to teach less and the learner to learn more."

Different people view the development and use of a modem Educational Technology in different ways. Some acclaim it as the basis of a revolution in the Educational system aimed at improving the effectiveness and efficiency of education at different levels. Some castigate it as a movement aimed at replacing the traditional teacher from the educational scene by sophisticated machines and gadgets. They argue that with the advent of Educational Technology gradually the role of teachers and students would be reduced to that of mechanical robots. The subject of Educational Technology has rarely been treated by either professional educators or by laymen in a scientific manner, which would provide an answer to what ***Infomercial Technology (I.T.)*** is and how it could be useful for educational, training and extension work.

The term technology implies the application of science to art. When we apply the science of learning and communication to teaching we evolve a technology. The interaction of physical sciences with education provides us with traditional aids, tools, hardware such as, paper, ink, books, Radios, lingua phones, films, televisions and more sophisticated modem hardware like computers, space-satellites, language laboratories etc. Stoluraw (1963) argues that there are three major factors that emphasize the linking of Infomercial with technology:

(a) The exploding world population.
(b) The exponential rate at which new knowledge is being generated.

(c) The changing science and technology of our current society.

Meaning of Infomercial Technology

In his book "The New Industrial State" J.K. Galbriath has given two main characteristics of every technology. These are:—

(1) Systematic application of scientific knowledge to the practical tasks, and

(2) The division of the practical tasks into sections and sub-sections.

Any subject who meets these two norms of the characteristics is called ***Instructional Technology.*** Educational technology does not determine the educational objectives. Political thinkers and philosophers keeping in view the wider aspects of society and values carry out this function. Educational technology defines teaching objectives in behavioural terms. It is that science, on the basis of which various methods and techniques are, developed and constructed in order to achieve predetermined teaching objectives. When the teaching objectives get determined, then educational technology comes in existence to achieve them. It creates conditions by interpreting the input during the teaching process. It selects and applies the appropriate strategy for achieving the teaching objectives. Finally, looking at the output or abilities of the pupils, it is evaluated whether the teaching objectives have been achieved or not. If not, then what changes should be brought about in the teaching strategy or strategies so that the teaching objectives may be achieved.

Infomercial Technology, today is widely accepted as the application of systems approach in the systematic design of a learning system, and as a method or approach combined with the appropriate and necessary media and material to bring about improvement in teaching-learning-evaluation process. It may, however, be noted that Educational Technology is neither an end in itself nor a concept that embraces all of education. Rather it can be considered as a means to accomplish some predetermined, clearly defined and unambiguous educational and instructional objectives.

Infomercial Technology is neither technology in education nor technology of education but both and all pervasive which pervades the whole teaching-learning process to make it meaningful for the teacher who teaches and the learner who learns and modifies his behaviour for his own betterment and the betterment of mankind. Infomercial Technology should not be confused with teaching or instruction or education or learning or engineering but it should be taken as a sum total of all such aspects, which go a long way in shaping the personality of the learner in a meaningful context. It is an aggressive invention in education which has a promising future in the hands of all those who are constantly engaged in the pursuit of knowledge otherwise it will remain an Orwell Ian nightmare.

DEFINITIONS OF INFOMERCIAL TECHNOLOGY

1. G.O. Leith - " Infomercial Technology is the application of scientific knowledge and learning and the conditions of learning to improve the effectiveness and efficiency of teaching and training."

2. S. S. Kulkarni - "Infomercial Technology may be defined as the application of the laws as well as recent discoveries of Science and Technology to the process of education."

3. John P. Detecco - "Infomercial Technology is the form of detailed application' of psychology of learning to practical teaching problems."

4. Robert A. Cox - "Instructional Technology is the application of scientific process to man's learning conditions."

5. Richmond - "Infomercial Technology is concerned to provide appropriately designed learning situations which, holding in view of objectives of the Teaching or Training, being to bear the best means of instruction."

Nature of Infomercial Technology

1. Its basis is science.
2. It studies the effect of science and technology upon education. Science and technology are used under educational technology. Hence; it is the practical aspect of science.
3. It is a continuous dynamic, progressive and effect producing method.

4. Due to it new conceptions have been possible such as programmed learning, micro-teaching, simulated teaching, interaction analysis, video-tape, tape-recorder, projector and computer etc.
5. It accepts school as a system. In this system, the school building, furniture and teacher act as input while various methods, techniques, strategies and the teaching and examination with the help of audio-visual aids' function in the form of a process. Lastly, the output is in the form of ability of the pupils.
6. Engineering Technology is not the educational technology because the engineering technology has manufactured radio, tape-recorder, video-tape and T.V. etc., which are used in teaching as audio-visual aids, but still engineering technology is different from educational technology. In education, it is accepted as hardware approach only.
7. Audio-visual aids cannot be termed as Instructional Technology. It is because its concern is only with the process-aspect of educational technology and not with the input and output aspects. But if these A.V. aids are used to achieve educational objectives, then it can be put in the category of educational technology.
8. Programmed Instruction is also different from Educational Technology. The student learns himself during the programmed instructions. It does not allow interaction between pupil and teacher. Hence, it can be used only for limited objectives and limited subject matter. Therefore, programmed instruction is merely a part of educational technology.
9. It cannot solve each and every problem of education. It can be used successfully in teaching and instructional system only.
10. It can never replace the teacher, because of three aspects of Instructional technology. (1) Input, (2) Process and (3) Output. Input is the teacher's job and therefore, educational technology cannot snatch the place of a teacher. In spite of this, Instructional technology develops cognitive domain only and not the affective domain. Affective domain can only be developed when an interaction between teachers and pupils takes place. Hence, educational technology

cannot replace the teacher. However, a teacher can provide benefits to the large groups of students with the help of radio, tape-recorder and television etc.

KINDS OF INFOMERCIAL TECHNOLOGY

Infomercial Technology can be divided into the following three components:—

1. Behavioural Technology
2. Infomercial Technology
3. Teaching Technology

1. Behavioural Technology

Behavioural technology is an important component of educational technology. It puts emphasis on the use of psychological principles in learning and teaching so that the behaviour of the teacher and pupils may be modified in accordance with the teaching objectives. As the present education is child-centred, therefore, every teacher should possess the knowledge of child psychology i.e., the age, standard, mental capacity or capability and individual variations etc. Only in that case, he can acquire the desired behavioural changes by creating learning experiences in the pupils in order to achieve teaching objectives. In short, behavioural technology intends to expand, progress and develop in the field of behaviour and learning.

B.F. Skinner designated teaching an interaction, which exchanges the contents between teacher and pupils. Hence, we can divide teaching into:

(1) Content and

(2) Communication.

The contents can be presented before the students either by the teacher or through the programmed instructions, at the three levels (1) Memory, (2) Understanding, and (3) Reflective. The different objectives, different methods and techniques of presentation and different evaluation methods are required to present the contents at the three levels. At the time of presenting the contents before the pupils, where the teacher is required to be active on the one side, it is also required that he (teacher) should provide complete freedom to the pupils for the expression of their ideas in order to bring about the changes in the behaviour of the pupils on the other side. In other words, for successful teaching, a frequent interaction between the teacher and the pupils is must:

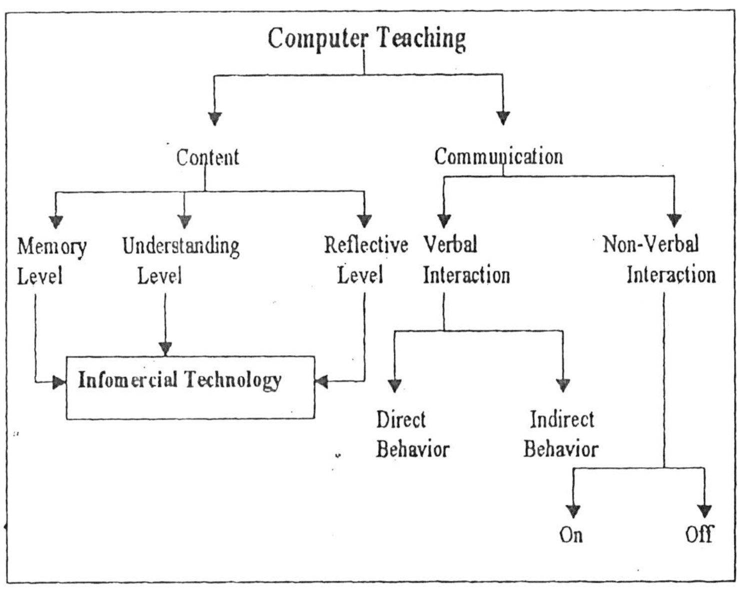

The above description suggests that the communication of the contents or the behaviour of the pupil and the teacher may be ***(1) Verbal, (2) Non-verbal.*** Asking the questions by the teacher and responding to them by the pupil is said to be the verbal behaviour. But, contrary to it, the nonverbal behaviour is symbolic in which the teacher and the pupils contribute in the development of the lesson though their facial expressions, gestures displaying the body-parts and any sort of signals. A skilled teacher succeeds in making the education clear and alive through his non-verbal, behaviours. In U.S. A. some tools have been constructed as a result of many research works in order to measure objectively the verbal and non-verbal behaviours of the teacher and pupils with the numerical and qualitative methods. With the help of these tools, by gaining knowledge about pupils and teachers behaviour and after slight adjustments in their study methods, techniques and strategies; some desired modifications in their behaviours could be brought about.

At one hand, educational technology tells us how the desired changes may be sought in the pupil's behaviours while at the other hand; it also describes the observation of teacher's classroom behaviour, its analysis, interpretation and techniques of its development. Everybody is not an inborn teacher. Mahatma Gandhi, Ravindra Nath Tagore, Shri Aurbindo Ghosh and Viveka Nand etc. were inborn teachers. But these handful inborn teachers cannot educate all the pupils of any democratic nation, Hence, these persons who are not inborn teachers are trained, as teachers in training institutions. Behavioural Technology suggests how such desired changes can be sought after going through the behaviours of such teachers in order to develop, teaching skills. The contents of behavioural technology for bringing about the changes in the behaviour of the teacher is the following:

1. Meaning and definition of the teacher-behaviour
2. Principles of the teacher-behaviour
3. Observation method of teacher-behaviour
4. Analysis and Nature of teacher-behaviour
5. Evaluation and Norms of teacher-behaviour
6. Models of teacher-behaviour
7. Various techniques of developing teacher-behaviour such as:
   (i) Programmed Instruction,
   (ii) T-Group training,
   (iii) Interaction Analysis Techniques,
   (iv) Simulated Social Skill Teaching,
   (v) Microteaching.

All these techniques are being used with much interest in the universities and schools of America with the purpose of bringing about changes in the teacher-behaviour. Initiative is being taken in India also.

Assumptions of Behavioural Technology

1. Teacher's behaviour is social and psychological.
2. Teacher's behaviour is observable.
3. Teacher's behaviour is measurable.

4. Teacher's behaviour is modifiable.
5. Teachers are not in born only they can be produced even.

Characteristics of Behavioural Technology

1. Its basic foundation is psychology.
2. Reinforcement and feedback are emphasized in it.
3. The teaching acts are evaluated from the objective point of view.
4. It is more focused on psychomotor objectives.
6. It is based upon software approach.
7. It is more used in the teacher's training institutions.
8. Its attention can be focused upon individual differences of pupil teachers.

2. Infomercial Technology

In instructional technology, the presentation of the contents is described in or out of the class. The pupils are motivated for learning in both, instruction and teaching but still there is much difference between these two. Instruction means communication of information. Other persons and methods than a teacher can do this. For example, various types of audio-visual aids can guide the students. The correspondence course and open university may accomplish the task of instructions successfully through press and television. Actually instructional technology is based upon Hardware Approach. It includes teaching material prepared on the basis of machines like tape-recorder, record player, television and projector etc. With the help of this, large groups of the students may be provided with the knowledge in minimum time and expenses.

Instruction is helpful in making teaching easy, precise, interesting and effective, but instructional technology cannot replace a teacher because the teacher can perform the teaching job only. Interaction between teacher and pupils is a must in teaching while in instructions, especially in programmed instructions, the pupils can learn himself. Instruction is used in teaching and hence teaching can be named as instruction but instruction cannot be termed as teaching because interaction between a teacher and pupils is not essential in instructions' Instruction can develop cognitive domain of the pupils only, while affective and cognitive domains may also develop by teaching. Thus, the basis of instructional technology is the machine system. It provides assistance in teaching work through machines prepared with the help of science and technology. In the words of S.M. McMurrin, "Instructional technology is a systematic way of designing, carrying out and evaluating the total process of learning and teaching in terms of specific objectives, based on research, on human learning and communication and employing a combination of human and non-human resources to bring about more effective instruction."

Thus, the instructional technology motivates learning process. The instructional material is selected keeping in view the objectives. Simultaneously, various methods, techniques, strategies and audio-visual aids are used for presenting the lesson so that the objectives may be achieved. In the end, the achievement of the objective is evaluated. If the objective is not achieved owing to any reason, then again the decision regarding any proposed change is taken so that the desired change in the pupils' behaviour may be brought about.

Assumptions of Infomercial Technology

1. A pupil can learn according to his needs and capacities.
2. A pupil can learn even in the absence of the teacher.
3. Reinforcement can be provided by using instruction continuously.
4. Learning objectives can be achieved through instructional objectives.
5. The subject-matter can be divided into its various elements or sections and each section can be taught independently through this technology.

Characteristics of Instructional Technology

1. It is helpful in achieving cognitive objectives.
2. It can meet the shortage of effective teachers.
3. With its help, the pupils can learn according needs and speed.
4. It can control the individual differences.
5. Conditioned Response Theory of Learning is also used.

6. Analysis of contents in depth is carried out in this technology, which encourages optimism regarding the impressive presentation of the contents.

3. Teaching Technology

Teaching is an art. Teaching technology makes this art more easy, precise, practical and objective by using scientific principles. Teaching has two elements—

(i) Content, and

(ii) Classroom behaviour or communication.

Teaching technology, include both contents and communication. Hence, teaching technology includes both instructional technology and behavioural technology. But neither does it add in itself only the major aspect; i.e., neither programmed instruction nor its studies only some contents like various principles of teaching behaviour, techniques of behaviour development and classroom behaviour models in behaviour technology. Even the observation of classroom behaviour, analysis, interpretation and evaluation are considered the contents of teaching technology.

Teachers have to develop professional sensitivity which makes the reaching so much active and dynamic that all the pupils of the nation become brave, intelligent, scholar and of high character citizens by achieving the objectives through existing resources. The learning system helps the teacher in making correct decisions as well as develops responsible professionalism. It makes necessary changes in the concept of teaching, training of the teacher, strategies and tactics of teaching, functions of the teacher as a manager etc. I.K. Davies has stressed upon the pupil learning in place of teacher's teaching and has supported this new learning management.

Functions in Teaching-Learning

In teaching management, teacher functions himself not as on aid of teaching, but as anger he determines teaching objectives. He defines those objectives in clear terms so that he may come to know what changes are to be brought in the pupils regarding their development through these determined objectives. After co-determining and defining teaching objectives, he creates an environment in which acquiring appropriate learning experiences; pupils experience desired behavioural changes and achieve predetermined and defined objectives successfully. I.K. Davies has divided the functions of the teacher as a manager into the following four steps : -

1. Planning
2. Organization
3. Leaaing
4. Controlling

(1) Planning

In this phase, the teacher analyses the content, determines, and defines the learning objectives and writes those objectives in clear terms. He performs three activities in this phase—

(i) task analysis,
(ii) identification of teaching objectives,
(iii) writing learning objectives.

In the words of I.K. Davies, "In teaching planning in the work a teacher does to establish learning objectives."

(2) Organization

In this phase, teacher creates an effective environment by selecting teaching methods, strategies, tactics and essential aids. Acquiring proper experiences pupils gain learning objectives while living in such an environment. In the words of I.K. Davies, "Organization is the work a teacher does to arrange and relate learning resources, so as to realize learning objectives in the most effective, efficient and economical way possible."

(3) Leading

In this phase, the teacher motivates the pupils so much at each and every step they start showing interest in the teaching and the learning objectives are achieved. In this connection, I.K. Davies has written, "Leading is the work a teacher does to motivate, encourage and inspire the students, so that they will readily achieve the learning objectives."

(4) Controlling

In this phase pre-determined and defined objectives of learning remain the same. No change is brought about in these objectives. But, the teacher observes the extent to which the organization and leading activities have achieved the pre-determined objectives. To accomplish this great task, the teacher seeks the help of various techniques of evaluation and measurement U he concludes that the learning objectives have not been achieved, then he should bring necessary changes in the activities of "organization" and "leading" phases, I.K Davies writes, "In teaching controlling is the work a teacher does to determine whether his plans are being carried out effectively, organization is sound, realizing is in right direction and that how far these functions are successful in realizing the set objectives."

FORMS OF INFOMERCIAL TECHNOLOGY

As Lumsdane suggests Instructional technology has the following three forms:

1. Hardware Approach
2. Software Approach
3. System Analysis

1. Hardware Approach

The use of engineering machines in teaching is called Instructional Technology-I. It is to be remembered that physical science and engineering technology have given birth to Instructional Technology-I, Davis has said clearly that Instructional Technology-I or Hardware Approach is the application of physical science in education and teaching with which the teaching process is being mechanized gradually so that maximum pupils may be educated in minimum time and at low cost. Thus, Instructional Technology includes cinema, gramophone, radio, tape recorder, projector, computer, closed circuit television (CCTV) and electronic vide-tape etc. all the teaching machines the use of which makes the teaching more and more effective in order to achieve the teaching objectives. Human knowledge has three aspects: ***(1) Preservation, (2) Transmission and (3) Development.*** The history of preservation of the knowledge is believed to exist since the printing machines started. The knowledge is preserved with these machines in the form of books, which are shelved in the libraries. The knowledge is also preserved through tape-recorder and films. Another aspect of human knowledge is its expansion or transmission. A teacher can himself impart knowledge to his pupils but such direct benefitters happen to be small in number. Now-a-day, transmission or expansion of the knowledge is supported by machine like mike, radio and television etc. With these, thousands of pupils enjoy home-delivery of such benefits. Surprising changes have occurred in the process of equation due to educational technology. The correspondence courses and Open University are the gifts of Instructional technology-I.

The third aspect of the human knowledge is its development. Provisions are made for research work for this aspect. In the research programs, the main function is the collection and analysis of data. For this purpose, the researcher uses the electric machines and computers. Hence, all the three aspects of knowledge allow the use of machines. Thus, now the teaching process has been mechanized. This mechanization of teaching process is termed as Instructional Technology-I or Hardware Approach.

2. Software Approach

It is also known as Educational Technology-II or Software Approach is also named as Instructional Technology or Teaching Technology of Behavioural Technology. Instructional Technology-II does not allow the use of engineering machines, However, psychological principles of teaching and learning are utilized so that desirable changes may be brought about in the behaviour of the pupils. If the 'machines are used, this is done only to make the subject matter effective. Hence, the Educational Technology-II is concerned with the teaching objectives in behavioural terms, principles of teaching, methods of teaching and techniques, reinforcement of instructional system, feedback devices and evaluation. In nutshell, in Instructional Technology-II or Software Approach, it is tried to develop all the three aspects i.e., Input, Process and Output.

While Instructional Technology-I or Hardware Approach means the use of machines in teaching, Educational Technology-II or Software Approach means the use of teaching and learning principles. Thus, there is close relationship between Instructional Technology I and II.

3. System Analysis

Instructional Technology-III or System Analysis is also known as Management Technology. Developed after World War-II, it has provided a scientific basis to the decision-making regarding the problems associated with administration, management, commerce, industry and army. Instructional Technology-III helps to study the problems of educational administration and management in a scientific and conclusive way. By using it we can make the educational system, educational administration and management effective. In short, Instructional Technology-III helps in the development of educational administration and formulation of instructional out line. Educational administration and management can be made more effective and less costly by using in educational system. Hence, these days the Instructional technology-III occupies an important place in the field of teaching.

SCOPE OF INFOMERCIAL TECHNOLOGY

The scope of Infomercial Technology depends upon in what context the term Instructional Technology is used. In the first case, if Instructional Technology is used as the Audio-Visual, Aids, mechanical and electric gadgets, the scope is limited, to improve the educational messages.

If the term, Infomercial Technology, is used as the process oriented technique, then it scope is limited to production of teaching learning material. The rigorous task analysis specification of direct behaviour, the determination of prerequisites and the gradual development of the program ensure that the teaching-learning material developed on this style will be most useful to the learner. Thus, in this sense Instructional Technology is basically the technique of developing software. To this is added the concept of management and organization of man-material resources, for specific objectives. This covers both planning as well as implementation phases and is the most accepted concept all-over the world.

If this aspect is forgotten, Infomercial Technology will become a futile exercise if the planners start with the availability of a few media as for example films, television, radio and then think how to employ them in education. The correct step should be to outline educational problems. Once educational problems are outlined, rigorous thinking should go into:

1. Availability of Resources at home.
2. Resources that can be managed by external assistance.
3. Clear specification of the problem.
4. The constraints, which hinder the probable solution.
5. How different resources interact with one another.

To a teacher who is willing to change Instructional Technology, promises a big help learning, in a non-technical sense, can be thought of a pursuit, which is somehow related to the following functions:

1. Informative function (staling, processing and retrieval).
2. Calculative function (in a way this too is a part of an Informative function).
3. Concept development.
4. Performance Improvement (Psychology domain).
5. Development of interests, attitudes, etc. (Affective domain).

The computer promises to take away the burden, which can be attributed to the first two functions. It is a fact that a major burden of the traditional learning would be taken away almost dramatically. Rote memorization would lose its traditional status and the process of learning would be more meaningful and less cumbersome.

ASPECTS OF INFOMERCIAL TECHNOLOGY

Instructional Technology has three major aspects:

(A) Input
(B) Process
(C) Output

(A) Input: It involves the entering behaviour of the learner.

1. Includes previous achievement; abilities of student and level of motivation.
2. It concerns with the comprehension level of the learner,
3. It involves the skill of teaching and awareness of teaching and training methods.
4. It considers availability and skill for teaching aid.

(B) Process (Teaching-Learning Process): It involves the means and devices of learning experiences.

1. To generate situation for presenting the subject matter systematically.
2. To select and use appropriate teaching strategies and tactics for desired learning structures.
3. To employ appropriate teaching aids for desired behavioural change.
4. To identify and use suitable communication techniques for the comprehension of the subject matter.
5. To use suitable schedules of reinforcement for effective learning.
6. To establish report with students for effective teaching.
7. To evolve appropriate school environment by developing good relations among students.

(C) Output: It includes mainly the terminal behaviours of the learner.

1. To identify the characteristics of content.
2. To clarify the objectives achieved through the content.
3. To analyse the stimuli.
4. To determine the characteristics of students desired activities.

Objectives of Infomercial Technology

The *Educational Commission (1964-66)* has recommended that the curriculum should be improved in the light of the fundamental objectives or preparing teachers for varied responsibilities in evolving system of education on the basis of a task analysis and that the relationship between different subjects should be worked out so that they could be taught in the integrated manner.

Alvin Toffler points out that even the most modernized industry today stands on the threshold of 'super-industrialism' and that education, till recently an instrument of change, is itself caught up in the agony of change. Peter Drucker tells us that we are living in an age of discontinuity'. This discontinuity is dangerous, no doubt, but it is not impossible to work for humanized technology. Technology, they say, is an "opium of intellectuals". It is perhaps to guard against this possibility that Alvin Toffler talks of 'responsible technology' and in this light we can think of the objectives of Instructional technology which may be enumerated as under:

1. To determine the goals and formulate the objectives in behavioural terms
2. To analyse the characteristics of the learner.
3. To organize the content in logical or psychological sequence.
4. To media between content and resources of presentation.
5. To evaluate the learners' performance in terms of achieving educational objectives.
6. To provide the feedback among other components for the modification of learners.

So Infomercial technology is not just an innovation, rather it is a bundle of many disquieting innovations put together. In order to understand this; let us have fresh look at what actually happens in a normal classroom situation. A teacher enters the classroom with an idea of giving a chunk of the subject matter or say, 'Archimedes Principle'. This chunk is generally passed on to the students almost as a bucket, perhaps, without a question. At the most, they answer the questions from the teacher but rarely do they question the answers given by the teacher. They keep that since the bucket is to be returned at the time of examination. The teacher receives back the bucket as if it is a registered parcel to be acknowledged. The students generally avoid disturbing the bucket because they know that teaches like to receive back the 'undisturbed' parcels very much. In this situation, the students do not see the need to think for themselves because Archimedes was good enough to think on their behalf.

> **"The mind is not a vessel to be filled but afire to be ignited."**
>
> —*Plutarch*

If Infomercial technology answers these questions positively, it will certainly ignite a fire among the learner, which is the sole purpose of any meaningful education.

EXERCISE QUESTIONS

1. Explain the meaning, definition and nature of Infomercial Technology in your own words.
2. What kinds of Infomercial Technology used in education? Write in 200 words.
3. What do you understand by the Forms of Infomercial Technology? Explain.
4. What is the main Scope of Infomercial Technology in the field of education? Also describe the aspects of Infomercial Technology.
5. What are the main Objectives of Infomercial Technology? Write in your own words.

Chapter 2

OBJECTIVES OF TEACHING COMPUTER SCIENCE IN SCHOOLS

- Introduction
- Aims of teaching Computer Science in our schools
- Difference between the Terms Aims and Objectives
- Meaning of the term "Instructional Objectives"
- General aims and objectives of Computer Sciences
- Taxonomy of Instructional and Educational Objectives
- Writing Objectives in Behavioural Terms
- Guidelines regarding writing of instructional Objectives
- All Illustration of writing Instructional Objectives
- Exercise Questions

INTRODUCTION

While starting to work on any mission it is essential to think before hand about the motives and purposes of undertaking that mission. Consequently the work on this mission is always planned in view of the various advantages anticipated to be drawn through it. The same holds good for the study of a particular subject. The advantages that can be drawn or purposes that can be served by the study of that subject generally become the aims for its study.

It is in the same tune and spirit that we are apt to think about the aims of teaching computer as a subject in our schools. Naturally, these aims are likely to be based on the various advantages or values drawn or purposes served by the study of computer as sciences. Keeping this thing in view, the various aims for the teaching of computer sciences in our schools may be briefly outlined as below.

AIMS OF TEACHING COMPUTER SCIENCE AS A SUBJECT IN OUR SCHOOLS

1. **Utilitarian aim:** To enables the students to make use of the study of computer sciences in their day-to-day life activates.
2. **Intellectual or mental development aim:** To develop the intellectual or mental abilities of the students.
3. **Disciplinary aim:** To help the students in making their minds and habits disciplined.
4. **Cultural aim:** To help in the process of preservation, promotion and transmission of culture.
5. **Moral aim:** To help the students in the development of moral values devoid of false notion, superstition and miseries.
6. **Aesthetic aim:** To helps the students in the inculcation of aesthetic sense and artistic values.
7. **Social aim:** To help in the process of the development of society and inculcate social virtues and ideals among the students.
8. **Vocational aim:** To helps the students in preparing them for the future professions or occupations.
9. **Inter Disciplinary aim:** To help the students in utilizing study of computer sciences for the study of other subjects of the school curriculum.
10. **Problem Solving aim:** To help the students to acquire problem solving ability by training them in scientific method or approach.

DIFFERENCE BETWEEN THE TERMS "AIMS AND OBJECTIVES"

The terms "aims and objectives" are usually taken as synonymous terms and used interchangeably. However, in a deep sense both differ significantly.

Values and aims are quite interrelated and interdependent. We aim at a thing because we value it. The values or advantages that can be drawn by achieving a thing become our purposes or aims. We strive for the realization of the values or advantages by setting our goals and aims. Therefore, what can be expected in the form of advantages or values from the teaching of computer sciences make the very basis of the aims of teaching computer sciences. These may be taken as the broader purposes, goals or targets that can be roughly anticipated through the teaching of computer sciences. These are like ideals, the high expectations, realization of which may or may not be possible to the expected extent. They need a long term planning and some serious function able efforts on the part of a teacher.

In order to proceed for the realization of the aims or broader purposes, these are usually divided into some definite, functional and workable units named as objectives. These objectives may be termed as short-term immediate goals or purposes that may be achieved within the specified limited resources and time by a subject teacher. They can be easily evaluated through the expected behavioural changes or learning outcomes.

Objectives, in this way are the ways and means of achieving the aims in a more practical and definite way. The aims of teaching computer sciences may thus be broken into some specified objectives for providing definite learning experiences to bring desirable behavioural changes. Consequently, objectives of computer sciences teaching thus provide certain clear cut well defined short-term purposes or tasks before a science teacher at the time of teaching a particular topic or providing a particular type of learning experiences.

MEANING OF THE TERM "INSTRUCTIONAL OBJECTIVES"

At the time of imparting instruction i.e. teaching learning of a particular lesson unit or sub-unit of the object computer sciences, a teacher has to place before him some definite and very specific objectives for being attained within a specified classroom period and resources in hand. Through these so specific classroom teaching-learning objectives, known as instructional objectives, a teacher tries to bring desired changes in the behaviour of his pupils. In this way, the term instructional objectives in relation to the teaching of computer sciences may be defined as a group of statements formulated by the teacher for describing what the pupils are expected to do or will be able to do once the process of classroom instruction is over. In fact, instructional outcomes is the teaching learning product in the form of behavioural changes in the pupils that a teacher expects as a result of his instruction related with a particular lesson/ unit or sub-unit of the subjects. Instructional objectives are thus nothing but descriptions of the pupils terminal behaviour expected out of the on going classroom instruction.

GENERAL AIMS AND OBJECTIVES OF TEACHING COMPUTER

In comparison to general aims and objectives of teaching computer sciences, instructional objectives are quite narrow and specific. They are definite, tangible, precise and functional. They are pre-determined and are always formulated in such away that their attainment becomes quite practicable through the usual classroom teaching within the stipulated period of fixed duration. They are desired learning or teaching outcomes and are always stated in terms of expected pupil's behaviour or desired behavioural changes. They are, therefore, may be termed as teaching-learning objectives for behavioural objectives. The main purpose of these objectives is to provide statements of skills; concepts of the behaviour learners are expected to demonstrate after going through a particular instruction.

Objectives of teaching Computer Sciences fall midway between Goals of aims of teaching Computer Sciences and instructional objectives. They are more specific and definite than the general aims or goals but less specific and much wider that the classroom instructional objectives.

In fact classroom instructional objectives, objectives of teaching Computer Sciences at a particular or entire stage of school education, and general aims or goals of teaching Computer Sciences represent a hierarchical order as shown below.

The above figure may well illustrate that instructional objectives are the fundamental and basic targets that could be

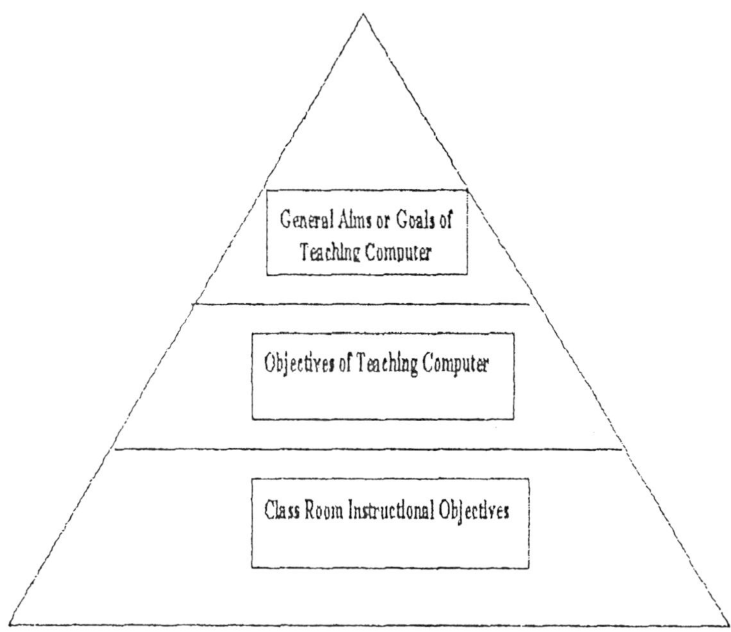

Fig. 2.1 : Hierarchical order of Aims and Objectives

easily achieved within the limited period and means while general aims or goals of teaching Computer Sciences are quite broad based, lofty and quite difficult in their attainment.

Their narrower or broader viewpoints or arising influence may be further illustrated as shown in the diagram below:

According to the above view, classroom instructional objectives may be sub merged in the reservoir of general objectives of teaching Computer Sciences at a particular school stage, which in turn are further submerged in the ocean of general aims and goals of teaching Computer Sciences.

TAXONOMY OF EDUCATIONAL AND INSTRUCTIONAL OBJECTIVES

"Taxonomy" means a system of classification and in this sense taxonomy like Bloom's Taxonomy presents a system of classification of the objectives in the similar way, as Dewey's

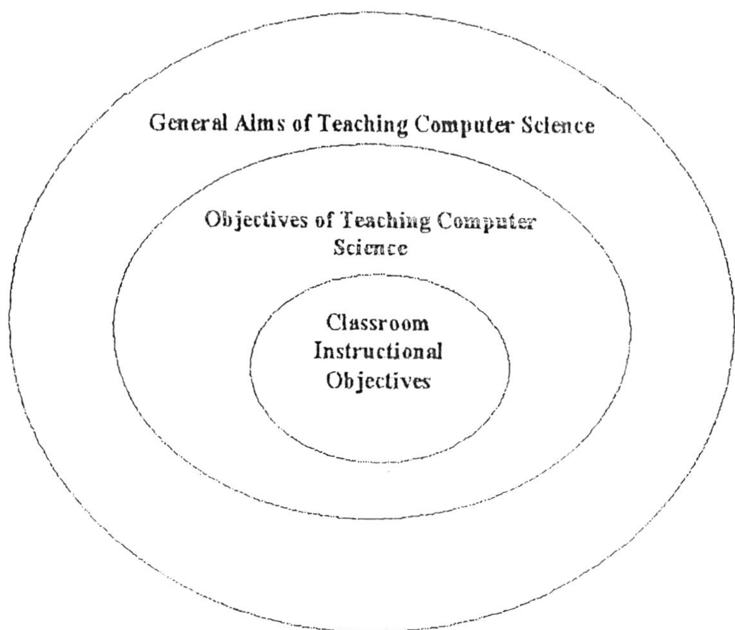

Fig. 2.2 : A diagrammatic view of Aims and Objectives

Decimal system tends to classify a number of books in a library.

The taxonomy of educational and instructional objectives has been worked out on the assumption that the teaching-learning process may be conceived as an attempt to change the behaviour of the pupils with respect to some subject matter or learning experiences. Behaviour is divided into three domains-Cognitive (knowing), affective (feeling) and psychomotor (doing). The taxonomy of educational and instructional objectives has also been considered to be belonging to these three domains.

The taxonomy related to cognitive domain has been presented by Bloom (Bloom, et. al., 1956), the second related to affective domain by Krathwohl, Bloom and Masia (Krath Wohl, et, al. 1964) and the third related to psychomotor domain by Harrow (Harrow, 1972) and Simpson (1966).

Taxonomy of objectives in the Cognitive Domain

Bloom and his associates have classified the objectives related to cognitive domain into six categories arranged from the lowest to the highest level of functioning as described below:

1. Knowledge

(a) Knowledge of Specifics,
   (i) Knowledge of terminology
   (ii) Knowledge of specific facts.

(b) Knowledge of ways and means of dealing with specifics,
   (i) Knowledge of conventions.
   (ii) Knowledge of trends and sequences
   (iii) Knowledge of classification and categories.
   (iv) Knowledge of criteria
   (v) Knowledge of methodology.

(c) Knowledge of universals and abstractions in a field,
   (i) Knowledge of principles and generalizations
   (ii) Knowledge of theories and structures.

2. Comprehension

(a) Translation
(b) Interpretation
(c) Extrapolation

3. Application

4. Analysis

(a) Analysis of elements
(b) Analysis of relationship
(c) Analysis of organizational principles.

5. Synthesis

(a) Production of unique communication
(b) Production of a plan or a proposed set of operations.
(c) Derivation of a set of set of abstract relations.

6. Evaluation

(a) Judgment in terms of internal evidence.

(b) Judgment in terms of external criteria.

Let us try to elaborate the above taxonomy of objectives of cognitive domain given by Bloom for its clarity and understanding.

1. **Knowledge:** It represents the lowest level of the objectives belonging to the cognitive domain and primarily aims for the acquisition of the knowledge concerning,

(i) Specific facts, terminology, methods and processes and

(ii) Generalized principles, theories and structures.

The knowledge objectives mainly call for the recall and recognition level of one's memory and therefore their evaluation is primarily made through a simple recall or multiple choice type questions.

2. **Comprehension:** Comprehension is based upon the knowledge. If there is no knowledge, there will be no comprehension. On the ladder of the acquisition of cognitive abilities its level is little higher than the knowledge. Specifically, it means the basic understanding of the facts, ideas, methods, processes, principles or theories, etc. as a result, what is communicated to a learner, he may -

   (i) Translate or summarize the communicated knowledge in his own words.

   (ii) Interpret i.e. cite examples, discriminate, classify, verify or generally and

   (iii) Extrapolate i.e. estimate or understand by use of knowledge and extend it to other subjects and fields.

3. **Application:** The knowledge is useful only when it is possible to make it employed. The application of an idea, principle or theory may be made possible only when it is grasped and understood properly. Therefore, the category of application automatically involves both the earlier categories i.e. knowledge and comprehension. Under this objective the learner is required to acquire the ability to make use of the abstract or generalized ideas, principles in the particular and concrete situations.

4. **Analysis:** Analysis refers to an understanding at higher level. It is a complex cognitive process that involves knowledge, comprehension as well as application of an idea, fact, principles or theory. Through the realization of these objectives the learner is expected to acquire the necessary skill in drawing inferences, discriminating, making choices and selection and separating apart the different components or elements of a concept, object or principle.
5. **Synthesis:** The objectives belonging to this category aim to help the learner to acquire necessary ability to combine the different elements or components of an idea, object, concept, or principle as to produce an integrated picture i.e. a figure of wholeness. As a result he may be expected to propagate or present a theory or principle by combining different approaches, ideas or viewpoints. He may arrive at something new or originate some novel thing or ideas after synthesizing all what is known to him earlier. In this way, it calls for the creativity aspect of the cognitive abilities and therefore may be considered definitely a higher level of learning involving knowledge comprehension, application as well as analysis.
6. **Evaluation:** This category of objectives aims to develop in the learner the ability to make proper value judgment about what has been acquired by him in the form of knowledge, understanding, application, analysis and synthesis. It represents definitely the highest level of the objectives belonging to the cognitive domain and involves all the five categories described earlier. As a result the learner is expected to take proper decision about the quantitative and qualitative value of a particular idea, object, principle or theory. He may arrive at an appropriate decision about the matter and methods by making use of all the cognitive abilities through the earlier categories of cognitive objectives.

Taxonomy of Objectives in the Affective Domain

1. Receiving (Attending)

(a) Awareness

(b) Willingness to receive

(c) Controlled or selected attention

2. Responding

(a) Acquiescence in responding
(b) Willingness to respond
(c) Satisfaction in response

3. Valuing

(a) Acceptance of a value
(b) Preference for a value
(c) Commitment

4. Organization

(a) Conceptualization of a value
(b) Organization of a value system

5. Characterization by a Value or Value Complex

(a) Generalized set
(b) Characterization

Let us try to elaborate further the above classification for its clarity and understanding as below:

1. ***Receiving:*** It represents the initial category for the objectives belonging to affective domain. For the inculcation of certain interests, attitudes, value or ideas it is essential that learner should be made to receive or attend the desired ideas events or objectives. This category points out towards this necessity and takes into consideration three types of following sequential activities:
   (i) Firstly, the learner is sensitized or made aware about the existence of certain stimuli.
   (ii) Then the desired intension or willingness for receiving or attending the stimuli is created in the learner.
   (iii) Lastly, the efforts are made for the control of the attention of the learner. He may be trained to pay selective attention and sustain it for a desired period.
2. ***Responding:*** It represents the second level of the objectives for the categories belonging to affective domain. Once a learner receives or attends to particular ideas, event or thing he must be made to respond to it as actively as possible. The response here do not confine itself in just

paying attention or arousal of a simple intention or desire of getting a thing, as in the first category or receiving but manifest themselves in the active behaviour like obeying, answering, reading, discussing, recording, writing, and reaching to a stimulus, etc.

3. ***Valuing:*** When one attends as well as responds to a particular thing, idea or event he is naturally drifted towards taking value judgment about that thing; idea or event. Therefore, this category of valuing depends upon both the former categories i.e. receiving and responding. Here the learner is expected to imbibe a definite value pattern towards different ideas, events and objects. In practice the objectives belonging to this category are usually concerned with the development of typical value pattern attitudes, etc.

4. ***Organizing:*** The category of objectives concern with the construction of relatively enduring value structure in the learner by organizing and synthesizing the different value patterns imbibed by him time to time. Ultimately this category of objective leads the learner to form a set value structure or philosophy of life.

5. ***Characterization by a value complex:*** It is the highest level category of the objectives belonging to the affective domain. Up to this stage, the learner is able to imbibe all the essential affective behaviour i.e. various interests, attitudes, values, value complex or value patterns, a permanent set value structure and therefore, all the earlier categories are automatically involved in the objectives of this category. At this stage, the learner is destined to imbibe typical characteristics of his individual character i.e. life style of his own. In fact it is the end point or ultimate goal of the process of education.

Psychomotor Taxonomy

The classification of psychomotor objectives was first product by Simpson (Simpson, 1966) and latter modified by Harrow (1972). These given by Harrow are being described in the following pages under six different categories arranged from lowest to the highest level of functioning.

1. ***Reflex Movements:*** Reflex movements may be considered as the involuntary motor responses to the various stimuli

in the environment. Examples of such reflex movements or actions are: the jerking of hands, the closing of eyelid, stretching of the arms, etc. These movements represent the lowest level of the psychomotor behaviour. They are largely controlled by the autonomous nervous system. However, they are very much essential not only for the development of psychomotor abilities but also for the survival of the human beings.

2. ***Basic Fundamental Movements:*** These fundamental movements are just a step ahead of the simple reflex movements. They are not so inborn and innate as the reflex movements but a child may be seen to demonstrate such movements in his very early days of life. Their movements in the form of kneeling, creeping, stumbling, walking, jumping, moving hands, neck, head, etc. may be named as basic fundamental movements. They represent the simple basic movements of the body almost requiring no serious attempts or skilled practice for their occurrence. In the later years of our life, these movements are made as a result of obeying certain kinds of orders.
3. ***Perceptual Abilities:*** The development of motor abilities related with the phenomenon of perception belongs to this category of objectives. When some meaning is attached to sensation, it is termed as perception. As a result, the learner is able to derive useful meaning out of the exposure of their senses to various stimuli in the environment. His bodily movements are then governed and controlled by his perceptual abilities. Whatever he perceives through his senses becomes an ignition point for the motor behaviour. Such type of behaviour is learned behaviour. It is always acquired through experience and systematic training.
4. ***Physical Abilities:*** For an effective motor behaviour, there is an urgent need of the development of desirable physical abilities. If one has adequate physical stamina and abilities, he may go ahead in the task of improving his psychomotor behaviour. Therefore, this category of objectives aims to develop the various physical abilities of the learners like tolerance to bear and stand against rough weather; to do hard labour, to carry the large load, to bend an article, to demonstrate one's physical power in starting, stopping or running an object or machine, etc.

5. ***Skilled Movements:*** Skilled movements are those complex bodily movements which help in performing the skilled tasks. These movements are to be acquired through an organized and systematic learning process. Their acquisition requires an intelligent understanding and sufficient drill or practice work on the part of the learner. The art of dancing, diving, driving, playing the musical organs, skating, typing, swimming, tailoring, etc. represent such skilled movements. The development of the abilities concerning such skilled movements depends upon the development of the motor abilities described under all the earlier four categories.
6. ***Non Discursive Communication:***This category represents the highest level of the psychomotor behaviour. The movements are hereby integrated with the inner feelings and affective behaviour of the learner. In this way, the non-discursive communication may be defined in terms of the overt behaviour activities related with the communication of affective behaviour feelings or emotions. This communication may range from a simple behaviour expressible through posing or facial expression to a complex behaviour performed through a highly sophisticated classical dance, sketching, painting or acting.

An Alternative Taxonomy of Psychomotor Objectives

An alternative taxonomy in the psychomotor domain has been proposed by Dr. R.H. Dave (1969) in the shape of a working hypothesis as below:

1. Imitation

(a) Impulsion

(b) Overt repetition

2. Manipulation

(a) Following direction

(b) Selection

(c) Fixation

3. Precision

(a) Reproduction

(b) Control

4. Articulation

(a) Sequence

(b) Harmony

5. Naturalization

(a) Automatism

(b) Interlamination

Let us have a necessary explanation for the above steps—

1. ***Imitation:*** For the burning of psychomotor activity i.e. drawing or surveying skill in mathematics, the task begins with the imitation of observed acts. The child observes the demonstrated behaviour related to drawing of a line angle or circle, etc. He feels an inner push or an impulse (by having an inner rehearsal of the psychomotor activities) to imitate action. It is followed by the over repetition (imitation) of the demonstrated behaviour.
2. ***Manipulation:*** This second category of psychomotor objectives emphasized manipulation on the part of the learner for the acquisition of skills by following directions, performing selected action and fixation of performance through necessary practice.
3. ***Precision:*** In the third category of psychomotor objectives learner is able to perform skilled acts or motor activities with a desired level of precision (accuracy, exactness and right proportion) and as such may be said to reach a higher level of refinement in reproducing a given act or skilled task.
4. ***Articulation***: It is the fourth category in the hierarchy of learning the psychomotor activities or skills. At the stage learner becomes capable of coordinating a series of acts by establishing appropriate sequence and accomplishing harmony or internal consistency among, different acts.
5. ***Naturalization:*** It is the highest stage reached in terms of the development or proficiency acquired in the learning of a skill or psychomotor act. One can now perform a single act or series of articulated acts with a greater refinement, ease and convenience as automatic and naturally as possible.

WRITING OBJECTIVES IN BEHAVIOURAL TERMS

The major weakness about the taxonomies of objectives given above lies in the fact that they do not state objectives in terms of terminal behaviour i.e. what the learns will be able to do or what will be their behaviour at the end of teaching a particular unit or topic. Let us therefore describe various methods and approaches of writing objectives in behavioural terms. But before discussing these methods or approaches let us make us clear about the terms terminal behaviour and entering behaviour essential for the specification of behavioural out comes through a particular piece or attempt of instinct ion.

CONCEPT OF ENTERING AND TERMINAL BEHAVIOUR

Entering behaviour

The behaviour of a learner at the point of entity i.e. before entering into the process of gaining learning experiences through a piece of instruction or teaching is termed as entering behaviour or simply entry behaviour of the learner. In this way the starting point with respect to one's behaviour in a process of instructions is called his entering behaviour. It is that initial behaviour which one is supposed to demonstrate before subjected to the process of tutoring, teaching or self-instruction.

In this way by the term entering behaviour of a learner in context with the teaching/instruction of a particular unit/topic on the subject Computer Sciences we will have to ascertain, test or evaluate the performance of a learner for finding out—

- The level of his knowledge and understanding regarding the learning of the topic/unit.
- The skills possessed by him for helping him in the study and learning of the topic/unit.
- The interests and attitudes possessed by him for helping him in the study and learning of the topic/unit.

In brief, we have to make a search for the level of potential possessed by a learner in terms of his knowledge, understanding, application, interest and aptitudes (covering all the domains of his behaviour before of his entry to the process of our instruction or teaching. The result or output of our search is thus being named as the entry behaviour of the learner in reference to that particular piece of instruction or teaching.

The evaluated out comes in terms of the entry behaviour of the learner should be essentially stated in specific behavioural terms for the required clarify about the potential of the learner. As illustration, it may be written as under—

"Before going through the present piece of instruction/ teaching of a particular unit or topic, the learner is able to .... read/write/define/calculate/observe /tell/explain/illustrate/ verify/infer/............ with...........efficiency or in..................... .... circumstances etc."

Terminal Behaviour

The behaviour of learner at the end of rccciving or undergoing through a piece of instruction or teaching a particular unit or topic is termed as his terminal behaviour. In fact entering behaviour help us in setting out our instructional objectives with reference to a piece of instruction of teaching of a particular topic. Through these objectives, we plan for the behavioural changes that may be expected from an individual learner in relation with the level of behaviour exhibited by him through his entering behaviour. A bright child in relation to his creditable entry behaviour may be expected to show better out put in terms of his terminal behaviour or he will be more benefited through a piece of instruction or attempts in teaching. In fact we have to set instructional objectives, instructional process and out teaching endeavours well with in the terms of the entering behavioural input of the learners. How far our efforts have got success may then be ascertained through the testing measurement and evaluation of the terminal behaviour of the learners.

In this way terminal behaviour represents that final or end behaviour of a learner which is demonstrable by him after going through a particular piece of instruction/studying a particular unit or topic.

It is nothing but a collection of the statement made through a number of instructional objectives set for the instruction/ teaching of a particular topic or unit. Through such statements we try to depict the nature of the terminal behaviour i.e. end behaviour or behaviour outcomes expected to be demonstrated by a learner after going through a piece of instruction or studying a particular topic or unit. In this way, the terminal behaviour is generally found to provide the information about the gains made by an individual learner to his entry behaviour in reference to-

(i) Level of knowledge and understanding with reference to the instructional unit or topic,

(ii) Ability to apply the received knowledge and gained insight,

(iii) Learning and acquisition of new skills or modified and improvement in the old skills,

(iv) Changes in outlook, interest and attitudes.

How the statements regarding the terminal behaviour of a learner are given, thus actually forms the essence of writing objectives in behaviour terms. How this is done let us understand through the various methods and approaches adopted for the writing objectives in behaviour terms. Although there are several methods of writing objectives in behavioural terms yet here we are going to discuss only the following three approaches—

1. Robert Mager's Approach
2. Robert Miller's Approach
3. RCEM Approach.

1. Robert Mager's Approach

According to Robert Mager (Mager 1962), instructional objectives are best described in terms of the terminal behaviour expended from the learners. He recommends the following things for the writing of the objectives:

1. Identification of the terminal behaviour or performance and its naming
2. Description of the important conditions under which the behaviour is expected to occur.
3. Specification on the criteria of acceptable performance (desired terminal behaviour) by describing how goods a learner's performance must be for being acceptable.

Mager's approach has adopted Bloom's Taxonomy as a stalling base for the writing of objectives. He has sought the help of the associated action verbs for stating be different objectives. The verbs help in describing the outcomes of learning or terminal behaviour of the learner in a well-defined way (observable and testable).

Table 2.3 : List of associated action verbs for the Cognitive Domain.

Objective (Based on Bloom's Taxonomy)	*Associated Action Verbs*
1. Receiving	Ask, Accept, Attend, Beware, Catch, Discover, Experiment, Identify, Favour, Follow, Observe, Prefer, Perceive, Receive, Select, etc.
2. Responding	Answer, Assist, Complete, Derive, Discuss, Develop, Help, List, Label, Name Obey, Present, Practice, Record, Select, State, Write, etc.
3. Valuing	Accept, Attain, Complete, Choose, Decide, Demonstrate, Discriminate, Develop, Increase, Indicate, Influence, Participate, Prefer, Recognize, etc.
4. Organizing	Add, Associate, Change, Compare, Complete, Coordinate, Correlate, Determine, Find, Form, Generalize, Integrate, Judge, Project, Prepare, Relate, Select, Synthesize, Characterize, etc.
5. Characterizing	Accept, Change, Characterize, Decide, Discriminate, Demonstrate, Develop Experiment, Face Identify, Judge, Prove, Revise, Serve, Solve, Verify, etc.

In case we strictly follow the Mager's approach for the writing of objectives in behavioural terms we would have to adopt the following procedure for writing an instructional objective in behavioural terms.

1. First state conditional under which the performance is to occur likes "Using a Doctor's thermometer the Students are able to or will be able to..."
2. Then use an action verb for telling what telling what students will be able to do like measure/read/identify, etc.
3. Finally, state a criterion for success like "Using a Doctor's Thermometer the students will be able to read the

Table 2.4 : List of Action Verbs for Affective Domain

Objective (Based on Bloom's Taxonomy)	*Associated Action Verbs*
1. Knowledge	Define, List label Measure, Names Recall, Recognize, Reproduce, Select, State, Write, Underline, etc.
2. Comprehension	Change, Classify, Distinguish, Explain, Formulate, Identify, Illustrate, Indicate, Interpret., Justify, Judge, Name, Resent, Select, Summarise, Transform, Translate, etc.
3. Application	Assess, Change, Choose, Conduct, Construct, Compute, Demonstrate, Discover, Explain, Establish, Find, Generate, Illustrate, Modify, Predict, Perform, Select, Solve, Use, etc.
4. Analysis	Analyse, Associate, Compare, Conclude, Contrast, Criticize, Differentiate, Identify, Justify, Point Out, Resolve, Select, Separate, etc.
5. Synthesis	Argue, Conclude, Combine, Derive, Discuss, Generalize, Integrate, Organize, Precise, Prove, Relate, Restate, Select, Summarize, Synthesize, etc.
6. Evaluation	Defend, Determine, Evaluate, Judge, Identify, Recognise, Relate, Select, Summarize, Support, Verify, etc.

temperature of the body of their fellow students with cent per cent accuracy".

By following such procedure an instructional objective related to the topic "Computation of kinetic energy" may be written as under:

"Given a mass 'm' and velocity 'v', the students are able or will be able to compute kinetic energy of a moving body by using the formula K.E.=½ v^2 with cent per cent accuracy".

Limitations of Robert Mager's Approach

Mager's approach although quite popular in the development of programmed instruction suffers from the following limitations.

1. Mager's approach is a behaviour approach but human learning cannot be confined merely to simple S-R learning.
2. It concentrates on cognitive and affective domains and neglect the psychomotor domain of the learner's behaviour. Therefore, its use is limited for the writing of cognitive and affective objectives.
3. For the writing of objectives it gives emphasis on action verbs designating behaviours and does not tell anything about the related mental processes or mental abilities. Therefore, it does not even save the purpose of writing cognitive and affective objective in an appropriate way.
4. The overlapping of action verbs in different categories of the cognitive as well as affective objectives creates confusion in the use of appropriate action verbs for writing particular instructional objectives.
5. Moreover the list of action verbs provided is too long and unwieldy to have any meaningful application to classroom teaching.

2. Miller's Approach

Mager in his approach badly neglected the cognitive domain or psychomotor aspect of the behaviour, Robert Miller (Miller, 1962) for meeting the requirement or writing. Psychomotor objectives put forward his scheme based on skill analysis by outlining the following procedure—

1. Description of the indicator, indicating the relevant activity.
2. Description of the indication or stimulus, which calls for a response.
3. Controlling of the object, which is to be activated.
4. Description of the activity to be performed.
5. The indication of the adequacy of responses of feed-back.

Like Mager, he also tried to enlist associated action verbs for the psychomotor objectives.

For the purpose of using Miller's Approach a list of appropriate action verbs is being provided in the following table based on the classification of psychomotor objectives pointed out by Harrow (Harrow 1972).

Table 2.5 : List of Action Verbs for Psychomotor Objectives

Objective (Based on Harrow's Classification)	*Associated Action Verbs*
1. Reflex Movements	Bite, Harden, Jerk, Lengthen, Loosen, Make, Small, Relax, Stop. Straighten, Stretch, etc.
2. Basic Fundamental	Befall, Catch, Creep, Drink, Hold, Jump, Kneel, Move, Reach, Run, Walk, etc.
3. Physical Abilities	Begin, Bear, Bend, Conduct, Increase, Lean, Reform, Smash, Start, Stop, etc.
4. Perceptual Abilities	Balance, Bend, Catch, Discover, Eat, Explore, Feed, Identification by touching, seeing, smelling, or hearing, Memory Tracing, Small, Throw, Write, etc.
5. Skilled Movements	Dance, Big, Dive, Drive, Knit, Play the musical organs, Row, Skate, Shoot, Swim, Type, etc.
6. Non-Discursive Communication	Mimic, Pose, Sit, Sketch, Smile, Stand, Tease, etc.

(3) RCEM Approach

Both Mager's and Miller's approach have remained unsuccessful in the task of writing all instructional objectives belonging to all three domains of behaviour. Where Mager's approach serves the purpose of cognitive and affective objectives, Miller's Scheme is meant for psychomotor objectives. Thus none of these approaches lay emphasis on associated action human behaviour. Moreover both of these approaches lay emphasis on associated action verbs (which are more often overlapping within and among the objectives of the domains) designating behaviours for writing a particular in the learning process. On account of these limitations both these approaches have come into severe attack in our country and now being replaced by a more reasonable approach known as R.C.E.M. approach developed by Regional College of Education, Mysore.

This approach makes use of mental processes or mental abilities in place of action verbs in the writing of instructional objectives. It makes use of its own taxonomy of objectives, known as R.C.E.M. Taxonomy of objectives, which is somewhat, a modified form of the Bloom's Taxonomy. Here there are four categories in place of six given by Bloom. For doing so the last three category, Analysis, Synthesis and Evaluation of the difference lies in naming the Bloom's Comprehension Category as Understanding in the R.C.E.M. approach. These objective categories of R.C.E.M. approach, along with the associated mental processes or abilities, are given ahead in Table 2.6.

Table 2.6 : Objectives and Mental Processing in R.C.E.M. Approach

Objective (Based on Harrow's Classification)	*Associated Action Verbs*
1. Knowledge	1.1 Recognize
	1.2 Recall
2. Understanding	2.1 Seeing relationship
	2.2 Cite Example
	2.3 Discriminate
	2.4 Classify
	2.5 Interpret
	2.6 Verity
	2.7 Generalize
3. Application	3.1 Reason out
	3.2 Formulate hypothesis
	3.3 Establish hypothesis
	3.4 Infer
	3.5 Predict
4. Creativity	4.1 Analyse
	4.2 Synthesize
	4.3 Evaluate

Note : For comparison of Bloom's objectives with the RCEM

The four categories of objectives, as may be evident from the above table, have been divided into seventeen mental processes or abilities. These processes or abilities are used for writing the objectives in behavioural terms. For this purpose RCEM approach lays down the necessary outline of the seventeen frames or statements given ahead.

1. Knowledge Objectives

1. The learner is able to recognize.........
2. The learner is able to recall.............

2. Understanding Objectives

1. The learner is able to see relationship between.......and........
2. The learner is able to cite example of......and.........
3. The leaner is able to discriminate between..... and.....
4. The learner is able to classify.........
5. The learner is able to interpret...
6. The learner is able verity...
7. The learner is able to generalize...

3. Application Objectives

1. The learner is able to reason out...
2. The learner is able to formulate hypothesis for..........
3. The learner is able to establish hypothesis for.............
4. The learner is able to infer about...................
5. The learner is able to predict about............

4. Creativity Objectives

1. The learner is able to analyse...........
2. The learner is able to synthesize...........
3. The learner is able to evaluate...........

How to Write Objectives in RCEM Approach

The procedure may be sequenced as below:

1. First of all, have in mind the entry behaviour of the learner.
2. Try to think over the element of content, topic or the learning experiences to be given to the learner.
3. Try to think over the teaching or learning objective or objectives.

4. In view of the entry behaviour, element of content and the particular objective, try to select appropriate processes or mental abilities for writing the objective in questions.
5. Try to make use of the seventeen frames or statements of the RCEM approach given earlier in this chapter and fill in the blanks in view of the entry behaviour of the learner and learning experiences given to him.

Let us now try to illustrate the RCEM approach of writing objectives with an example:

Example 1. Subject : Computer Science
Topic : Laws of Floating Bodies

1.2 The learner is able to recall the laws of floating bodies' (Knowledge)

2.6 The learner is able to verify the laws of floating bodies' (Understanding)

3.1 The learner is able to reason out why does a big ship float in the sea while a small needle sinks. (Application)

4.3 The learner is able to evaluate the application of laws of floating bodies in his day-to-day life. (Creativity)

Guidelines Regarding Writing of Instructional Objectives

The discussion held so far may help the pupil teachers in the task of formulating the desired instructional objectives related to the topics or sub units of their daily lessons. They have to bring desired behavioural changes in their students. These changes are to take place in all the three domain-cognitive, affective and co-native of their behaviour. The taxonomies related to these three domains along which the approaches adopted for writing these objectives in behavioural terms thus may provide desired help to the teachers in the task of planning and writing of instructional objectives. The question however arises in actual practice and in the existing conditions available for teacher training, what type of behavioural changes can be actually expected in the behaviour of the students through the teaching of the lessons in Computer Sciences. These changes falling in the different domains of their behaviour may generally be summarized as under:

1. Students may acquire the knowledge and understanding of the facts, principles, processes and idea related to the topic and units of the different branches of the subject Computer Sciences.
2. They may learn about the various skill related to the processes and products of Computer Science like manipulative and experimental skills, drawing skills, mathematical skills, problem solving and inventive skills.
3. They may be able to utilise the knowledge, understanding and skills related to the subject Computer Science in their day-to-day life as well as in the study of other subjects.
4. They may development proper positive attitude for the learning as will as way of acquiring knowledge and skills in the subject Computer Sciences.
5. They may develop proper interest and appreciation for the process and products of the subject Computer Science.

In the tight of the above types of expected changes in the behaviour of the students, the subject teachers may consider the following types or categories of instructional objectives for the planning of the lessons in the subject Computer Sciences.

1. Knowledge and understanding objectives.
2. Skill objectives.
3. Application objectives.
4. Attitude objectives.
5. Interest and appreciation objectives.

By adopting the above five categories of institutional objectives, how should the pupil teachers plan and write instructional objectives for a particular teaching learning unit or lesson may be made clear through the following illustration.

AN ILLUSTRATION OF WRITING INSTRUCTIONAL OBJECTIVES

Topic: Our Solar System (Presentation with the help of Computer and Software of Solar System)

Knowledge and understanding objectives (After showing the learning software)

1. The pupil recalls the names of the planets of the solar system.

2. The pupil tells the name of the planets which lie at the nearest and farthest distance from the earth.
3. The pupil recognizes the names of planets and satellites.
4. The pupil recognizes the position of the planets, moon, sun and other members of the solar system in a map or diagram of the solar system.
5. The pupil identifies planets and satellites.
6. The pupil explains the difference between a planet and a star.
7. The pupil detects error in telling the comparative size and distance of the member of the solar system.
8. The pupil illustrates the meaning of the terms Light year, Earth year and Moon year etc.

Skill Objectives

1. The pupil draws accurate and neat diagram with the help of computer using the software paint and brush and showing the solar system and the occurrence of solar or lunar eclipses.
2. The pupil calculates the time taken by the light from the members of the solar system to react earth and also their relative distances from the earth.

Attitude Objectives

1. The pupil does not accept the mythical stories for giving the reasons of lunar or solar eclipse.
2. The pupil accepts his mistake in judging planets and other stars as small as they appear from earth.

Interest and Appreciation Objectives

1. The pupil shows keen interest in visiting planetarium.
2. The pupil builds a model or solar system.
3. The pupil writes an article on solar system and eclipses in the science bulletin.
4. The pupil reads scientific literature concerning solar system and universe in the library.
5. The pupil derives pleasure in knowing about the solar system and its place in universe.

6. The pupil shows thrill and excitement in knowing the scientific facts about the members of the solar system and their impact on our life.
7. The pupil admires the contribution of ancient astronomers and scientists in finding out the secrets about the solar system and universe.

Note: Instead of repeating the word the pupil in all sentences we can write it on the too like. After studying the topic "our solar system" the pupil is expected to demonstrate the following types of behavioural outcomes.

EXERCISE QUESTIONS

1. What are instructional objectives? Discuss their relationship with general aims and objectives in relation to the Computer Sciences teaching.
2. What do you mean by the term taxonomy of instructional objective? Provide the taxonomies of objectives in cognitive, affective and psychomotor domains of behaviour.
3. What is Bloom's taxonomy of instructional objectives? Name some of the popular taxonomies.
4. What do you mean by the term taxonomy of educational objectives in the term of teaching computer. Name some of the popular taxonomies.
5. Explain the term "Writing objectives in behavioural terms". What is its need? Name a raw important methods or approaches of such writing.
6. Describe in detail the Mager's approach of writing objectives by presenting suitable examples Discuss its limitations also.
7. What is the Miller's approach with regard to the writing of objectives? Illustrate it with an example.
8. What are instructional objectives? Point out clearly how will you proceed for the writing of instructional objectives related to a particular topic in the teaching of Computer Sciences.

CHAPTER 3

COMPUTER AND ITS APPLICATION

- Introduction
- First step in Computing
- History of Computers in India
- Importance of Computers
- Limitations of Computers
- Classification of Computers
- Classification of Generation
- Classification by Principle
- Computer in Education
- Exercise Questions

INTRODUCTION

In the ancient time men lived in jungle like animals. But to complete his requirements he started to think. And effort made men superior from animals. This was the straiten step in the history of progress. In this development process some inventions changed the life of men. These inventions were Fire, Wheel and Electricity. These three inventions increased the speed of progress and made human life much easier. But to maintain this speed he felt the necessity of a machine which could store the large volume of data and could perform large calculations at very high speed, because this as becoming the big problem. And finally he found the computer which has machine which has changed the life of men and has become the best machine of not only of this century, the best one amongst all the machines which are invented by men up to this time. But this machine was not invented in one or two years, this is the result of many hundreds of even thousands of years of research.

FIRST STEP IN COMPUTING

The computer is the most significant contribution of man in the present century. The present era is the era of devices of science and computer is one out of them. It has wide applicability in the human life. It has made human life faster and precise.

Meaning and Definition

The computer is known as electronic brain. It is a speedy electronic device, which is designed to accept and store dates in the form of information. When we give the instruction to the computer its process the data and create a report for us as program is given for that particular work or task.

The term computer is the origin from the Latin word computer. It is a calculating device. The letters of "**Computer**" have some specific meaning i.e. **C-Calculate, O-Operate, M-Memorize, P-Print, U-Update, T-Tabulate, E-Edit and R-Response.**

It is an electronic device, which organizes and controls the data. The computer analysed the data in short time accurately. A computer is considered as a machine, which performs number of operations.

Development of Computer

It all started; about in 3000 B.C. a simple instrument called 'Abacus' was invented. The word Abacus is made from the Latin word 'Abac' whose meaning is the plain surface of sand. This was the first instrument used for computing. This simple instrument changed the world of computing. There is no record form where the abacus was invented. But the earliest form of this was used in Mesopotamia. Many countries are still using this instrument these days. Some of these countries are China and many countries of the western world. Basically it is a frame with several wires across it, on each of which are strung a number of beads.

Abacus can perform the calculations of addition and subtraction very well, but it is difficult to perform the calculations of multiplication calculations like addition, subtraction, multiplication and division of numbers.

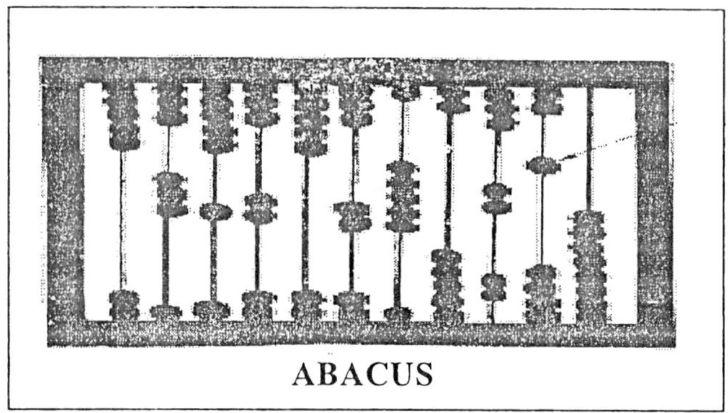

ABACUS

Shikard's Calculator

In 1630 a German mathematician Wugekn Shikard designed a mechanical calculator, which was able to do simple arithmetic calculations like addition, subtraction, multiplication and division of numbers.

Pascal's Calculator (Pascaline)

After years of Shikard's calculator a famous philosopher and mathematician Blaise Pascal of France invented a calculator, which was known as 'Pascaline'. Blaise Pascal made many changes in this instrument but this instrument couldn't get success. The reason was its high cost.

Lebnitz's Calculator

In 1671 Blaise Pascal's Pascaline' was further improved by the great German scientist Gaut Fraid Lebnitz. This machine was able to do arithmetic calculations very simply. After the invention of this calculator there was a long dark period of about one hundred and fifty years. In this dark period no such serious effort was made.

Babbage's Engine

In 1823 A great British mathematician Professor Charlse Babbage of Cambridge University, Britain Began work with the help of British Government and developed a machine called 'Deference Engine'. This was a mechanical machine and was able to perform algebraic, arithmetic and statistical calculations. This Deference Engine incorporated four parts.

- An Input/Output device for inputs and outputs
- A memory unit for storage
- A mill for process
- A sequential program controller to control the process.

Modern computers also use the similar concept. For his pioneering concept, he is known as the 'Father of Computers' in computer world. But the main drawback of this machine was that it was very difficult to understand by other scientists due to its complicated structure, Charles Babbage was not satisfied with his 'Deference Engine' so he made many changes and after ten years he invented a more advanced machine called Analytical Engine. This was the first step in the automation of computing and is an ideal for today's computer scientists.

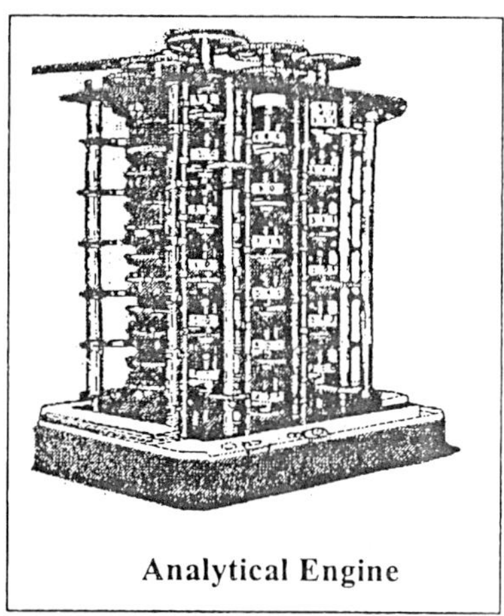

Analytical Engine

Stage of Computer Development

If we judge according to the time frame and electronic components used for the growth of computer industry we will get different generations of computers. Study the following paragraphs to know about the different generation of computers.

IBM-Mark1

In 1938-39 Professor Howard A. Aiken, Director of mathematics department Howard University, U.S.A. and an American company IBM (International Business Machine) Corp. signed an agreement to design an automatic machine. In this

IBM's Founder: Thomas J. Watson Sr.

agreement the role of IBM was to arrange the money and laboratory for research. This dream came true in 1944. They named it A.S.C.C. (Automatic Sequenced Controlled Calculator), which was later known, as 'IBM-MARK11'. This was an electro-mechanical machine rather than mechanical. Punched cards were fed into the machine and result were output onto a punched card machine or electronic typewriter– connected to the machine.

ASCC was a very large machine and was able to perform all types of mathematical calculations. The name of the machine indicates that this was the calculator but actually this machine was able to take decisions independently.

ENIAC

In 1945 Sir Ambrose Fleming developed the Vacuum tube, which were used as electronic switches. Vacuum Tubes were electronic devices and made of glass tubes. After the invention of vacuum tubes two American scientists J. Presper Eckert and John Mauchly started their work at Moore School of Engineering, University of Pennsylvania. Research of these two scientists was based on Vacuum tubes.

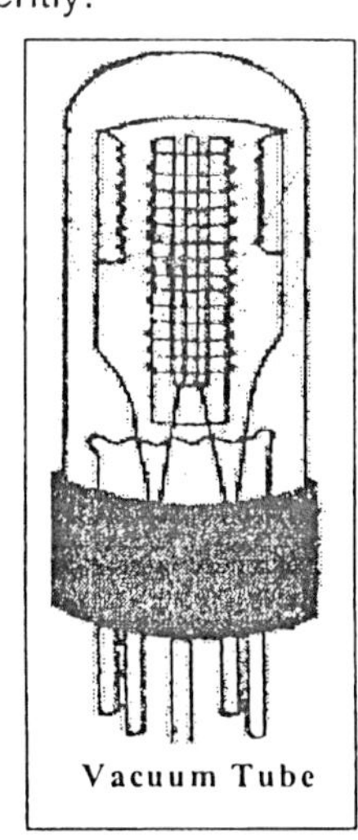

Vacuum Tube

And was aided by U.S. Department of Defence. And in 1946 they developed the world's first electronic computer. They named in ENIAC (Electronic Numerical Integrator And Calculator.) ENIAC contained about 18,000 Vacuum tubes and about 6000 switches. Each Vacuum tube could hold one bit and representation of one character required 6 bits. This machine was about 5000 times faster then the IBM-MARK1. But mere were many disadvantages of this machine like, the size of machine was very large while the memory was very small. This machine consumed very high power (in many Kilowatts.) Major disadvantage of this machine was that it produced a large amount of heat, due to this everyday one or more tubes burnt and the replacement of these tubes was very difficult. Also it was very difficult to work on this machine for a long time continuously due to heat. To eliminate the problems created due to overheat it air-conditioned environment.

IBM-7090

In 1948 a new type of technology was invented by a team of three scientists of AT&T Bell Laboratory of, U.S.A. They named it Transistor technology. These transistors changed the world of electronics. The working of these transistors was similar to Vacuum tubes in many ways. Transistors consumed very low electricity and reduced the size of different instruments. Vacuum tubes were made of glass and used different gases inside it, whereas transistors were made of solid metal, so it was very easy to transport instruments based on transistors rather man Vacuum tubes. Hence the electronic instruments based on transistors are also known as 'Solid State'. Transistors also reduced the size of electronic instruments very much in comparison to instruments based on Vacuum tubes. To use this technology

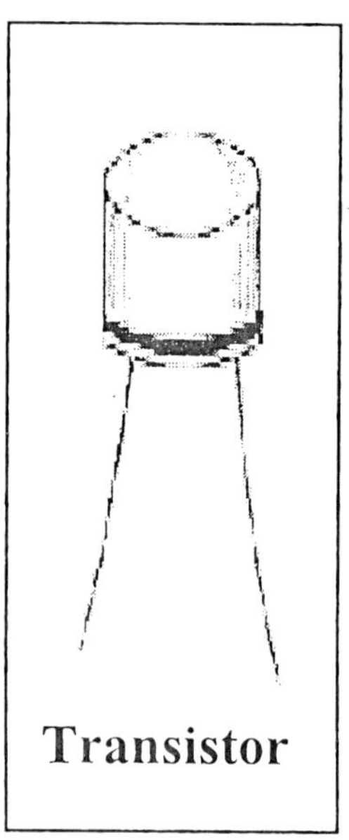

Transistor

IBM Corp. Developed the world's first computer, completely based on transistors. IBM corp. named it 'IBM -7090'. This computer was smaller in size in comparison to earlier computers and was able to for lier computers and was able to for run many hours continuously.

After the invention of transistors many scientists started their research. The aim of research was to reduce the size of various electronic instruments. In this race, a scientist J.S. Kilvi of Texas Instruments Co. of U.S.A., invented integrated Circuit (IC) Chip in 1958. These IC chips are very smaller in size than the transistors. These chips are further improved and known as LSI (Large Scale Integration) and VLSI (Very Large Scale Integration). Today's computers are completely based on these chips.

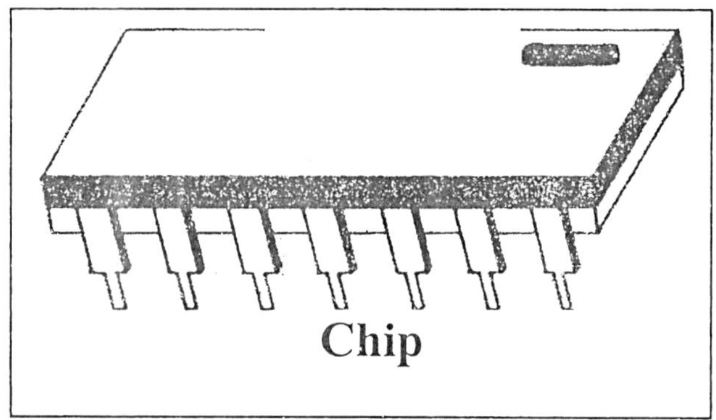

Chip

HISTORY OF COMPUTERS IN INDIA

The arrival of computers is in India is not very old. The first computer system, which came in India, was a mini-computer. Name of the computer was HEC-II purchased by Indian Statistical Institute (ISI), Calcutta. This mini computer as installed in 1955 which was supplied by Hollerith India Ltd. Second computer was also purchased by the same institute of Fundamental Research, Bombay established computer centres in 1963, and 1964 the first Indian computer ISIJU was jointly designed and developed by Indian Statistical Institute (ISI) and Jadavpur University, Calcutta. This computer was installed in Jadavpur University.

The period between 1960 and 1972 saw only 186 computers installations in the country. In those days Electronic as an industry was not familiar to the country. To get self-sufficiency in the production of computer-ECIL (Electronics Corporation in Indian Ltd.), Hyderabad started producing TDC-12 mini computer in 1973. TDC-12 was designed by Bhabha Atomic Research Centre (BARC) Bombay. After some time ECIL produced two modified versions named TDC-312 and TDC-316. At this time private industries were not involved in the manufacturing of computers in India. PSI was the first Indian manufactures which obtained a license in the private sector. The small-scale industries in the private sector made its debut in the field of microcomputers in 1980.

Up to this time most of the commercial computers available were restricted to the Research & Development (R &D) and large educational institute. In fact, till as late as 1982, out of the top 100 companies in the country, only a 6 had any sort of EDP department at all. The period between 1978 and 1981 saw the market place expanding slowly with Hindustan Computers Ltd. (HCL) was sitting firmly on the top of the commercial segment.

In 1980, the government began to play a more positive role for the industry. The year it compelled the LIC (Life Insurance Corp) union to install computers at the branch level as replacement for their earlier accounting machines. It was also announced to computerize on other sectors of government as well.

Between 1981 to 1983 the market had expanded considerable and 8-bit machine which had become a standard by then, were slowly on their way out and the 16-bit systems built around Inter chips were trying to enter in the market.

Indian Computer Industry began to feel the necessity of P.C.'s. In 1984 the new computer policy was released. Government opened the country to a virtual flood or systems, both in terms of numbers and technology. Finally PC revolution started from here and new companies sprouted in all comers of the country.

IMPORTANCE OF COMPUTERS

Almost a century ago when the first industrial revolution began, then within a short span of time many countries became industrialized. Now we are in the beginning of another industrial revolution. The major cause of the second industrial revolution is the invention of computers. Man has invents many electronic devices but computer has made a greater impact on society than any other single electronic device. Now a question arises that what are a computer and what function computer can perform?

What is Computer?

Computer is a device, which can compute. In the starting computer was able to perform only mathematical calculations but now it can do a variety of tasks. So we can say that computer is an electronic device, which works under a set of instructions, automatically accepts the supplied data, process and analyse the data and produces the information.

Capabilities of Computers

Computer has affected the human life very much, because it can do a variety of tasks easily, which men cannot do easily. These days computer has entered in all parts of human life. Few of these capabilities of computer are enough to show the importance of computers.

1. Speed

Fast speed of computer is one of the importance characteristics. It can do calculations in micro or even in nano-seconds. Modem computers are able to process millions or even billions of instructions in a second. We can imagine the high speed of computer from this fact while the human brain can take 40,000 instruction per second, computer may take up to 140,000 million instruction pre-second. Also human brain transmits binary pulses (signals) ten billion times slower than a microcomputer.

2. Accuracy

Computers do not lose the accuracy even if they work at very high speed. If a person increases the speed, chances of errors also increase. This is the major difference between human brain and computers. Due to this characteristic human can depend on computers. While the computers are highly accurate machines, these machines can also errors. But these errors mainly depend on user, not on the machines. Also these machines can do repetitive tasks without any error as many times.

3. Data Storage

Storage capacity of computer is very high. It can store large amount of data in a very little space. It uses many devices to store the data such as floppy disks, hard disks, optical disks, magnetic tapes etc., we can just imagine the storage capacity of computer from this fact that one optical disk can store many encyclopedias in it. Today's research is mainly concentrated on speed and storage capacity.

4. Power of Remembering

Power of remembering of the computer is hundred percent. A man can forget the information as the passes but the computer retains the information several years without losing the quality of information or data. Unlike man every piece of information can be recalled as and when required. A computer forgets or loses certain information only when it is asked to do so. So, it is entirely up to the user to make a computer retain or forget particular information.

5. Activeness

Unlike human beings, computer does not feel tiredness and carelessness. After a long period of continuous work human loses its concentration and decreases the efficiency, but the computers are free from types of problems.

6. Versatility

Computer's enormous speed, memory and accuracy has made it the most popular machine. Another reason of its popularity is that computer can do a variety of jobs well. Engineers and scientific make use of the high speed computing capability of computers to solve their complex research and design problems.

In business and commercial organization, computers are used to systems. These are extensively used in manufacturing and process control, airline and railway reservation system, in banking, weather forecasting and also in sending mails.

Today space technology complete depends on computers. To make use of computer man has reached the moon and is trying to reach other planets. We can imagine the role of computers in space technology from this incident in U.S.A., just before the final countdown, space shuttle Columbia was abruptly stopped for sometime. The reason was difference by a few milliseconds noticed between the computers aboard the spacecraft and the ones at the mission control of Houston.

These are some of the fields, which are making full use of computers. Computers are also playing an important role in many other fields.

LIMITATIONS OF COMPUTERS

Even the computer is a machine, which can perform a variety of tasks, but it has also some limitations. Some limitations area—

1. Lack of Intelligence

Computer is a man made machine, but it has no brain by itself. Computer cannot think by itself. This machine works under the detailed step-by-step instruction of a stored program which automatically accepts the supplied data, process data and produces information. If any problem occurs at the time of execution or any logical error on program then it cannot detect them easily. Thus, to operate computers trained personal are required.

2. Lack of Sense

Computer has no intuition. It can do only those jobs defined by the programmer. Unlike humans it cannot jump any step without executing them. This is a machine, which carries out the instructions defined by the programmer no matter they are right or wrong. Also computer cannot learn from its experiences.

CLASSIFICATION OF COMPUTERS

Since computer has become very popular, there are various types of computers available these days. These computers can be classified in various categories as follows—

1. Classification by generation
2. Classification by principle
3. Classification by size
4. Classification by application

Classification by Generation

Computers can be classified in five generations. These are—

A. First generation (1946-59)
B. Second generation (1959-65)
C. Third generation (1965-70)
D. Forth generation (1970 - latest)
E. Fifth generation (under Development)

A. First Generation

First generation computers used value technology (I.e. vacuum tubes). The development of vacuum tubes led the use of very high speed vacuum switching devices in place of the electromechanical devices. These tubes consumed very high power and produced large amount of heat. These computers used low level programming languages like machine language or assembly language. Some computers of this generation were—

ENIAC

This was the first electronic computer of the generation. ENIAC stands for Electronic Numerical Integrator and Calculator. This computer was introduced in 1946 at the More School of Engineering of the Pennsylvania USA. A team of engineering led by John Mauchly and Prospect Eckert constructed this. ENIAC contained about 18,000 vacuum tubes. Each tube could hold one bit and a set of six bits needed to form a character. This was the first large-scale value based electronic computer. This computer was hundreds of time faster than the earlier computers, but the major problems with this machine was its huge size and large amount of heat.

EDSAC

In 1949, Professor Maurice Wilkes of Cambridge University, England developed a computer named EDSAC (Electronic Delay Storage Automatic Computer). This machine was able to perform different mathematical calculations in microseconds.

EDVAC

Almost simultaneously with EDSAC, in 1952 Dr. John Von Neumann of the Pennsylvania University developed another computer named EDVAC (Electronic Discrete Variable Automatic Computer). This was a refinement of ENIAC computer. This computer was based on a new concept of "stored program" developed by Dr. Von Neumann. The basic idea behind the stored program concept is that is sequence of instructions and the data can be stored in the computers memory for the purpose of automatically directing the flow of operations. Dr. Neumann also used first time storing and manipulating data and instructions in the binary form. All modem digital computers (except supper-computer) are designed on Von Neumann design.

IBM-701

In 1952, IBM Corp developed a computer IBM-701. This was an electronic computer. This computer used magnetic drum for data storage. This consisted of a cylinder coated with a magnetic recording material. This device could access data hundreds of time faster than the punched cards. But the major problem with these drums was that they could not be removed from the drive unit and capacity was very limited.

UNIVAC

After the invention of ENIAC computer, developers of this computer Eckert and Mauchly left the Pennsylvania University and formed their company. They developed a new computer and named it UNWAC (University Automatic Computer). This computer used magnetic tapes first time for input and output. This computer became very popular due to its smaller size and had very low cost than the earlier computers. UNIVAC computer was widely used in business and commercial fields. Some other computers of this generation were LEO, IBM-700 series.

Manufactures of first generation computers

Manufacture	*Computer*
Pennsylvania	ENIAC
Cambridge University	EDSAC
Pennsylvania University	EDVAC
IBM Crop	IBM-701

B. Second Generation

With the advent to transistor technology, second generation of computers came into existence. Transistors were usually made of silicon metal which is a semiconductor. Working of these transistors was similar to vacuum tubes, but these were smaller in size and generated less heat in comparison to vacuum tubes. Transistor technology ended the value industry. Seconds generation computers were more reliable and highly efficient. These were easy to transport due to its "solid state". These computers used High Level Language like BASIC etc. These languages are English language, which are easy to programme and understand. Second generation computers used magnetic tapes or magnetic drum for secondary storage purpose, Some of the second generation computers were WHIRLWIND-I developed at Massachusetts Institute of Technology (MIT), TDC-12 of Electronic Corporation of India Ltd. (ECIL), Hyderabad, IBM 7000, LEO MARK III, Honeywell series, UNIWAC-III etc.

C. Third Generation

J.S Killvi of Texas Instrument Co. introduced a new technology in 1958, which made possible to combine hundreds or even thousands of transistors, diodes and other components in a small single chip. This chip is known as Integrated Circuit (IC) chips, which is a solid state micro-electronic technology. Third generation computers were based on these IC chips. These computers were very low in cost and the speed was thousand of time faster than the first generation computers. These computers could process data and instruction in micro (10^{-6}) or even in nanoseconds (10^{-9}). Mini computer was first introduced in this generation computers used FORTRAN and COBOL languages which were also developed in this generation. Third generation computers made possible the multi-programming and multiprocessing concepts. These computers used improve input/output units and backing storage devices. Third generation became very popular in many colleges, universities, laboratories etc. Some third generation computers were -IBM -360 series, IBM-370 series, and TDC-312 developed by Electronic Corporation of India Ltd. (ECIL), Hyderabad etc.

D. Fourth Generation

IC chips, which are used in third generation computers, contained hundreds or even thousand of transistors and other components on a single chip. These chips were also known Scale integration (SSI) and Medium Scale Integration (MSI).

Invention of MOS (Metal Oxide Semiconductor) technology made possible to put million of components on a single chips known as Large Scale Integration (LSI) and Very Larger Scale Integration (VLSI). These VLSI techniques made possible to combine the ALU (Arithmetic and Logical Unit) and CU (Control Unit) on a tiny square chip. This was the "microprocessor", which was the used first time in this generation's computers. Intel Crop developed the first microprocessor chip. Of U.S.A. the Invention of microprocessor chip made a revolution in the computer industry. Fourth generation computers are much faster and cheaper than the second-generation computers. These computers have greater data processing capacity and can process data at the second. These computers can be connected with communication lines to form a communication link from one part to the other part of world. Fourth generation computers use different high level language and many application packages for different type of application such as Computer Aided Design (CAD) for designing purpose, Dbase, FOXPRO for data based management. Some fourth generation computer manufactures are—IBM, Hewlett-Packard, Apple etc.

E. Fifth Generation

Fifth generation computers are expected to have capabilities like recognition of voice, response of voice. These computers will be able to learn and think. For these types of ability a new technique, Artificial Intelligence has been developed.

Voice recognition is a technique in which a computer will be able to recognize the human voice. In these types of system, computer consists of a microphone, which recognizes the user's word, translate it into digital form, then this translated signal is analysed with a dictionary of patterns stored in the computer's memory. Recognizes words are matched steps-by-step and the computer uses when a match is found then corresponding words. Voice response is a techniques in which a computer will be able to talk with the user. In this system input data is processed and output is converted to appropriate sound.

These computers will be very small in size and will have the tremendous data processing speed and storage capacity. This fifth generation computer will use different and much improved memory devices such as bubble memory and optical disk.

Classification by Principle

Based on their working and electronics computers can be classified into three categories—

1. Analog Computer
2. Digital Computer
3. Hybrid Computer

1. Analog Computer

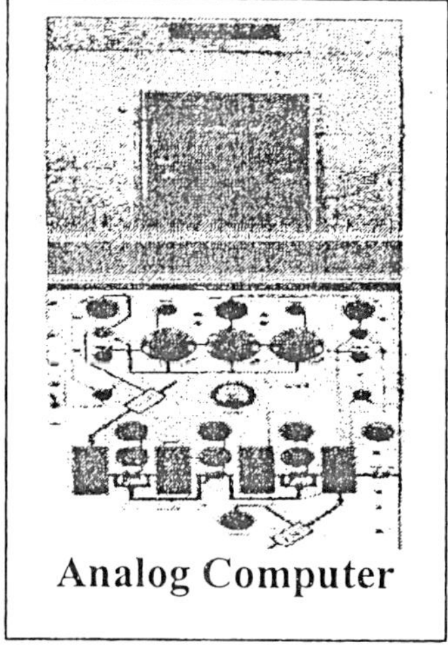
Analog Computer

Analog computer operates at continuous voltage or current. This name is derived from the Greek word "Analog" which means to find out similarity between two quantities. These are mainly used to solve manufacturing, design and scientific problems. These computers have to be construed to perform only specific task. An example if this is the constant monitoring of the Electronic Cardiogram of a patient. Polyp emus were the first fully electronic analog computer, which was developed by George Phil brick. Analog computers are less accuracy of these computers can be up to 99 per cent.

2. Digital Computer

Digital computer operates on electric inputs that have only two states on and Off (i.e. binary Ones and Zeros). The word computer is generally used for these binary digital computers. Digital computers are useful for evaluating arithmetic expressions and manipulation of data. The accuracy and speed of digital computers are very high in comparison to analog computers. These computers are cheaper and smaller in size in comparison to analog computers. Digital computer are the most popular computers all over the world these days.

3. Hybrid Computer

In some applications both digital and analog features are used to solve problems. So a new types of computer is developed which is party digital and partly analog that means a computer which has the properly of both computers. Such computers are called Hybrid computers. Hybrid computers are not widely used.

Classification of Size

In this classification, computer is classified according to size (not the physical, size in terms of speed, capacity and other Functions). Computers can be divided as follows:

1. Microcomputers
2. Minicomputers
3. Mainframes
4. Supercomputers

1. Microcomputers

In the last fifteen years we have passed through a major revaluation - a revaluation is affecting the way all of us live. This is the electronic revaluation. This electronic revaluation introduced microcomputers. These are called microcomputers because these types are the smallest type in size, speed and capacity amongst all types of computers. Microcomputers have all the functional elements found in a large computer: These computers can used by only one person at a time. Microcomputers usually have a 8 bit or 16 bit or 32 bit microprocessor and have two types of memory -RAM (Random Access Memory) and ROM (Read Only Memory), Programs and data are held in RAM during processing whereas some permanent instructions are held on ROM. One of the earliest microcomputer kits was Atari 8800 designed by Ed Roberts of Micro Instrumentation and Telemetry System (MITS) in early 1975. Microcomputer can be further classified into three categories—

a. Home computers
b. Personal Computers
c. Lap-top Computers

a. Home computers

Home computers are the smallest in microcomputers in terms of speed and capacity. They use Television (TV) as a display unit and audiocassettes to store data and information permanently. 3½ inch size floppy diskettes are also used for storing data. Families to store its daily information like daily expenses use home computers. These computers are also used for playing different types of computer games, and for educational purpose. The first home computer was "Atari VCS 2600' which was the developed by ATARI Corp. in 1978.

After this models many others modified models were introduced. But all these models were used for playing games only. In 1980 a British scientist Sir Clive Sinclair announced the first home computer, which could bc used for more than just playing games. This was the Sinclair ZX-80. Sinclair introduced many other modified models after ZX-80. Some of these were

Home Computer

- Sinclair ZX-81 with 1K RAM
- Sinclair Spectrum
- Sinclair QL contained a 16-bit microprocessor and was able to run software like graphics, spreadsheets, word processors and databases.

Due to the need of large software's and improved technology, home computers have been outdated now.

b. Personal Computer

It is the personal computer, which has deeply affected the human life. Personal Computers are commonly known as PC. Personal Computers are better than the home computers in every aspects (i.e. speed, capacity, memory etc.). These Computers use a separate TV like monitor as a display device and floppy diskettes usually 3½ inch, 5¼ inch, hard disk etc. as secondary storage device. Personal Computers are used for graphics applications, for Computer Aided Design (CAD) applications. Personal computers are also divided into three categories—PC (Advanced Technology). Amongst the three,

P.C's are the lowest in speed, capacity and memory whereas PC-AT are the fastest computers. PC-XT lies between these two. Personal computers have become,the most popular in all types of computers and are widely used by individual professionals - like doctors, chartered accountants and even in shops and restaurants.

More and more companies manufacture personal computers these days in large quantity. Some of the major companies involved in production are - Apple Computers Inc., IBM Corps, Digital Equipment Corp., Hewlett-Packard and many more.

c. Lap-top Computers

These computers looks like a briefcase. In the lap-top computers upper part contains the display unit and lower part contains the keyboard, CPU and floppy drive. These computers usually contain 3.5-inch floppy drive. These computers use very little power and can be run either by cells or main supply. Due to the use of cells these computers are portable. Another reason of portability is the light weight (only 2-3 kg) of these computers.

Laptop Computer

2. Minicomputers

Minicomputers are large computers in comparison to micro-computers. Micro-computers support only one user at a time whereas minicomputers can support more than one user at a time. These computers have large memory, speed and data storage capacity than the

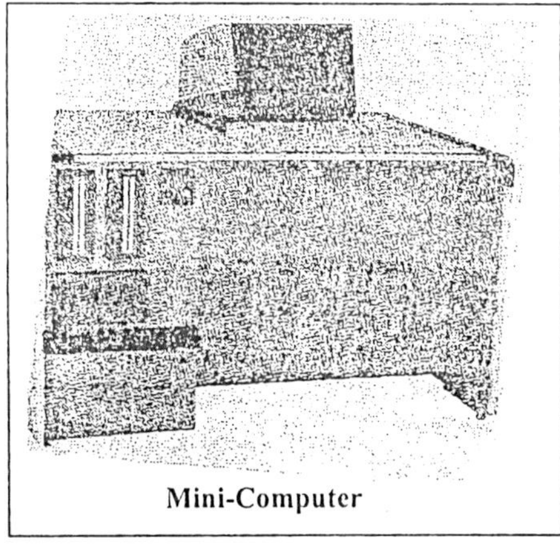

Mini-Computer

micros. The cost of minicomputers lies in 3-4 lakes these days. In 1959 Digital Equipment Corp. (DEC) developed the first minicomputer named PDP-8 and PDP-11. The speed and memory of those minicomputers were much smaller than today's microcomputers, but those machines were very popular in 1960's and 70's. These days minicomputers are widely used by medium size organizations, Research and development departments and by many other departments.

3. Mainframes

Mainframes computers are very large computers and have a great storage capacity and processing speeds. Mainframes use several microprocessors in place of single microprocessor used in micros or in minis. These computers can be linked into a network with many micros. Mainframe support many hundreds user. These are mainly used for commercial applications and by government department such as a railway and airline reservation systems. Mainframes use magnetic are IBM360 and 370 series, and CDS cyber series.

4. Super Computer

Supper computers are the most powerful among all the computers. All the computers are based on von-Neumann design but the super-computers use Non-von Neumann design. Super. Computers contain many processors and use parallel processing, These computers use more advanced devices for memory like bubble memory and can process billions of instructors per-second. Super computers are used for complex scientific applications such as weather forecasting. First supper computer was developed by Cray Research and Control Data Corp. of United States. Some other is CRAY-XMP24, CDC-205, Flow Solver developed by Center for Development and Advanced Computing (C-DAC) under the Department of Electronics, India.

Classification by Application

In this type of classification, computers are classified on their applications. These can be of two types—

1. General Purpose Computers
2. Special Purpose Computers

1. General Purpose Computers

General purpose computers are designed to solve a large number of common problems of different types. In a general purpose computer, instructions for another job can be loaded into the memory of computer for further processing. General purpose computers are, usually the digital computers and are used to prepare pay bills, manage inventories and so on.

2. Special Purpose Computers

Special purpose computers are usually analog computers. These computers are designed to perform special tasks or applications. The set of instructions required for the particular application are permanently stored in the memory of computer, so that it can perform the given task by a single command.

Use of A Computer

A computer is used in all human life. It has revolutionized all spheres of human activities. The most important areas have been given as follow:

1. ***Routine Job Handling:*** The routine classical and steno type jobs calculating and formality bitts, salaries, updating stokes, tax return, reservations records and information are stored by the computer carefully.
2. ***Traffic Control:*** Controlling traffic, traffic lights. Television cameras are used to maintain traffic light routine.
3. ***Electronic Money:*** Automatic teller machine (ATM) is very common in banks. You can deposit and with draw money with the help of ATM.
4. ***Industrial Application:*** It plays an important role in production controls. It bring efficiency in trade and industry.
5. ***Trade:*** In every trade computer is used successfully. It is used in Banks, Stock Exchanges, to control stocks and accounts.
6. ***Scientific Research:*** In every science the research work become economical from time energy and from the money point of view. A large data is analysed very quickly and successfully.
7. **Medicine:** There is wide use in medical sciences e.g. ECG, CAT Scan., Ultra Sound, etc. The proper and accounts

diagnosis is done with the help of computer. The medical apparatus are logically computerized.

8. ***Space science:*** The satellites are controlling the space with the help of computer. The information's are collected and after analysing, used to control the satellites. In this process the computer is playing a very important and vital role for the success of space research.
9. ***Publication:*** The composing work is speedily and economical with the help of computer. Computer also does the disfiguring work. The quality is maintained in publication by computer.
10. ***Communications:*** The computer is used for sending message e.g. Teleprinter, tax, e-mail, Internet etc. The import and export work is done on Internet.
11. ***Education:*** The computer is widely used in the field of education. An independent study field of computer science has developed which is very popular these days. All every stage computer education is compulsory. The distance education is using computer for instructional purpose as multi-media approach. The computer makes teacher-learning process effective by involving audio and visual sense of learners.

COMPUTER IN EDUCATION

One of the most significant forces, influencing change in education in the present century is the emergence of highly advanced communication technologies. The distance education system being and innovation in itself, is continuously influenced by these technological reforms. The distance education institutions in some developed countries have grown very much dependent on these technological advances. The media have become almost an indispensable part of the whole education system in those countries.

The fundamental premise of distance education is the assumption that it has to provide individuals 'Access' to the learning attained in it should not be inferior in any sense to the learning attained in a traditional institution. Knowledge about recent technological developments will help becoming critically aware of the new opportunities for increasing accessibility to education and maintaining the quality of education. Due to various constrains, at present developing countries like India are unable to benefit fully from these technological advances. But by becoming aware of the opportunities that are available, Indian educators can feel more confident that there are technologies that can help them to improve the quality of education and to increase the accessibility of education to masses. The following are the other non-print Media of education:

1. Computer as Non-print and Print Media,
2. Teleconferencing,
3. Videodisk, as Non-print and
4. Videotex Print Media.

1. Computer as Non-print and Print Media

Computer is an important technology used in distance education. During the past decade, the computer has become one of the most widely used aids to education instruction in the developed countries, chiefly because of its interactive capabilities.

A longer list of its advantages, besides its interactive capabilities can be drawn to prove that the computer is an asset to distance learning. A computer can record, analyse and react to student's responses, it can store and manipulate information on an extensive scale, can control and manage a wide variety of learning materials it can simultaneously cop with the learning requirements of many individuals. In addition, it can by itself, offer instruction of learners. It can, moreover, through its electronic circuit, accurately make a myriad of decision necessary to the planning and implementation of an individualized programme of instruction on a mass basis in almost no time.

Technical Description of Computer

A computer is an electronic device that accepts data, performs operations on that data in sequence (decided by a programme) and outputs the results. Computers are termed according to their side and thus we come across terms like mainframe computers, mini-computers and microcomputers. Besides size, specifications of the electronic devices (that differ from computer to computer) are also used to identify computer types. 'The specification includes details about the amount and type of storage, the capabilities of the central processing unit, and the type and the nature of the peripheral equipment (such as disc storage) that can be connected to the computer. The advent of microcomputers in the 1970s at comparatively cheaper price made the accessible to many people and made the possibility of using them for educational purpose a reality. The basic micro computed system consists of an input device (e.g., the keyboard), the central processing unit of the computer and storage devices (e.g., cassette tape player; floppy disc device) and the output device (e.g., and TV) display unit, or a monitor and printing terminals. The actual equipment of the computer system is called the hardware, while the term software refers to the instructions of the programmes that the computer carries out.

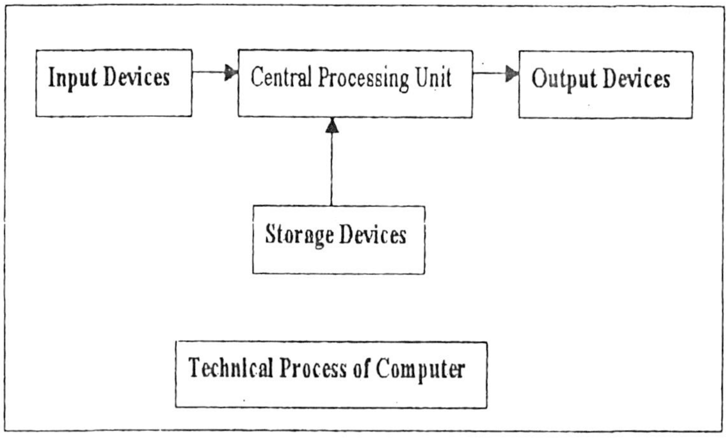

Technical Process of Computer

Application of Computer

Two types of application of computer is popular in India, These are as:

1. Administrative Applications of Computers.
2. Instructional Situations of Computer Application.

1. Administrative Applications of Computers

(a) Budgeting and monitoring of finances.

(b) Keeping students records.

(c) Maintaining Statistics.

(d) Student Billing.

(e) Preparation of payroll, bills and date ledger.

(f) Mailing of score.

(g) Monitoring materials production register and so on.

2. Instructional Situations of Computer Application

(i) Pre-testing of student's knowledge on enrolment

(ii) Planning and printing individualized programmes

(iii) Monitoring students progress and

(iv) Compiling test and scores etc. A number of such data files can be stored in the computer.

Advantages of Computer

The computer applications described above have certain remarkable advantages over the traditional 'print' medium of instruction. These advantages can be briefly pointed out in the form of the following hints:

1. The novelty of working with a computer raises the learner motivation;
2. Colour, music and animated graphics can add realism and appeal to drilling exercises, laboratory activities, simulations etc.
3. High-speed personalized responses to learner actions yield a high rate of reinforcement;
4. Memory capacity allows student's past performance to be recorded and used in planning the subsequent steps;
5. Step, can present a more positive and effective climate, especially for slow learner.
6. The record keeping ability of the computer makes individualized instructional feasible and individual prescriptions can be prepared for all students (particularly mainstreamed special students) and their progress can be monitored; and
7. The teacher's span of control's enlarged, as more information is put easily at the teacher's disposal.

Scope of Computer

Certain characteristics of computer-interaction can make computers well suited for distance learning. The features listed below make the prospects of computer-use look more promising:

1. Access to experts and respected peers
2. One-to-one and one-many communications
3. Active learner participation
4. Linking of new learning to concrete on-the-job problems
5. Follow up, feedback and implementation support from peers or experts
6. Self-direction-control over stop or start, time, pace and place of learning or communication activity.

Limitations of Computer

In spite of the advantages and the promising prospects, computers do differ from some disadvantages too. Some of the major limitations are:

1. Despite the dramatic reduction in cost of computer and computer use, computerized instruction is still relatively expensive. Careful consideration must be given to the costs and benefits of computers in education. Maintenance can also be a problem especially if the equipment is subjected to heavy use.
2. The design and production of computer specifically for instructional purposes has lagged being design and production for other purposes.
3. There is a lack of high quality direct-instruction matter for use with computers, especially for the microcomputers. Their use with computers, especially for the microcomputers.

There is also a compatibility problem-often the software developed for one computer system cannot be used with another. The ease with which the software-especially cassettes can be duplicate without permission has inhibited commercial publishers and private entrepreneurs from producing, and marketing instructional software (Heinich et al. 1982: 318).

2. Teleconferencing

Educational teleconferencing can be a valuable medium for interactive group communication by means of a two-way broadcast. Three main types of teleconferencing have been identified:

(i) Audio teleconferencing
(ii) Video teleconferencing and
(iii) Computer teleconferencing.

We discuss audio teleconferencing being the most commonly used technique in distance education institution in detail.

Till the early 1980 audio teleconferencing was at a experimental stage and was used occasionally. But during the past few years it grew to be a routing part of the delivery strategies of some distance education institutions. It was found that with the use of this means, the communication costs could be reduced and the quality of service to distant learners could be improved without compromising the academic integrity of the programmes the flexibility, and the low capital and operating costs of studio teleconferencing make it a communication—means of special interest of institutions serving students who live in small and widely separated communities. Today, the dependence on this technology is accelerating. The interest in using audio and related visual data that can be transmitted over regular telephone lines appears to be related to the growth of education.

Technical Description of Teleconferencing

Teleconferencing is an electronic means which can brings together three or four people in two or more locations to discuss or share the use of two-way and one-way video, both full motion and slow scan, electronic black of boards, facsimile, computer graphic, radio, satellite and Videotex. However the most essential part of all forums of teleconferencing is a good quality audio to help immediate interaction among the participates for information exchange.

Audio teleconferencing requires a multi-telephone line electronic switch or interconnection device called a bridge to which the used can attach a wide variety of data transmission devices and telephone. The normal practice is to connect device per line into the bridge. Audio equipments used with the bridge are the usual handsets, speakerphones, radio-telephones, and microphone speaker units (often caller 'conveners').

Audio teleconferencing uses regular telephone lines provided by local public telephone companies. If the quality of standard business or household line is good enough, virtually any line could be used.

Effective content environment

Occasional users normally purchases their service from the local telephone company, teleconferencing consultants or major user that is willing to sell available time on its system. Any specialized terminal equipment is usually rented for a including all necessary equipment long distance tool charges, and user training.

The costs for starting a university or college-based private audio teleconferencing system are not large if the local telephone system has:

(i) A relatively quiet line,
(ii) Ready accessibility, and
(iii) Acceptable local and long distance rates.

Advantages of Teleconferencing

There have been a few studies on the effectiveness of audio teleconferencing from the point of view of student learning. These studies show that the telephone was as effective a medium as face-to-face teaching. A study conducted in Canada (Roberston, 1986) found that upper level undergraduate statistics students taught on teleconference did as well as or better than most campus based students and had a drop-out rate of zero. Traditional correspondence institution on the other hand, average 40-60 per cent dropout rates. Satisfaction among the students was recorded high and remote learners though the course did not lack rigor or suitable contact.

During the 1984 International symposium on Teleconferencing mere as evidence for strong support for educational audio teleconferencing. The support was mainly due to the consideration of the following advantage:

(i) ***Effective support from remote learners:*** Teleconferencing can be very useful when most of the potential students are widely scattered among communities that are far apart and when each centre has them learner population, say less than ten students, on a given course or programme.

(ii) ***Cost effectives***: The cost for starting and operating an audio teleconferencing system is relatively low in comparison with other available methods of serving remote learners.

(iii) ***Flexible system***: The system used can be adjusted quickly to serve large or small group.

(iv) ***Familiar instructional mode***: The mode of instruction is simpler to that the seminar with the instructor being in charge of the discussion and able to stimulate multiplication interaction.

(v) ***Easy scheduling adjustment***: A scheduling adjustment can be made almost as readily as for no-campus classrooms.

(vi) ***Multi-vocational access-control:*** Access to the instruction or programmes can be controlled through a limited number of off-campus centres.

(vii) ***High quality instruction***: The quality of the instructional materials can be maintained high because of the need for careful and easy preparation.

(viii) ***Immediate feedback***: The teleconferencing system provides the facility to the learners for immediate feedback and to convey their reactions to the tutors.

Experiments in Teleconferencing

The potential of teleconferencing as a viable educational medium is being experimented in institutions the world over. The UKOU has been experimenting with its system of teleconferencing called CYCLOPS. As an interactive audio-visual aid the system has helped the learners and the tutors of the experimental groups to write electronically to each other over the telephone and have their words and pictures reproduced at the other and on a TV screen. It was found during the pilot stage of this experiment that nine different groups of leaner scattered hundreds of miles apart could be tutored simultaneously sharing a common picture display and linked by voice through loud speaking telephones. Experiments on teleconferencing are being conducted in India too. The Space applications Center, Ahmedabad, has undertaken some experiments in this direction.

The experiments abroad and within point to feasibility of using teleconferencing as an effective viable to promote education among widely scattered potential learners on low enrolment course.

3. Videodisc As Non-Print Media

Videodisc is comparatively a newer medium that has widened the scope of use of the television set, Videodisc players are available in two models:

(i) Consumer model, and

(ii) Educational industrial model.

The consumer model is basically a playback medium and is mostly used in homes. The educational/industrial model more versatile, it can provide interaction-individualized instruction. Sometimes, it is rendered more capable by means of a built in microprocessor. Videodisc can record materials from a verity of media, including film slides, audio and printed text. This makes rich the opportunities for individualized instruction for students learning at a distance.

(1) Technology of Videodisc

A videodisc system is made up of a videodisc on which the information is stored, a videodisc player and television set. Videodisc is used as information storage medium. A videodisc rotates on the turntable of the videodisc player at a high speed and is read by a stylus or laser. Microscopic pits, of varying length and density, contain information on the disc. The pits are in tracks or gross. The information read room these pits is displayed on a regular television set.

(2) Application of Videodisc

There are two major types of videodisc system: capacitance and optical.

(i) ***Capacitance Videodisc:*** Capacitance is a technical term for the electrical charge that can be collected on a plate. It may very player, which other. Thus, when the stylus rides over the disc (which contains the pits conversed with a plastic coating to even out the surface), the distance between the disc and the stylus varies, causing changes in capacitance to occur. These changes are translated into the video and audio signals which are displayed by the television set.

(ii) ***Optical videodisc:*** The optical videodisc is more useful than the capacitance videodisc. The potential of the optical videodisc lies in its enormous storage capacity and optical disc can store 108,000 tracks (54,000 on each side). Each of the 54,000 frames on a side is addressable with a five-digit number and can be randomly accessed in 5 seconds or less. The entire Encyclopedia Britannica could be stored on a single videodisc with room to spare.

In addition to the information stored onto the disc, there are two channels of accessible audio, the accessibility to the dual audio channels allows for use of a second language, i.e., for the use of one language with the content oriented for a audience of a different linguistic background. It can allow for the addition of stereo sound too.

The videodisc system is capable of fast forward, fast reveres, slow motion and stop frame movement. Individual images can be displayed indefinitely in freeze frame mode without a wear on the disc since there is no mechanical contact. But sound cannot be used in the freeze frame mode.

(iii) ***Intelligent Videodisc:*** The intelligent videodisc system (videodisc connected with computer), which is particularly useful for educations. Consists of a videodisc player under the direct control of a computer. This system permits interactive instruction for individualized learning. The videodisc is used simply as a storage medium for both still frames and video. The external computer programme may be used interactively to compare a student's response with a programmed correct response and can automatically move to a resigned number of material depending on the response. Thus by combining two powerful technologies the computer and the television—the videodisc can offer more individualized and interactive instruction for learners.

(3) Advantages of Videodisc

Use of videodisc is in expensive, when the discs are mass-produced. Besides, the discs require little storage room. These two factors make it possible to gather extensive library of courses on small discs, the discs also provide easy accessibility and retrieval of the material of our choice. The videodisc can be used to increase learner productivity through:

(1) More information in attractive presentation modes,
(2) Immediate access (forward and reverse) to different parts of the disc,
(3) Facility for repetition to achieve mastery,
(4) Higher motivation through simulations of actual events in living colours,
(5) Provision for immediate 'feedback',
(6) Automatic frame stop, and
(7) Provision for students.

(4) Limitations of Videodisc.

However, we have to bear in mind that the information on disc is permanently cached into the surface of the disc. One cannot record new material into a finished disc as one can with videotape.

4. Videotex As Non-Print Media

Video is a system for providing an interactive information retrieval service. This particular technological development is one further step of the 'information revolution' which many industrialized countries are now experiencing. There are three Videotex items prevalent today: British (Prestal), French (Antiope) and Canadian (Telidon).

Videotex allows the home television to function like a computer terminal that retrieves text information and graphics from a remote data. Thus, these technologies bring in the power into home at a reasonable cost.

(1) Technology of Videotex

The basic Videotex system consists of keypad or keyboard, a TV display unit, a decoder, a telecommunication link and a

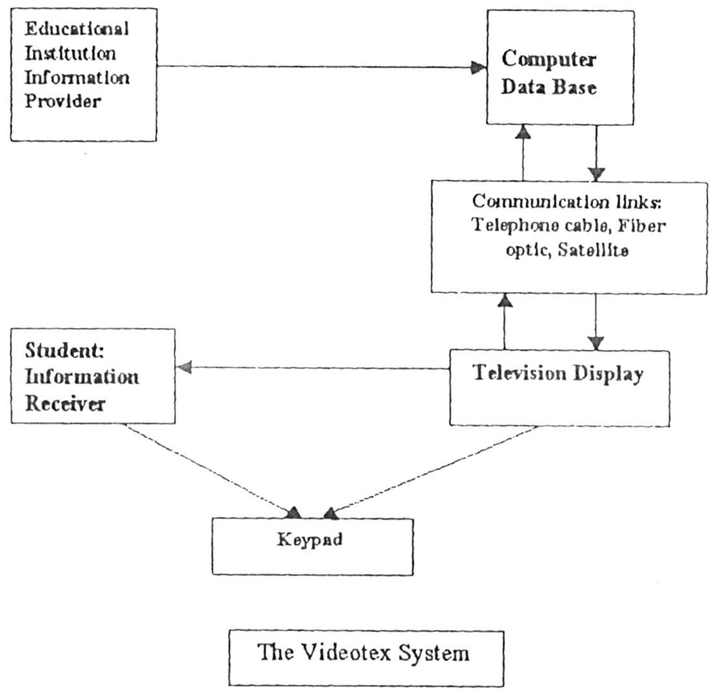

The Videotex System

central computer containing a database. Videotex uses television and telephone in order to provide access to the computerized information. The keypad, a small frame with number-buttons on it, is used to request pages of required information from a remote computer.

The television is connected to the computer by telephone and it is adapted by means of a decoder to display the recordings on Videotex when it is played. Thus the home television set is turned into a terminal. As a television set is already present in most of the homes of developed countries this device promises a wide range of social and educational utility.

The decoder can be wired directly into the television set during the manufacturing process or can be fitted on externally at a later stage. The decoder allows a TV set to display text and graphics from digital transmitted down the telephone line and to transmit back to information entered through keypad. A modem (modulator-de-modulator) enables the computer and the decoder to communicate in digital form over telephone lines designed for the speech.

Videotex offers advantages over other time-bound communication media like radio, television of telephone because it is free from a time schedule. If a keyboard could be added to the user terminal, a Videotex can offer computer-assisted instruction also. Two-way interaction between the teacher and the taught is also possible with alphanumeric keyboard (i.e., a keyboard with number-buttons). This interaction resembles an electronic main, and learner can address questions to the tutor and receive immediate feedback. It is definitely faster than the post and has an advantage over telephone because this kind of interaction does not have to wait for a mutually convenient time for discussion. In the long run it may also prove to be cost-effective.

(2) Application and Advantages of Videotex

Most Videotex application is currently at initial phases, number of applications for Videotex has been tested which as work game teaching a second language, instruction to deal etc. In distance education Videotex can be used for the transmission and to-way interaction on general or specific information courses.

A Videotex system is very useful in disseminating general information about courses and programmes available, in raising the level of awareness of potential learners about education opportunities available.

The system with a substantial database can be very helpful to learners in remote areas as they could have access to the kind and the volume of information currently available to learners in areas with large libraries.

(3) Limitations of Videotex

However, while the Videotex system provides graphic capabilities, there is no provision for including audio. So Videotex would work better if it is used as a part of a multi-media system in providing instructional material. As it is still at an experimental stage, its cost-effectiveness could not be determined. Thus Videotex system provides means for delivering instructional material to those individuals who have chose to learn at a distance.

However, there are, at present few instructional programmes, which are being delivered by this method. To date, most educational applications of Videotex and teletex (a system using a similar technology as that of Videotex and is discussed below) systems have as their information base a catalogue listing the courses available or services provided by the institution.

Teletext—A System Related to Videotex

There are two system that deliver words and graphics to a modified television set-one. Videotex which uses the telephone to connect the user to the data base: two the broadcast version known as Teletext in which pages of information are broadcast in a cycle (usually 400 pages) and - when the requested page comes up in the cycle, it is grabbed, and displayed on the, screen.

With the Videotex the amount of material available for retrieval is limited only by the storage of the host computer. This is in contrast to the Teletext, which has limit on the amount of material that can be transmitted.

Teletext Application in India

The Teletext service in India was formally inaugurated by the doordarshan, Delhi on November 14, 1985. It is known as 'INTEXT' (Meaning Indian teletex). Teletext uses the medium television for transmitting information. The data are organized into pages, which contain text and graphic, symbols. Six colours can be used in creating these graphics. The information is polled and transmitted on a few predetermined lines in vertical "blanking" interval of television signals. The information is in the form of magazines, each of which contains about 100 pages. The details of contents of the magazine are given on the first page.

The news items, sports events, financial trends, timings of arrival and departure of important trains, weather forecast, city engagements, AIR and TV programmes to be telecast, etc., are given through Teletext service. The information is collected through for hot-lines connecting Teletext information-room to:

(i) The meteorological department

(ii) The northern railway central enquiry,

(iii) The Indian Airlines enquiry (for international arrivals) and

(iv) The Air traffic control (for interactional arrivals)

The using the existing Television broadcast, additional information can be transmitted in the form of Teletext service. Efforts are being made to provide the Teletext service on a large scale. In addition, work has been undertaken to develop necessary software for creating pages with characters from different Indian languages. Non-effort has so far been made to use teletex service for educational purpose. In advanced countries also the educational application of telex text has been largely on experimental basis so far.

Use of Computer in India

Computers have been put to a widespread use for educational purpose in the advanced countries. Especially with the advance of the relatively cheap micro-computer, the technology has become more popular with the instruction (CAI) has already been used in Canada and at the Open University in Britain to provide diagnostic feedback remedial help; and revision aids in 1986. The projects in the area of Remedial English in Indian education are a new phenomenon but we have made a beginning in using computers in our school system.

Computer Literacy in India

The Ministry of Human Resource Development in collaboration with the Department of Electronics initiated the project in India in 1983-84. The main objectives of the CLASS project were to demystify computers and acquaint the students and teacher with the computer application and it potential as a learning medium.

CLASS was launched in 248 selected secondary and higher secondary schools representing all geographical areas. Preferential term tent in selection was given to Government schools with limited resources and, whose student population that came largely from the lower socio-economic status. After on, 501 more schools were added in the project. It is proposed to include another 590 schools in the year 1987-88.

The software and hardware components for the project were obtained for the United Kingdom. Since the inception of the project, 3180 teachers have been trained at 10 resource centres. After conduction a study in 250 schools, the Space Applications Centre, Ahmedabad has claimed that the task of demystification of high technology and creation of computer climate had been achieved. NCERT also noted that the programmed had, generated a great interest among the students and the teacher. By 1990, the NCERT hopes to have spread its CLASS programme, to nearly 14,000 higher secondary schools in the country.

Suggestions

As the Videodisc/Videotex are relatively new media, the opportunity of these media to serve distance education are yet to be fully realized. The greatest advantage of the videodisk is its dense storage capacity. The interactive medium can provide educators with a highly effective delivery system for learning at a distance. The use of Videotex is still at an experimental stage but it is believed that Videotex system (such as Telidon, used in Canada) can be an educational medium in his or her own right with a potential to deliver educational material to any participant in the system, at any time and in any location.

Although the use of new technology in the Indian context raises certain issues for educators to reflect upon, it also presents them with new opportunities for overcoming barriers of distance and time.

In spite of the media boom in the field of distance education because of the availability and accessibility of the technological instruments and their great potentiality, it is unfortunate that very few institutions in the world use them to a large extent. Printed material seems to be the main stay of education institutions. Some Australian institutions use audio-cassettes with the printed materials, telemetric, etc., some European institutions use videocassettes; the Open University in Pakistan uses several media successfully. Students enrolling on their computer courses are sent a microcomputer each for their use at home on a loan basis. Some of the distance education institutions in India use radio and TV for their courses. The Indira Gandhi National Open University is pioneering the use of computers in home study. More and more institutions should start using computers for non-instructional purpose to begin with, so that more and more people are educated about the use of computers.

India, as we know, is one of the leading manufactures of computers in the world. Computer process is coming down (pre-budget-estimate). The Government is also coming forward to help educational institutions with computers. Why don't the education institution make use for the opportunity and provide the benefits of the wonder matching for their students? Let us hope that more and more institutions take on the computer in future.

EXERCISE QUESTIONS

1. Define the term 'Computer'. Explain the main characteristic of a good Computer.
2. Indicate the types of Computer. Point out the uses of Computer.
3. Justify Computer as print and Non-print media. Describe the uses of Computer in education.
4. Indicate the stages (Generations) of computer development.
5. Describe the role of computer in individualized instruction and teaching learning.
6. Explain the term 'Computer Assisted Instruction' and its use in education.

CHAPTER 4

DATA REPRESENTATIONS AND PROCESSING

- Introduction
- Data Representation
- Codes Used in Computer
- Data Processing
- Real Time System
- Distributed Data Processing System
- Exercise Questions

INTRODUCTION

The word 'data' is derived from the Latin word 'datum' that means the fact. Hence the data can be said as a collection of facts. In a foot ball match names of all players goals made by each player and many other details regarding to the players and teams is data, because these details show facts about the match.

Collected data is not very useful, so this data is to be processed through a certain method, either by hands or by computers. Processing involves various types of calculations, comparisons etc.

In our example, counting total number of goals made by each team, maximum number of goals made by any player of either side is the example of data processing.

The reason for data processing is to convert data into some useful results. This useful result is called information. In the example of football match, result of match and the best player of the match is information.

DATA REPRESENTATION

We have studied that data is collection of facts. These facts may be in the form of numbers, characters or in pictures. Numeric data is made up of numbers only like 1024, 8.9×1028,100.50 etc. Character or text data may be made up or alphabets only or a combination of alphabets, punctuation marks and digits. Pictures and graphs are made up of lines, curves etc. Computers can process all types of data efficiently to produce meaningful information. But computers cannot understand this data in its usual form. The every data, which is to be processed by computers, firstly transformed into the machine code. This code is made up of 'bit', which is the smallest and most fundamental unit of data represented in computers. Bit is an acronym of Binary digit T. Bit has only two distinct values -0 and 1. Bit serves as a building block with which we can construct and work with larger and more meaningful amount of bytes in pair. This pair of bytes forms 'word'. It means 32-bit computers can process a word of 32-bit or 4-bytes at a time.

In binary number system, if only 3 bits are used then 8 (i.e. 23) combination of 1's and 2's are possible. These can be

000
001
010
011
100
101
110
111

Each could represent a unique character. In other words 8 different characters can be represented using 3 bits. Similarly if we have bits (1 byte) the number of possible distinct combination of bit settings in a byte is 2^8 (i.e. 256) different values or bit combination.

CODES USED IN COMPUTERS

While the computer can understand data in binary form, the user needs to use numbers, letters and other symbols in order to get information out of them. Computers use some codes for input and output units. These codes also allow manufacturers to standardize various input/output devices like printers, keyboard. VDU etc. Two most popular codes are—

ASCII

EBCDIC

ASCII

ASCII is an acronym of American Standard Code for Information interchange. This is the code used by many non-IBM computer manufacturers. ASCII has 256 different codes ranges from 0 to 255.

All the ASCII characters are divided in two parts.

1. ASCII proper character set
2. ASCII extended character set.

ASCII proper character Set

ASCII proper character set contains codes from 0 to 127, and is divided into two parts—first part contain first 32 characters with decimal code 0-31. These are called 'control characters' and have very special use. Control characters are non-printable characters and used by programmers to pass special information to printer or to another computer through a telephone line and sop forth.

ASCILL Extended Character Set

These codes are not used to pass data itself, but to provided action commands, formating signals and communication control codes. Second part of ASCII proper contain character codes with decimal 32-127. This pat of ASCII proper contains all the alphabets, digits and punctuation marks.

ASCII Extended Character Set

This half of ASCII codes contains the higher various foreign (non English) characters, drawing character and scientific characters.

EBCDIC

EBDIC is an acronym of Extended Binary Codes Decimal Interchange Code. EBDIC is used in IBM and IBM compatible

128	€	160		192	À	224	à
129	□	161	¡	193	Á	225	á
130	‚	162	¢	194	Â	226	â
131	ƒ	163	£	195	Ã	227	ã
132	„	164	¤	196	Ä	228	ä
133	…	165	¥	197	Å	229	å
134	†	166	¦	198	Æ	230	æ
135	‡	167	§	199	Ç	231	ç
136	ˆ	168	¨	200	È	232	è
137	‰	169	©	201	É	233	é
138	Š	170	ª	202	Ê	234	ê
139	‹	171	«	203	Ë	235	ë
140	Œ	172	¬	204	Ì	236	ì
141	□	173	-	205	Í	237	í
142	□	174	®	206	Î	238	î
143	□	175	¯	207	Ï	239	ï
144	□	176	°	208	Ð	240	ð
145	‘	177	±	209	Ñ	241	ñ
146	’	178	²	210	Ò	242	ò
147	“	179	³	211	Ó	243	ó
148	”	180	´	212	Ô	244	ô
149	•	181	µ	213	Õ	245	õ
150	–	182	¶	214	Ö	246	ö
151	—	183	·	215	×	247	÷
152	˜	184	¸	216	Ø	248	ø
153	™	185	¹	217	Ù	249	ù
154	š	186	º	218	Ú	250	ú
155	›	187	»	219	Û	251	û
156	œ	188	¼	220	Ü	252	ü
157	□	189	½	221	Ý	253	ý
158	□	190	¾	222	Þ	254	þ
159	Ÿ	191	¿	223	ß	255	ÿ

Fig. 4.1 : ASCII Proper Character Set.

machines. EDBIC also contain 256 character and similarly divided into two parts. Various code grouping in EBDIC differs from ASCII code set.

DATA PROCESSING

Data processing is the processing of collection data, verifying it and recording it in proper form so that any required information can be easily retrieved later.

Today data processing is done by either—

1. Manual method
2. Computerized method

I. Manuai Method

In manual data processing all the steps involved in data, and producing it into meaningful information are done without using electronic or electromechanical devices. In other words hands and mechanical devices do manual data processing.

A clerk in library maintaining the details of books, like book issued, book returned, calculation of fine due to late return of book by student etc., in various registers by hand is an example of manual data processing.

Manual method is the older method and losing its popularity day by day. The reason is that manual method has more disadvantages than advantages. In manual Data processing, changes of mistakes are too high. This is very slow method and repetition of any task makes it much slower.

2. Computerized Method

The data processing method, which uses computers and other electronic devices, is called Electronic Data Processing (EDP). Electronic data processing may be partly manual and partly electronic.

Computerized method has many advantages over manual methods. Computer method reduces the chance of mistake and increase the speed of data processing.

Data Processing Systems

Various types of data processing systems are used for data processing. Few of this are—

1. Batch processing system
2. On-line system
3. Distributed data processing system

1. Batch Processing System

Batch processing is the most appropriate method for those applications in which it is not important to update records immediately, like payroll. This system is based on automatic job-to-job translation facility provided by most operating systems. Batch processing system contains several steps. First, a computer operator collects the source transaction programs, which are capture on forms. These forms are then put together in a batch and a batch slip is attached with the batch, which contains information about the batch like description of the documents, amount, total etc. This batch is than sent to the data processing centres for processing their jobs. Collected batch are then checked against the batch slip. After checking the batch, data is stored on any storage device like disk or tape. In the next operator loads the validated batch of programs into computer where they execute one after another. This execution updates the master file and produces the final reports. Finally these printed reports are collected by the operator and distributed among the respective users.

Batch processing system reduces the idle time of computer system because transition from one job to another does not require operator intervention. This system allows to process a large volumes off data together. The drawback in batch processing system is that system makes each job wait in line at each step and often increases the turnaround time.

2. On-Line System

On-Line system is also called 'Random Access' or 'Direct Access' system. In this system, the data to be fed into backing storage device from the point, where data originated through the on-line terminals. These terminals are linked to the main-computer. When the data is fed into computer then all the steps of batch processing are used for data processing. On-line system has several advantages over batch processing system. On-line system reduces the data entry errors and validates automatically whereas in batch the operator does processing system validation. Also the retrieval of any record is faster in on-line system than the batch processing system.

3. Point of Sale (POS)

One good example of on-line system is Point of Sale (POS) terminal. A POS acts both as a cash register and a data collection terminal. This system is very popular in many countries and frequently used by super markets, banks and retail stores.

POS terminal contains a keypad and operator through keypad enters the details of an item. Every entered detail is sent to the main-computer where the master files are updated regularly.

A bar code system can also be used with POS system to reduce the data entry error and to speed up the work. Barcode system consists of bar code patterns, bar code reader, synthesizer, printer and a host computer. Bar codes are some vertical parallel bars, which can be seen, or the back of many items like books, greeting cards etc. These are actually machine-readable code, which contains various details related to that item. The information contained in the barcodes are determined by its pattern of varied width of bars and spaces between bars.

Bar code reader is an optically scanning device which reads the bar patterns. It generates electrical signals in relation to the pattern, Bar code decoder receives electrical signals from the bar code and converts then into message characters. Bar code synthesizer creates barcode pattern and printer prints bar code patterns. The principle of barcode system is that pulses produced by the reader are compared with standard codes stored in the host computer. If a match is found then the details regarding the item are printed out on a receipt. Master files are also updated at the same time.

POS terminals eliminate the tedious job of price marking of each item. This also eliminates check-out errors due to human errors or illegible/inaccurate price marks. These terminals help to maintain an accurate and updated inventory account.

REAL TIME SYSTEM

Some applications need such type of system that the input data must be processed quickly enough so that further Action can then be promptly taken on the result. Real-time system fulfills the requirement of such type of applications. Real-time is actually an on-line system. The only difference is time take in accessing of record or in updating file is very low in comparison to the on-line system. Railway/airline reservation system, air traffic control system, reservation system used by hotels is the example of real-time systems.

Since in a real-time system input data must be processed quickly and always shows the current status hence a system crash can be disastrous. To save from difficulties an alternative procedure is provided with real time system.

DISTRIBUTED DATA PROCESSING SYSTEM

Distributed data processing is sometimes called 'Distributed computing'. In a distribute system several independent computers can be connected by a telecommunication network to the main computer. Each computer is used to process data separately, and allows several user to sit and work far away from each other. In distributed system messages and data can be transmitted between the terminals.

In a distributed system the access of data is very fast at low cost. But has the drawback of lack of proper security controls for protecting the confidentiality and integrity of the user programmes and data stored or transmitted.

EXERCISE QUESTIONS

Write the answer in your own words

1. What is Data?
2. What do you understand by Data Processing?
3. Explain the Data Information in 100 words.
4. Data Representation
5. What is the use of Codes in Computer?

Fill in the blank

1. Word data is derived from the Latin word..........
2. ....is a collection of facts.
3. Computerized method of data processing is also called.
4. BIT is an acronym of................
5. Two popular codes used in computers are.........and....
6. ASCII character set is divided into...and.........
7. POS is an example of........system.

True/False

1. Electronic data processing may be partly manual and partly electronic.
2. BIT is the smallest and most fundamental unit of data riper scented in computers.
3. ASCII character set contains 255 different characters.
4. Control character is printable character.
5. EBDIC character set is also divided in two part like ASCII character set.
6. EBCDIC code is used in non-IBM computers.
7. A bar system can note used with POS.

Pick the correct one

1. 1.3E+3 is a

   a. Number b. alphanumerical string

   c. String d. None of the above

2. Byte is a collection of—

   a. 1 bit b. 4 bit

   c. 8 bit d. none of the above

3. 64 bit word equivalent to—

   a. 4 byte word b. 8 byte word

   c. 2 byte word d. none of the above

4. Control character are—

   a. 0-31 b. 32

   c. 128-255 d. None of the above

5. ASCII extended character set consists—

   a. Foreign character b. Drawing character

   c. Scientific character d. All of the above

6. 4 bit allows maximum possible combination of 1's and 0's are

   a 16 b. 4

   c. 8 d. All of the above

7. Alphabets and digital are in between—

   a. 0-31 b. 128-255

   c. 32-127 d. None of the above

CHAPTER 5

COMPUTER HARDWARE

- Introduction
- Central Processing Unit
- Main Memory
- Arithmetical and Logical Unit
- Control Unit
- Magnetic Ink Character Reader (MICR)
- Exercise Questions

INTRODUCTION

Hardware of computer refers to all the physical components (i.e. memory of computer, microprocessor, different peripherals etc.) of the computer system. These components can be mechanical, electrical or electronic. These days all digital computers have similar hardware. Computer hardware can be divided into parts.

- Central Processing Unit
- Peripherals

CENTRAL PROCESSING UNIT

Central Processing Unit is the heart of computer system and usually called as CPU. All Peripherals are connected to CPU. Which send or receive data and instructions to and from the CPU. CPU has three parts. These are—

- Main Memory
- Arithmetical and Logical Unit
- Control Unit

MAIN MEMORY

Main Memory is also known as Immediate Access Storage or Primary Storage. Main memory is made up of thousand tiny storage locations. Each location is known as "Cell". These are arranged in rows and columns. Main memory is organized into units of byte. Each byte can hold 256 distinct values, which form the characters. Same memory byte are used to store instructions, numeric data or alphabetic data. Each byte of memory has an address. This address of each cell is unique. First address is identified as zero and increased consequently. Giving the address of that location can access any location in the memory.

Main memory is used to storage data and instruction temporarily. This is the main memory where data and instructions held which are to be processed. Intermediate and final result are also stored in main memory before the permanent storage. Computer uses Main memory first because this is thousand of time faster than the secondary memory Computers use different types of memories. These are—

1. RAM
2. ROM
3. Cache Memory

1. RAM

This is the abbreviated form of the Random Access Memory. Main memory is usually referred to RAM. RAM holds programs and data while the computer works. This is a volatile memory that means data and instruction retains in it only as long as the computer runs. The name of this memory indicates that any location of memory can be access randomly, and read or rewritten in the same amount of time. Because this memory allows both operations (i.e. read and write), hence this is also known as read/write memory. RAM chips are not much expensive.

2. ROM

ROM is the abbreviated form of Read Only Memory. This is a special kind of memory and is different from Random Access Memory. This is a permanent memory and does not lose data when computer is turned off. Some programs are hard wired on these chips cannot be written to or changed by programs, hence this is also known as "non-volatile memory". ROM chips are used by manufactures to supply some certain essential programs, which helps in bootstrap process of computer. Various types of ROM chips are—

PROM

PROM stands for Programmable Read Only Memory. ROM chips and PROM chips are very similar, both are read only memories, and both are used to store some essential programs. Different between both the chips is that ROM chips are programmed at the time of manufacturing whereas PROM chips are supplied without any programme. User can programme PROM chips once and after that these work like the ROM chips.

EPROM

EPROM is the abbreviated form of Erasable Programmable Read Only Memory. Programmes store in ROM or PROM chips cannot be changed, EPROM chips the programmer to erase and reprogrammed. This is done by ultra-violate rays.

EEPROMS

This memory stands for Electrical Erasable. Programmable read only Memory. These types of memory chips are erased and reprogrammed by special electrical circuits in place of ultra-violate rays.

3. Cache Memory

Speed of microprocessor in comparison to main memory is very high, so it decrease the performance of microprocessor. This make use of the full performance of microprocessor, a small memory between CPU and main memory whose access time is close to the processing speed of CPU is used these days. This memory is called "cache memory". This memory is expensive than the main memory.

ARITHMETICAL AND LOGICAL UNIT

Arithmetical and Logical Unit is usually known as ALU. This is the unit where all the mathematical calculations (i.e. less than, greater than etc.) are made. Data stored in main memory is transferred to ALU. Finally ALU process data and then information is released to output unit.

CONTROL UNIT

Control Unit (CU) controls the entire operations of Arithmetical and Logical Unit. Control Unit picks and instruction from main memory and transfers to ALU one by one. ALU responds to these instructions. After processed by ALU it transfers the information from ALU to main memory and finally on to output.

PERIPHERALS

Peripherals devices are those devices, which are connected to Central Processing Unit, and allow it to communicate with user. These devices transfer data and information to and from the CPU. Peripherals can be classified into two categories:-

1. Input-Output Devices
2. Backing Storage Devices

I. Input-Output Devices

Input-Output devices are used to make communications between user and CPU directly. On the basis of working these can be of three types:—

- Some devices can be used only for input data and instructions into the computer. These data and instructions are then converted into binary form for processing.
- Some devices can be used only for output information from the computer. These devices take the generated information from the computer and convert it into a human readable form.
- Some devices can be used for both purpose (i.e., input and output)

Few of these devices are—

- Keyboard
- Magnetic Ink Character Reader
- Light Pen
- Mouse
- Input Tablet
- Printers

- Plotters
- Microfiche
- VDU

Keyboard

Keyboard is the most popular input device. Sometimes it is also called as keyboard. Keyboard is similar to a typewriter's keyboard expect that it contains some additional keys. Operations of computer keyboard's key are much softer than the typewriter's keys. The speed of entering data through keyboard is very slow because user directly operates it. Earlier keyboards contains of 84 keys whereas today's keyboards contain 101 keys. These keyboards are pronounced as 'one-zero-one' keyboard.

Computer keyboard can be divided into three sections: -

- Alphanumeric keys
- Function keys
- Special keys

Alphanumeric keys are similar to typewriter's keys and cover most of the space. Alphanumeric contain digits (0-9), Alphabets in upper cases (A—Z) and lower cases (a—z) and some other characters like

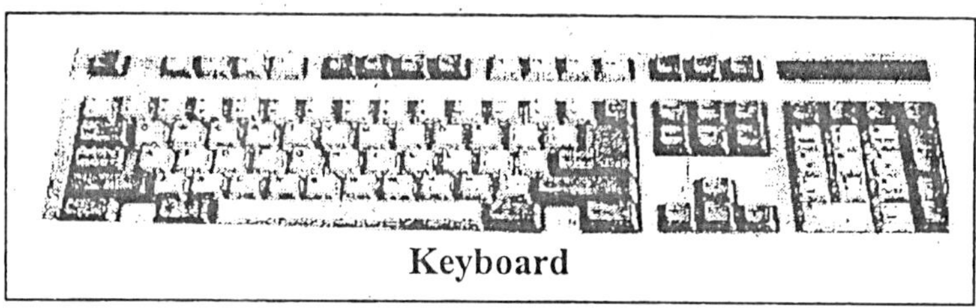

Keyboard

Function keys are used to perform a specific task through a single keystroke. For example, usually all the software's use F1 function key for getting help at any time. Function keys are twelve (named F1-F12). These function keys are located on the upper first row in some keyboards or on the left side in two rows on some others.

Special keys also performs some special task such as when CAPS Lock key is ON all the letters typed through keyboard are converted into upper case letters, RETURN key is used to transmit the keyed command or data as a whole the cursor is currently positioned. BACKSPACE key deletes one character left from the cursor. Keyboard contains many other and special keys for different purpose. Some other keys are—Num Lock key, Tab key, Ctrl key, Alt key, Ins key, Shift key etc. in most of the keyboards some special keys are duplicate. These are only to speed up the typing speed.

Keyboard contains 101 keys but it is possible to generate maximum 256 characters. Rest of the characters can be generated using different key combinations of these keys. A company 'key Innovations'., USA, has introduced a new type of keyboard. This keyboard contains three additional keys. Through these new keys, cursor can move one whole word in either direction or deletes a whole word.

MAGNETIC INK CHARACTER READER (MICR)

Magnetic Ink Character Reader (MICR) is a device, which is widely used by banks to process Cheque number; branch number and some other important information's are printed on the Cheque. Customer prints this information's with special INK, which contains magnets able particles in bank MICR detects the characters and compares the scanned characters with standard characters. If a match is found then characters are sent for further processing. The advantages if MICR are that is speeds up the processing and roughly handled, or folded Cheque can be easily read with the same accuracy. MICR can read about 3000 Cheque per hour.

Optical Mark Reader (OMR)

Optical Mark Reader (OMR) is an input device. OMR is used to detect the presence or absence of mark. OMR scans the marks with a photo electronic device. Light is focused onto the mark then the reflection of light is sensed by OMR. If a mark is there then lesser light is reflected. This reflected light pattern is then compared with the stored mark. If a close match as found the mark is recognized. OMR is widely used in examination. Questionnaires are designed in a special manner such that questions are asked with a choice of multiple answers. These marks with the marks as mentioned in questionnaires. Marks put by led pencil are best suited for sensing. The advantage of OMR is that it reduces changes of human errors.

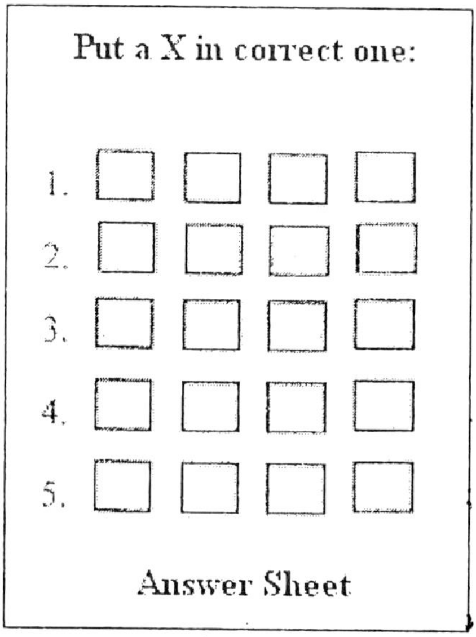

Put a X in correct one:

1.
2.
3.
4.
5.

Answer Sheet

Optical Character Reader (OCR)

Optical Character Reader works in a similar fashion and can recognize the characters. OCR contains all the characters in place of marks. The reflected light pattern are converted into electrical pulses and transmitted to recognition logic circuits. There they are compared with the stored characters. OCR devices are also widely used in examinations.

Light Pen

A light pen is an input device, which is used for graphical purpose. Light pen is also known as "Electronic Pen." This is used to draw lines and curves, which is not easy through keyboard. Light pen looks like an ordinary pen and consists a stylus, which is connected through a cable to the video display terminal. When the user puts this photosensitive device on the cathode ray tube (CRT) a dot appears on the screen. Similarly the movement of light pen on Cathode Ray tube can draw the desired image.

Mouse

Mouse is also an input device. Mouse is a small device which contains a tracking ball in its bottom and two or three buttons on the upper side. This can be put on any plain surface. When the user rolls the mouse across the surface, tracking ball at the bottom also moves and causes the movement of cursor on the screen. After positioning the cursor on the screen a click or mouse's button points that position or selects the required option from menu. Some software also allows drawing lines and curves on the screen with the help of mouse. Since it is very easy to control the cursor through mouse so the popularity of mouse is increasing day by day.

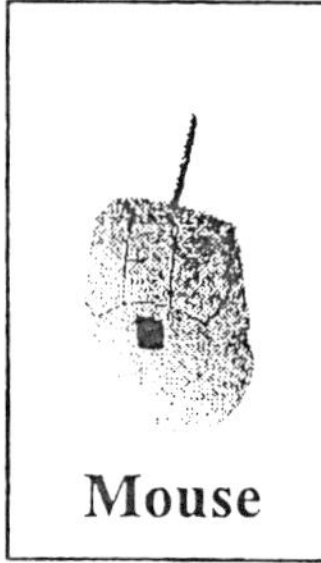
Mouse

Input Tablet

It is also known as "Graphic Tablet" or digitizer Tablet. It contains a square surface like a drawing board and a light pen connected to tablet. This board contains a grid of horizontal and vertical copper wires inside it. When the light pen is put on the surface of tablet this grid receives electrical pulses and send to central processing unit, which finally display the designed image on the screen input tablet is mainly used for engineering and scientific images.

Printers

Printers are the importance and commonly used devices. Printers generate the output on papers. Printers take information from central processing unit either in binary or hexadecimal form, which is to be printed. Since the printing speed of printers are very slow in comparison to central processing unit, so printers first store the incoming information in it's own buffer. This buffer is known as "Printer Buffer".

These days various types of printers are in use. These can be divided into following three categories:—

1. Character Printers
2. Line Printers
3. Page Printers

1. Character Printers

Character printers are those printers, which print one character at a time. Some character printer's are—

1. Golf Ball Printers
2. Daisy Wheel Printers
3. Dot Matrix Printers
4. Inkjet Printers

1. Golf Ball Printers

Golf ball printer is an impact printer. This is slowest type of printer. This is also the oldest one, which was introduced by IBM Corp. In this type of printer, characters are marked on a print head, which looks like a golf ball. A ribbon is mounted between paper and the print head. This print head strikes a ribbon and prints the character on the paper. Major disadvantage of golf ball printer is its speed, which is not more than 25-30 characters per second (cps).

2. Daisy Wheel Printers

Daisy wheel printer is an example of impact printer. These are faster than the golf ball printers. In daisy wheel technology, daisy wheel is a circular wheel like mechanism that has many petals and each petal has a printing head. Character is embossed on these head. This wheel is rotated by a motor.

When signals are sent from the system to print characters the motor rotates the daisy wheel to the correct position. Once the desired character is positioned to be printed the hammer strikes the character. When the hammer strikes character a ribbon, which is mounted between the paper, and daisy wheel prints the desired character on page. One of the major drawback of these printers are that one daisy wheel cannot print in different fonts. For a printing of different fonts one has to change different

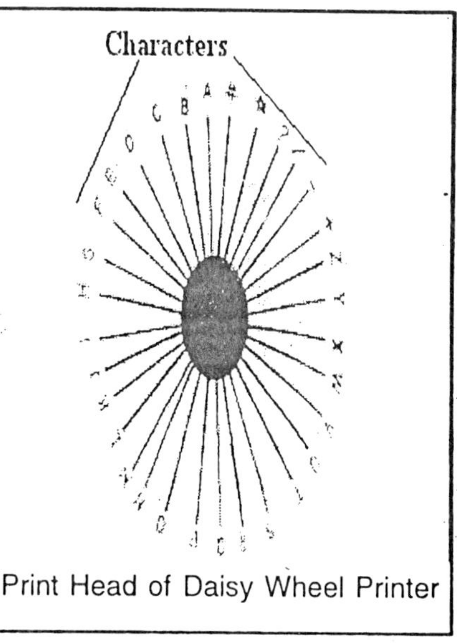

Print Head of Daisy Wheel Printer

daisy wheels, which can be changed any time easily. The letters qualities of daisy wheel printers are fine. These printers work at the approximate speed of 90 characters per second (cps).

3. Dot Matrix Printers

These days various types of printers are in use but the dot matrix printers are most popular printers. Dot matrix printers are widely used for mailing labels, multiple forms, high volume draft printing and continuous printing. The stationary, which those printers use, are the form of continuous strip of paper perforated at regular intervals where the paper can fold. The paper between the two folds forms a page Depending on the length and width of the paper, a fixed number of lines can be printed on one page, and a fixed number of character per line. In dot matrix printers the characters are formed as a combinations of dots.

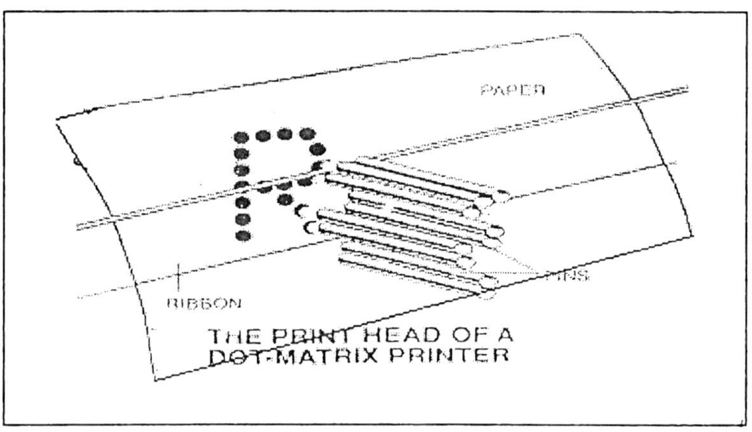

In dot matrix printers the print head consists a matrix of needle like hammers. A ribbon is mounted between the paper and print head when CPU sends the signals for printing, the needles strikes the ribbon and creates a character. Only those needles strikes, which are required to produce character. In a dot matrix printer standard characters are produced in a 5 × 7 (5 pin wide and 7 pin high) or 7 × 9 (7 pin wide and 9 pin high) matrix. High quality dot matrix printers use 18 or 24 pins, but these are costlier than the 9 pin printers.

Dot matrix printers have the drawback of letter quality printing. Characters printed by dot matrix printers are in the form of dots so the quality of letters is not good. To produce a letter quality printing most dot matrix printers allows the printing in double strikes mode. In double strikes mode dot matrix printers produce high quality printing but reduce the printing speed up to a level of half of normal speed. Another big problem with these printers in noise that at the time of printing, dot matrix printers produce much noise, which creates problem.

4. Inkjet Printers

Inkjet printers are not the impact printers. These are the non-impact printers, which uses other techniques for printing. Droplets of ink are fired through a nozzle. These droplets are then guided to the proper position on the paper by electrically charged deflection plates. Ink used by these printers is also electrically charged before leaving the nozzle.

Inkjet printers produced high quality output and can print different colours or in monochrome. These printers can print on various types of papers. The speed of these printers lies between the dot matrix printers and laser printers. That means these are faster than dot matrix and slower than laser printers. On limitations of inkjet printers and other non-impact printers is that these printers cannot produce multiple carbon copies of a document in a single printing. Some other non-impact character printers are also available. These are—

1. Thermal Printer
2. Chemical Printer
3. Electrographic Printer

2. Line Printers

Line printers are usually with mini computers and mainframe computers. The similarity between line printers and the character printers is that both are impact printers, but the difference is that character printers print one character at a time whereas line printers print one complete line at a time. Line printers are of three types. These are—

A. Drum printers
B. Chain printers
C. Band printers

A. Drum printers

Drum printers use a print head very similar to a drum on which characters are embossed in 64 lines parallel to head's axis. Drum moves at a rapid speed past the printing positions. Hammer behind the head strikes the head and ribbon mounted between print head and paper helps to print the desired characters.

B. Chain Printers

Chain printers and Band printers are very similar to Drum printers in mechanism. The only difference is that these use either a chain or a band on which the different characters are embossed.

The letter quality of line printers is very fine. These work at the speed of 300 lines per minute approximately, and suitable for heavy-duty printing. But the one drawback with these printers is that, these printers cannot print graphic images, diagrams or printing in different fonts.

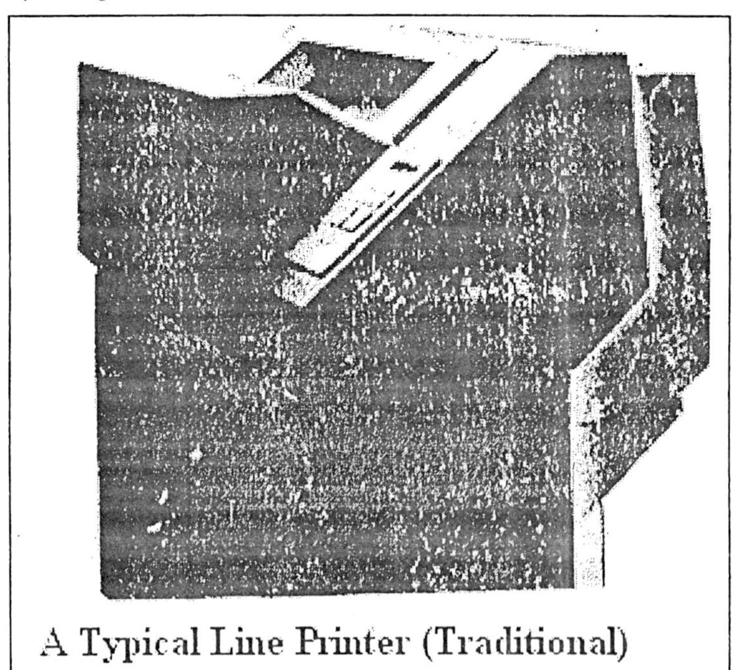

A Typical Line Printer (Traditional)

C. Page Printers

Page printers are the fastest printers. These are also non-impact printers. These are called page printers because these print one page at a time. Laser printer is an example of page printer. Laser Printer prints by using a combination of laser light, electrical charge and a back powder known as 'toner' similar to Xerox machine. Laser printer contain a revolving drum having a light sensitive surface. Scanned image or file to be printed is broken up in to a series of dots and projected onto photosensitive drum by a laser beam. Then toner is sprinkled onto these dots and form the image. Finally this image is transferred to page. Laser printer prints the output in approximately 600 dots per inch (dpi). Higher the dots per inch means higher the quality. Laser printer works at a speed of 8-15 pages per minute. These printers are costlier than dot matrix printers.

Interfaces

Any printer either it is impact or non-impact can be connected in two different ways with computers. Either with parallel interface or with serial interface.

Parallel port is specially designed for printers only hence this port is also known as Printer port.

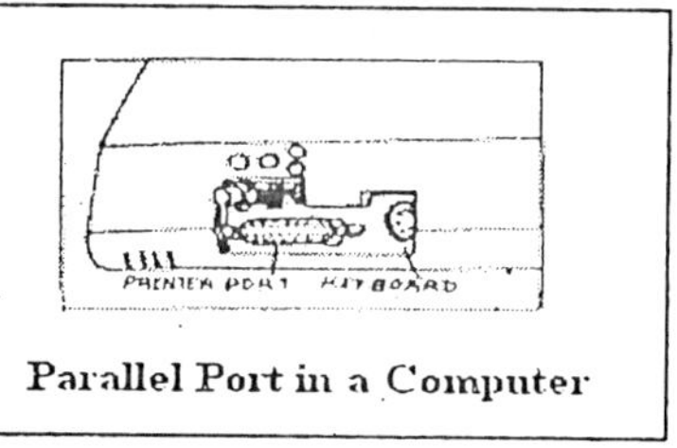

Parallel Port in a Computer

This interface is called parallel because it is designed to transmit data one byte at a time. That means all bits of a byte passing out to the printer at the same time, moving out through eight separate wires, in parallel.

Serial interface can be used for various purposes, and a printer is only one of them. Serial interface is fully two-way path while parallel interface allow one-way path for data to be transmitted to the printer. In serial interface data is sent one bit at a time. The communication parameters are a set of specifications, which establish how each serial port will work. The serial communication parameters begin with a baud rate, which determines how fast the interface will run in a measure, called baud (bit per second). Baud rate vary from 110 to 9600.

Plotters

Plotters are also used for hard copy outputs, but are used for complex tool designs, architectural design and other types of technical diagrams. Plotters are highly accurate devices. There are two types of plotters. These are—

- Drum type
- Flatbed type

In a drum type plotter paper is mounted on a drum, which moves the paper along its length, and the pen moves along the width. In flatbed plotter pen is moved by motor in a table of plotter drum plotters produce more accurate diagrams.

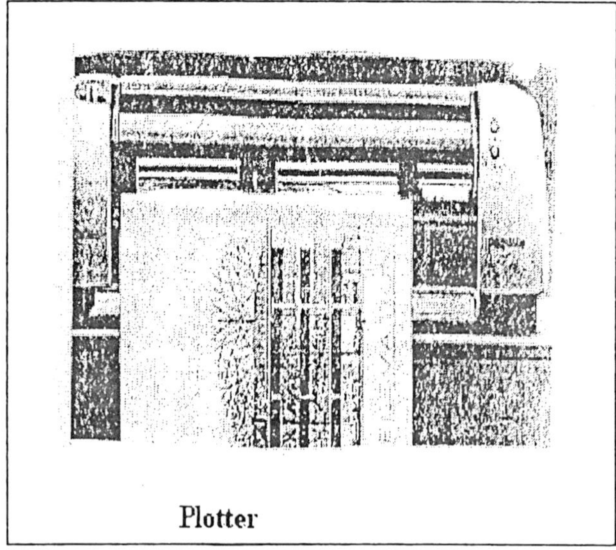

Plotter

Usually plotters use one pen so the output comes in one colour, but more advanced plotters are in use these days, which use more than one pen for the colour output. Plotters work at the speed of 20 inches per second approximately.

Microfiche

Microfiche sometimes known as Computer Output Microfilm (COM). In this technology image of complete page is sensed at a time and is recorded information is used to produce output.

Microfiche devices are capable of holding many hundred pages of information. Some more advanced devices are also available called Ultra fiche can store thousand pages of information at the same space. Another advantage of microfiche is that this device can produce about 48 times smaller or large images. Microfiche devices are used to store and produce different types of images.

VDU

Video Display Unit (VDU) is the most popular input/output device for all computers. VDU contains a screen similar to a TV screen and a keyboard. The video system of VDU consists of two basic components—

- Video display adapter
- Video screen

Video display adapter

Video display adapter takes the signals from CPU and sent it to video screen to produce the images. Video adapter consists two parts—

- Video memory
- Circuitry

CPU writes information to be displayed on video screen into VDU memory (This VDU memory is called as Video RAM or VRAM), whereas the adapters circuitry transfers this information from video RAM onto Video screen. Each character, which is to be displayed on the screen, occupies two byte in Video memory. The first of these bytes contains the attribute in which the character is to be display and the second byte contains the actual character the actual character. The display adapter circuitry repeatedly reads information from Video memory and places it on the screen, making the image displayed on the screen clear and steady. This process is called as 'Refreshing the screen' and the rate at which the display adapter refreshes the screen is called as 'Refresh rate'. Some

Video adapter which are in use these days are—

- Monochrome Adapter (MA),
- Colour Graphics Adapter (CGA),
- Enhanced Graphics Adapter (EGA),
- Video Graphics Adapter (VGA),
- Hercules Graphics Adapter (HGA)

Monochrome adapter can operate in text mode only and supports only one colour. However the text produced by monochrome adapter is much sharper. CGA, EGA, and VGA, can operate in both text and graphics mode. Also these three adapters support many text and graphics mode. Also these adapters support many colours. CGA, EGA and VGA consists different resolutions, HGA contains the graphics capabilities of these graphics adapter and high quality text display of monochrome adapter. But HGA does not support colour display.

Video screen (also called monitor) consists of Cathode Ray Tube (CRT), which is also called picture tube. In CRT an electron beam, which is controlled by the electronic circuitry, places dots in a specified series on the phosphorescent surface of CTR. These dots shine at the phosphorescent surface and forms the character or image. Some common monitors which are in use these days are—

- *Monochrome monitor*: These are designed to display high-resolution text, but cannot display graphics images. These works with monochrome adapters for graphics. But these monitors produce images in only on colour.
- *Composite colour monitors*: These monitors can display both text and graphics. But these monitors produce image in only one colour.
- *RGB monitors*: These monitor support high quality text display with the high resolution graphics and colours. These support only three colours— Red, Green and Blue.
- *TV Sets*: Sometimes television (either colour or b/w) is also used as monitors. These produce a lower quality image than the other monitors.

The entire adaptor support either text or graphics mode or even both. Text mode is used to display text characters only (i.e. ASCII value 0 to 255). The display resolution in text mode is defined text in 25 rows and 80 columns but may very from adapter to adapter.

Graphics mode I mainly used for complex drawing and graphs. However, text characters can be drawn in variety of fonts in graphics mode. In this mode images on the screen are made up of small dots (pixels). The displays resolution is defined by the number of rows (called scan lines) and number of pixels per scan line. Resolution various from adapter, but in general higher the resolution means a sharper and clear picture.

Motherboard

Motherboard is sometimes known as "System Board". This is the largest single electronic component in the computer. Motherboard holds most of the chips like microprocessor chip and memory chip and memory chips. It also holds some other components.

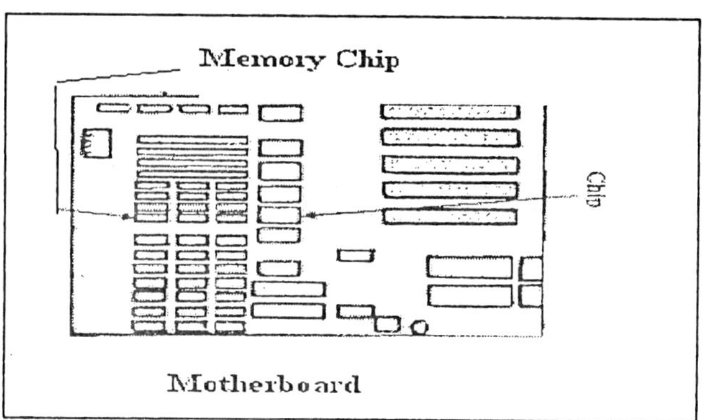

Motherboard

Backing Storage Devices

Backing storage devices are discussed in next chapter.

EXERCISE QUESTIONS

Write the answer in your own words:

1. What do you understand by the Central Processing Unit?
2. What is main memory?
3. Write about Arithmetical and Logical Unit in 200 words.
4. What is Magnetic Ink Character Reader (MICR)

Fill in the blanks:

1. First generation computers used.......... technology.
2. MOS stands for...........
3. ....generation computers will be able to recognize voice.
4. Digital computers operate on the electric input that have only two states...... and......
5. ....are the smallest in micro-computers.

True/False:

1. Micro- computers support more than one user at a time.
2. Generation purpose computers are usually analog computers.
3. Lap-top computers are portable computers.
4. Hybrid computers are partly digital and partly analog.
5. Home computers use TV as a display unit.

Pick the correct one:

1. Microprocessor was first introduced in—
   a. First Generation's Computers
   b. Second Generation's
   c. Third Generation's Computers
   d. Fourth Generation's Computers
2. Which computer is used for weather forecasting?
   a. Microcomputer b. Mainframe
   c. Mini computer d. Supper computer
3. Fourth generation computers use—
   a. Machine Language b. Assemble Language
   c. High level Language d. None of the above
4. In the voice recognition technique computer will be able to—
   a. Recognize voice b. Think
   c. Not recognize voice d. None of the above

CHAPTER 6

BACKING STORAGE DEVICES OF COMPUTER

- Introduction
- Punched Cards and Paper Tapes
- Magnetic Tapes
- Magnetic Disks
- Type of Magnetic Disks
- Hard Disk and Disk Pack
- Exercise Questions

INTRODUCTION

From the invention of computer till now backing storage capacity is one of the major research area for computer enthusiasts. Today's backing storage devices have enormous capacity than the earlier devices, but the increasing need of data and information has indicated, there is still a requirement to improve the capacity. Backing storage devices are also known as Secondary storage devices or Auxiliary storage devices. These devices are used to store data permanently. Good backing storage devices should have—

- High retrieval speed
- High storage capacity
- Low cost per bit capacity

Some backing storage devices to be discussed here are :

(1) Punched Cards and Paper tapes

(2) Magnetic tapes

- Cassette tape
- Spool

(3) Magnetic disk

- Floppy disk
- Hard disk and Disk pack

(4) Optical disk

(5) Bubble storage

PUNCHED CARDS AND PAPER TAPES

These are the oldest storage devices. Punched cards were invented in the 18th century, but before 1920 there was no standard. IBM Corp. Standardized the punched cards of 19 cm. × 8.3 cm. These punched cards were made of cardboard which had the thickness of 0.17 mm. a punched card is divided into from the bottom are used to represent the digits, and alphabets are represent by the punching in 11th and 12th rows. Hence one punched card can store maximum 80 characters.

A special punching machine called 'Card Punching Machine' punches these cards. This card-punching machine contains a keyboard, a hopper in which the plain cards put together for punching and a stacker, which collects the punched cards. A card reader is used to read these punched cards. This cards reader also contains a hopper and stacker. Punched cards are put into the hopper, read station reads these cards one by one and stacker collects these cards.

A read operation always results in reading and transferring one card of data; hence files on punched cards always contain a record length of maximum 80 characters. Also file can be accessed sequentially only.

Punched paper tape is similar to punched cards the only difference is that an entire file can be stored on a single tape whereas many cards are used to store file. This tape is about one inch wide and has a length of up to several hundred feet. There is a line of holes in the middle of the tape for the purpose of moving the tape. Information is recorded as holes punched in row across the width, where one row represented one character. Paper tapes have advantage over punched cards that these take less space to store data and information in comparison to punched cards. Also tapes are easily transferable rather thân punched cards. But the main problem with the tapes is, if a wrong punching is made then first cut the wrong punched part and then paste the tape again, which takes a long time. Also both (tapes or cards) have a common problem; once these are punched then these cannot be reused (i.e. re-punched). These are not in use nowadays.

MAGNETIC TAPES

Magnetic tape is a popular media for storage of large files, which are sequentially accessed and processed. These tapes are made of long plastic ribbon, coated with magnetic material on one side. Electro-magnetic side of the tape-record data. Magnetic tape has advantage over paper punched tape that these are reusable, that means old data can be erased and new data can be written in the same tape many times. Two types of magnetic tapes are in use these days. These are—

1. Spool
2. Cassette

1. Spool

This form of magnetic tape is commonly used in large computers. This tape is about half inch wide and has a length of 500 feet to 2400 feet. Magnetic tape is wound on a spool of about 10.5-inch diameter. This spool can be mounted on a tape unit for reading and writing the tape. Tape drive rotates the spool and bring into a constant speed before the reading or writing operations. A head assembly of 7 or 9 heads is used to read and write the data. Each head is made of small electromagnet, which is separated from each other with tiny gaps, between the poles. At the time of reading, the magnetized patterns on the tape include pulses of current in the read coils and transmit as data into CPU. At the time of writing, electrical pulses flow through the write coils at appropriate tracks causing iron oxide coating of the tape to be magnetized in proper order.

Magnetic tape is divided into vertical columns and horizontal rows. These rows called as 'channels' or 'tracks' and Columns are called as 'frames.' Data is usually recorded on tapes in parallel tracks, where one column represents one character. Data is recorded in 7 or 9 parallel tracks. In earlier days a character was represented by 6 bits code with one parity bit (i.e. 7 track tape).

These days, one character is represented by 8 bits and one parity bit (i.e. 9 tracks tape). Parity bit is an extra bit generated by computer and recorded along with other bits. When the data is transmitted, this parity bit is also transmitted. At the time of reading the data computer checks for proper parity, if one bit is wrongly read an error is indicated by computer.

Earlier, records were stored on the tap separately in file. Each record was separated by some blank space, which called 'Inter Record Gap' (IRG). Since tape drive is a mechanical device, this takes some time to stop down or start up the tape. So if the IRG are not there then some information will be lost.

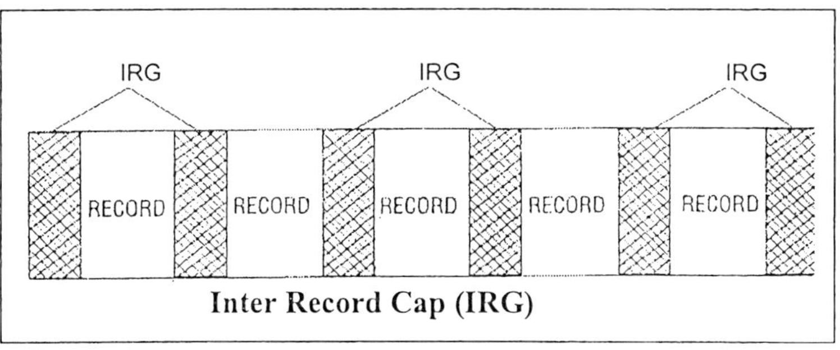

Inter Record Cap (IRG)

But the real problem in this case is, if the tape contains a large number of short records then most of the tape would remain blank due to these Inter Record Gaps. To solve this problem several short records can be combined to form a tape block. And these blocks are separated by some blank space. This blank space is called Inter Block Gap (IBG). A block may contain several numbers of records. Read or write operation to and fro the magnetic tape always transfer one block of data. This reduces the required time.

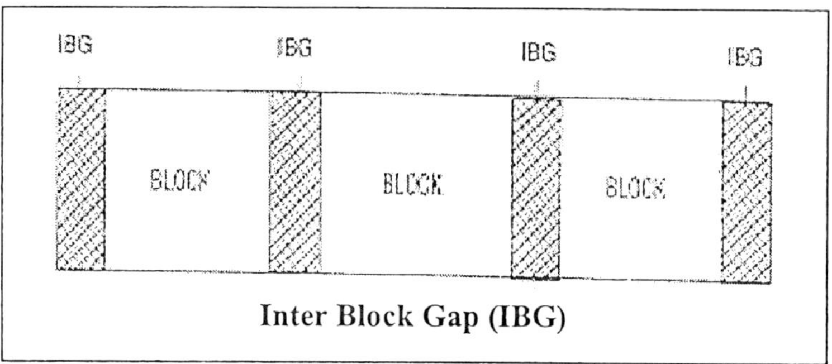

Inter Block Gap (IBG)

Usually the first few feet of the tape is left unrecorded for the threading of the tape and these magnetic tapes are marked on both ends with visible tags. Tag at the beginning is called 'load-point' and that of the end is called 'enc-of-reel'.

Between the load point marker and the first data block, a header control label is placed which contains the control information of tape file, such as name of the file, serial number of block on tape file, where the file has been ended or not and some other information.

The number of characters recorded per inch of the tape is measured in characters per inch (cpi) or bytes per inch (bpi) and is called as 'recording density'. This recording density of tape is very high and may be in thousand of characters per inch. The major drawback with the tapes is that these are sequential access devices. That means if a record in particular position is to be read the tape has to be moved to that particular position and the system has to scan through all the records sequentially up to that record.

2. Cassette

Cassette tapes are sometimes called 'Cartridge tapes'. These tapes are similar to spool. These are used by small personal computers. Cassette tape is smaller and similar in structure and looks like an audiocassette. The width of this tape is about quarter inch.

A tape drive is used to read and write to and from the tape. In this cassette a tape supply reel and a tape take-up reel is used to roll-up the tape similar to audiocassette spools. A head is used for read/write operation, which is similar to head in spool tape. The storage capacity of the cartridge tape is less in comparison to spool tape. Since it's lesser storage capacity these are less expensive.

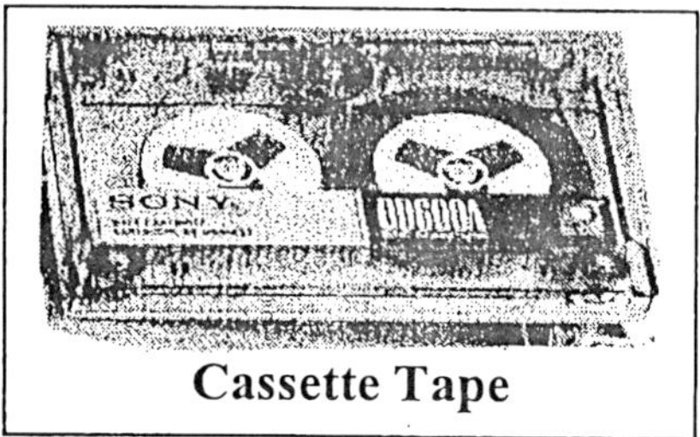

Cassette Tape

MAGNETIC DISKS

Magnetic disks are most popular backing storage devices these days. Basically all magnetic disks are made of circular platter coated with a magnetic material. Earlier when introduced these were made of metal platters. Those were faster than the magnetic once, but the real problem was once the power turned off all the data stored in it wiped out.

Data is stored on the disk in tracks and sectors. Tracks are the invisible concentric on the platter Their tracks start from the outer edge and continue towards the center. The outer track is counted as zero and increases one by one to wards the center. Each track in further divided into fixed number of sectors of fix size.

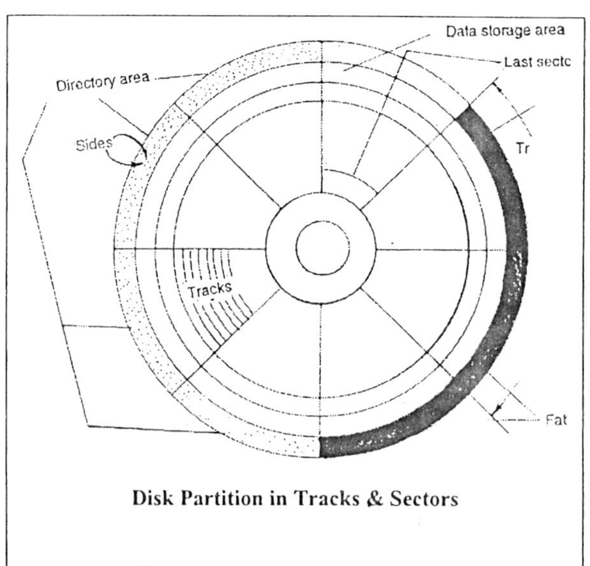

Disk Partition in Tracks & Sectors

Formatting the disk does the partition of disk into tracks and sectors, (i.e. Format is a process of dividing the disk into tracks and sectors). Any new disk has to be first formatted before storing any information to it. This division of disk speeds up the reading and writing operations to and form the disk.

The amount of information that can be stored on disk depends on the number of tracks, number of sectors and size of sector, which is under operating system's control. MS-DOS divides the disk into four major sections.

- Boot area
- FAT (File Allocation Table) area
- Directory area
- Data storage area

The boot sector contains disk bootstrap program. The purpose of this program is to load DOS files disk into memory.

FAT area contains information about the space and the space that is unusable due to defects in the disk. Since FAT contains very important information, duplicate copies of FAT are stored on disk.

Directory area contains information about file's size, it's starting location on the disk, it's data and time of creation, and name the number of sectors reserved for directory entries may very.

Data storage area is the area where the actual files and sub-directories are stored. It occupies the largest part of disk.

A disk drive is used for these magnetic disks. A disk drive is a mechanism that rotates the disk. It works in a start-stop motion and rotates the disk at constant and rapid speed. The number of read/write heads depends on the surface of the disks. These heads can be directly positioned to read the desired information. The address of this information is recorded by control program and supplied to the head mechanism. Due to this property disks are also called Direct Access Devices. These magnetic disks have many advantages over the magnetic tapes.

- Data stored on magnetic disk is more reliable than the magnetic tape.

- Data transfer rate of disk is very high than the tape.
- Any record stored on the disk can be directly accessed with out searching through previously recorded data, which is not possible in case of magnetic tapes.

Type of Magnetic Disks

1. Floppy disk
2. Hard disk

1. Floppy disk

Floppy disk are made of soft, plastic material, coated with magnetically material, either in one or two sides. Floppy disks are made of very thin platter, which can be easily moulded. These are enclosed in a special jacket to prevent from dust and moisture. According to the size floppies can be classified into three categories:—

Floppy with 8" (inch) diameter

Floppy with 5¼" (inch) diameter

Floppy with 3½" (inch) diameters

Standard floppy with 8-inch diameter is not much in use these days, this floppy usually contains 77 tracks per inch.

Standard 5¼" inch floppy disks are very much in use these days. These are also called 'mini floppy disks', and were jointly introduced by Apple and Radio Shack in 1978.

Disk has a central hole, just like the phonogram record. This is the hole where the disk drive grabs it. For locating a sector, a small hole on the floppy disk called 'sector hole' is made. This sector hole marks the location of the first sector, and all other sector are referred to with reference to this hole. The two small cuts on either side of the read/write slot are called 'stress relief notches'.

These make sure that jacket does't wrap. On one side a 'write-protect notch' is also present, which enable it to be write-protected. This means that if the notch with a uncovered the disk can be written onto, otherwise if it is covered with a plastic tape the disk can only be read from. According to the data density mini floppies are available in various density disks, quad density disks and high-density disks. The storage capacity of double density disk is about two times of single density disk, and contains 48 tracks per inch (tip). The storage capacity of quad density disk is the latest one and has greater capacity than any other disk. The type consists of 96 tracks per inch and 15 sectors per sector, whereas above three types of disks consist 9 sector per track.

31/2" Floppy

The 3½" floppy disk is the newest member in the floppy disks. These disks are also known as 'micro floppy disks' and were introduced by Sony Development Corp. Japan in 1982. These micro floppy disks are much safer than the mini floppy disks. These are completely enclosed in the jacket; hence reduce the chances of head crash due to dust particles and hairs. Microfloppies contain 135 tracks per inch and 15 sectors per inch. The storage capacities of these disks are 1.44 MB. 2 MB disks are also available now. These disks are little expensive than mini floppies but have higher capacity and are much safer. Due to these advantages microfloppies are becoming popular day by day.

Every floppy disk of any size needs some care. This care reduces the chances of data loss by taking some precautions. Few of these are—

1. Do not touch disk surface. It can be easily contaminated by dust particle, oil etc.
2. Do not put magnet or any magnetically material near the disk.
3. Do not use any solution to clean the disk except disk cleaner.
4. Do not bend or fold the disk.
5. Do not place heavy objects on the disk.
6. Do not place any type of food or drink near your disk. (Recently a floppy has been introduced which is safe from liquid. A material called 'Tafflon' coats this.)
7. Do not expose disk to excessive heat or sunlight.

8. Keep the disk in its envelope properly when not in use.
9. Keep each disk in the storage boxes and set the boxes standing up.
10. Keep the disk at about 10° C- 53° C temperatures and 32%-80% relative humidity.
11. During transpiration each disk should be stored in it's enveloped and placed in a protective storage box.

HARD DISK AND DISK PACK

Hard disk is a backing storage device, which has very large data storage capacity. This is one of the largest storage device used in PC. Hard disk is also called 'Fixed disk'. This is placed inside the computer permanently and cannot be removed like floppy disk. Hard disk gets their name from this fact that this made by the coating of magnetically material on aluminium platter. This looks like a gramophone in its' structure.

Both, the top and bottom of a hard disk is used for data storage. Two head are mounted on each arm to access data from both surfaces.

Another form of hard disk is called 'Winchester disk'. An air proof box covers the only differences between these, that Winchester. This box protects the disk from dust particles and other contamination, hence reduces the chance of head crash.

Hard disks are available in market, in different capacities. Capacity of this disk varies from 20 MB to 9 GB. Data stored

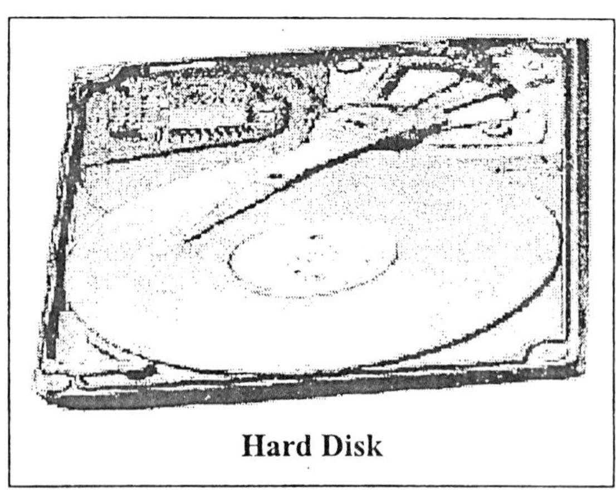

Hard Disk

on hard disk is much reliable than the floppy disk. Accessing of data is also much faster than floppy disk but these are relatively costlier devices. Since the storage capacity of hard disk is relatively large these allow the partitioning of disk. This means user can partition the disk space into many parts, one part of the disk space is for DOS and other part for other operating systems. Each partitioned data can be kept completely separate from the data in the other partitions, also each partition contains its own boot sector and operating system.

A disk pack is a device, which contains multiple numbers of magnetic disk platters in place of single device. The entire platter, sometime this is called as 'multi-disk' storage device. All the platters are mounted on same spindle separated from each other at a distance of about half inch. In disk pack data is stored on both sides of platters except the both outer sides, hence if the disk pack consist 6 circular platters then 10 surfaces are used to store data. A separate head is used for each platter but all these are connected at a common arm at the end.

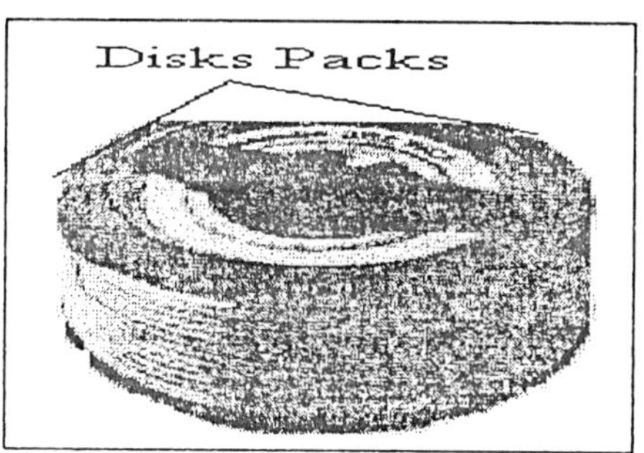

Same number of track on each surface in a disk forms a cylinder. At the time of reading, to calculate the address, cylinder number is used first, then track-number (i.e. surface number) and finally sector number. File on a disk pack in store is such a manner, that first same number of tracks of all surfaces is used. If the file is even large then the second cylinder is used and so on.

Disk packs rotate at very high speed, All the platters move simultaneously in the same direction and in equal speed. Storage capacity of a disk pack depends on many things—

such as number of platters, diameters of platters, number of cylinders, tracks per inch, sectors per inch, number of rotations per minute and some other factors.

Optical Disk

Optical disks are not much older. Coating of magnetizable material does not make these disks. Instead of magnetically material these use some other technique. This technique is the use of laser. The data which is to be stored on an optical disk is stored by a laser beam, burns the tiny holes on a thin coating of metal deposition of the disk platter.

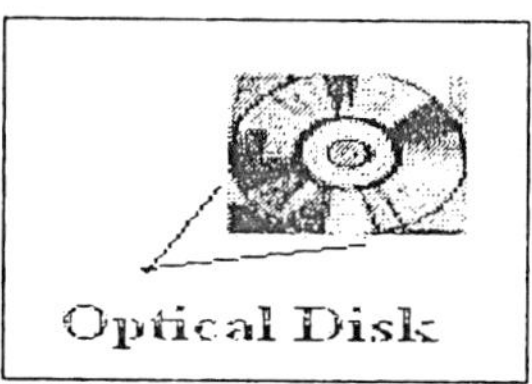

Optical Disk

Earlier when optical disks were introduced they had a major disadvantage that once data written on it could not be erased, hence the disk could not be reused. But these days' reusable disks are available.

The storage capacity of optical disk is enormous in comparison to magnetic disk. A single optical disk can store data in terms of gigabytes. This capacity can be imagined with this fact, that total characters of 33 encyclopedias can be stored in a single optical disk. These disks are removable like floppy disks. The chances of head crash or data corruption are relatively less than the magnetic media.

Bubble Storage

Bubble storage or bubble memory is the storage of future. This device is not much in use these days due to it's high cost. Dr. Andrew Bobeck of Graham Bell Laboratory invented bobble memory in 1996. In the bubble memory bubble like magnetic fields embedded on the surface of garnet wafers. The data is stored as the presence or absence of electronic bubbles on the device to register the binary pattern. Storage capacity of bubble memory is enormous and can store up to 65 lakh bits per square inch. This is non-volatile memory and can operate in harsh environment, whereas shock, dust or temperature might adversely affect magnetic disks tapes.

EXERCISE QUESTIONS

Write answers in your words:

1. What are Punched Cards and Paper Tapes? Explain.
2. Write about Magnetic Tapes in 30 words.
3. Explain the charactertics of Magnetic Disks in 100 words.
4. Write the type of Magnetic Disks and explain their uses in computer technology.
5. What is Hard Disk and Disk Pack? Explain.

Fill in the blanks:

1. Punched card's standard size is..................
2. A card punching machine contains.................... and..................
3. Spool is about..............inch wide and cassette is about............inch wide.
4. In magnetic tapes rows are called.............and columns are called..................
5. Data is stored on the disk in............ in...............and...........
6. The outer track on the disk in............ and...........
7. MS-DOS devices the disk into..................................... and...........
8. A disk pack consisting 4 platters use........... surface for data storage.
9. A single optical disk can store data in terms of...........
10. Bubble memory is a...........memory.

True/False:

1. Punched cards and paper tapes are reusable.
2. The record length of file stored in Punched cards can be more than 80 characters.
3. Magnetic tape allows random access.
4. Data can be recorded on the both side of magnetic tape.
5. Parity bit is used to check data transmission error.
6. One magnetic disk may curtain variable size sectors.
7. Floppy disk is made of soft plastic material.
8. Floppy with 5¼" diameter called mini floppy.
9. Hard disk does not allow disk partitioning.

10. Data corruption in optical disk is less than the magnetic disk.

Pick the correct one:

1. A good backing storage device should have—
   a. High retrieval speed b. High storage capacity
   c. Low cost permit capacity d. All of the above

2. Punched cards were standardized by—
   a. IBM Corp. b. Digital Equipment Corp.
   c. Apple Computers d. None of the above

3. Data stored on magnetic tape of 9 track consists—
   a. 1 bit code, 8 parity bits b. 8-bit code, 1 parity bit
   c. 5 bit code, 4 parity bits d. 6-bit code, 1 parity bit

4. A gap between two block on tape called—
   a. Inter Record Gap b. Inter Byte Gap
   c. Inter Block Gap d. None of the above

5. R/W operations to and from the magnetic tape always transfers—
   a. One byte b. One bit
   c. One block d. None of the above

6. Storage capacity of disk depends on—
   a. Number of tracks b. Number of sectors
   c. Size of sector d. All of the above

7. Disk bootstrap program is stored in—
   a. FAT area b. Directory area
   c. Boot area d. Data storage area

8. Number of copies used for FAT—
   a. Single copy b. Two copies
   c. Three copies d. Four copies

9. In a disk pack consist 8 platters, number of heads used for r/w operations would be—
   a. 8 b. 16
   c. 15 d. 14

10. Optical disk uses............ for data storage.
    a. Ultra-violet technique b. Laser technique
    c. Infra-red technique d. none of the above.

Chapter 7

COMPUTER TECHNOLOGY: MICROPROCESSOR

- Introduction
- Math Co-Processor
- Clock Speed of CPU
- Inside the Microprocessor
- Different Types of Microprocessor
- Major Chip Makers
- Pentium
- Motorola
- Exercise Questions

INTRODUCTION

We have already studied that CPU is the heart of computer system. All peripherals are connected to CPU, which send or receive data and instructions to and from the CPU. This CPU consists of three parts—

1. Main memory
2 ALU
3. CU

In which ALU performs the mathematical calculation and logical comparisons. And CU controls the entire operations of ALU. Due to VLSI technique available in 1970s, ALU and CU could be integrated on a single silicon chip. These is the microprocessor.

Microprocessor can do more than arithmetic. There are two main kinds of operations which microprocessor does. These are—

- Tests
- Conditional branches

Test involves the comparison of two data items for equality, greater than or less than type operations, while the conditional branches let the computer change the sequence of steps being executed based on test.

MATH CO-PROCESSOR

The execution of high precession arithmetical operations may involve a large number of complex steps to be performed. It could be inefficient for the microprocessor to dedicate itself to this task, because it will mean a waste of processor's time. So it is possible to attach another processor on the motherboard, which is dedicated to the task of handling complex arithmetic computations. This processor is called 'math co-processor' or 'auxiliary processor' and acts as slaves to the main processor.

CLOCK SPEED OF CPU

Two cycles are used during the processing of each program's instruction— the instruction cycle and the execution cycle. Both are synchronized by a specific number of electrical pulses produced by an electronic clock built into the microprocessor chip. This is the clock speed at which the instructions are executed. Thus is the speed with which an instruction is executed is also directly related to the chips clock speed or the number of pulse pre second. Clock speed is measured in millions of pulses per second (Megahertz or MHz.) So higher the clock speed means higher the execution speed of microprocessor.

INSIDE THE MICROPROCESSOR

The microprocessor consists of the ALU, the CU and some special purpose storage areas called 'registers'.

Use of ALU and CU has already been discussed above

During the operation of ALU and there is a movement of information between the various units of the computer system. In order to handle this process satisfactorily and to speed up the rate of information transfer, processor uses the registers. These are of various types and uses to hold the information temporarily. The number of registers various from processor to processor.

A 8-bit microprocessor has built in 8-bit line data or data bus. This means, the chip can only retrieve and process a single 8-bit (or 1-bite) of data at a time. An address bus is also built into every processor to determine the primary locations of the instructions and data that are needed. The maximum memory supported by any microprocessor chip can be calculated by the formula—maximum memory (in bytes)= $2^n - 1$, where n is the number of address lines supported by any microprocessor.

So if a microprocessor support 16-lines address bus, then it is possible for the chip to identify a maximum of $2^{16} -1$ or 65535 separate storage locations. Since an 8-bit microprocessor can manipulate only a single byte of data at a time and a 16-bit chip can handle 2 byte of data in the same unit of time. Hence, in general a 16-bit microprocessor chip will be faster than the 8-bit processor chip.

MAJOR CHIP MAKERS

Intel

Intel is not only America's but also the words number one chipmaker company. Intel also manufactures communication and networking products, various peripheral components and many other components used in computers, at large scale. This company has a wide range of microprocessor chips like 4004, 8080, 8086/8088, 80286, 80386, 80486, and Pentium. Intel has also introduced a range of math co-processors such as 8087, 80287 and 80387. There are also known as '87' chips.

4004

This was the first chip released by Intel in 1971. This was a 4-bit chip never used in computers. Firms like Texas Instructions, Hewlett-Packard and Sinclare Research put this processor chip was found in making digital watches. After the introduction of 4004 chips, Intel released many chips time to time.

8080

Intel 8080 was introduction in 1974 and contained about 6,000 transistors. The processor chip also contained an 8-bit internal bus. The first microcomputer kit Altair 8800 developed by Micro Instrumentation and Telemetry system (MITS) was based on this chip. The speed of 8080 chip was about 60 MIPS at a clock speed of 2 MHz.

8088/86

In June 1978 Intel released another chip named 8086. The datapath between 8086 and main memory is 16 bit wide, hence all operation to and from processor are done 2-bytes at a time. Once retrieved however, data is processed 16-bit chip.

This processor chip contains about 29,000 transistors and works at a speed of .33 MIPS, at a clock speed of 5 MHz.

8086 contains total 14 registers. These are—

- General purpose registers
- Flag registers
- Segment registers
- Index registers
- Stack segment registers and pointer
- Base registers
- Instruction pointer register

General-purpose registers are four. In theory, these can be used for anything. However, each register has certain special functions, and may be more efficient than other in some cases. These are—

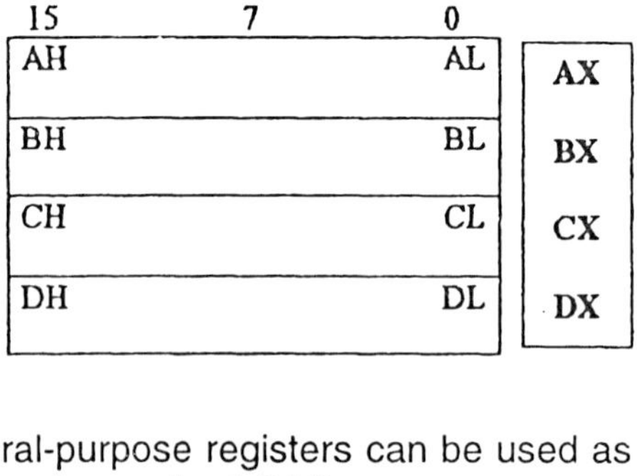

15	7	0	
AH		AL	AX
BH		BL	BX
CH		CL	CX
DH		DL	DX

General-purpose registers can be used as a whole 16-bit or in two parts, each of 8-bits.

- AX register is sometime called 'accumulator' and used in arithmetic operations.
- BX register participates in forming address in real mode.

- CX holds counts in loops and repeated operations.
- DX specifies/I/O addresses. It also works AX during multiply and divide instructions.
- Flag register is only one and contains a series of bits that determine the status of microprocessor. Programs usually manipulate this register with special instructions to set and clear bits.
- Four registers i.e. Code Segment (CS), Data Segment (DS), and Stack Segment (SS) and Extra Segment (ES) points to the current segment for Code (CS), Data (DS) and the Stack (SS). ES is an extra segment that helps transfer data between segments. These segments registers participate is address calculations.

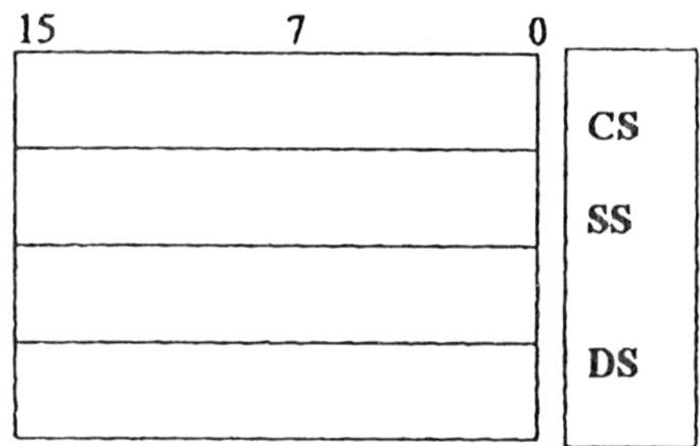

- Two index registers Stack Index (SI) and Data Index (DI), participate primary in forming addresses. Unlike the general-purpose register they cannot be spit in half.
- One Stack Segment Register and Pointer (SP), points to the top of the stack. Stack serves as a temporary holding area for data.
- One Base Register (BP) points to items on the stack.
- One Instruction Pointer Register (IP) is the offset in the code segment of the next instruction.

A stablemen of 8086 is 8088. Unlike the 8086, can internally process 16-bits of data in one operation and send or receive 8-bits of data in one operation and send or receive 8-bits data at a time. Thus it is a 8/16 bit microprocessor.

An expanded built in address bus with 20-lines permits both the 8086 and 8088 to identify about a million separate primary separate primary storage locations [2^{20}–1) = 1,048,575 bytes or 1 MB].

80286

Intel released 80286-microprocessor chip in the market. This chip has a 16-bit internal bus and 16-bit external datapath. 80286 chips contain about 1,34,000 transistors and works as a speed of about 1.2 MIPS at the clock speed of 8 MHz. It also contain a 24 lines built in bus which allows up to 16 MB of working memory. 80286 processor has the ability to work in two fundamental operating modes.

- Real mode or 8086 compatible mode.
- Protected mode

In real address mode 80286 does its best to behave just like its predecessors, 8080 and 8086. In real mode 80286 can only access 1 MB of memory even though the chip's internal circuitry allow to access up to 16 MB of memory. Another key characteristic of real address mode is that any program may read or write code at any byte in the 1 MB address space, simply by loading the desired address directly into processor's registers.

In protected mode, processor can access its entire 16 MB physical address space and prevent the memory access conflicts that occur all to frequently among DOS programs. In contrast to the 286's is real address mode; the memory locations each program can access are strictly controlled in protected mode. The protected feature prevents one programme from another, tempering with any part of the memory that does not belong to it.

80386

80386 are closely related to the 80286 processor in function design and software compatibility. In a general sense, 80386 are a stretched version of 80286. This 32-bit chip is about 10 times faster than 8088 and about 2-4 times faster than 80286 depending upon the clock rate 4096 MB (more than 1 GB) with it's 32 lines address bus. 80386 can run more than one operating system simultaneously or juggle separate programs. The most unusual feature of 80386 is its ability to act like several 8086s running simultaneously. An appropriate crafted operating system could permit the 80386 to run several conventional DOS applications at the same time. Hence the UNIX (multi-user operating system) cannot run below 80386 microprocessor.

80486

The next generation product, which Intel launched, is 80486-microprocessor chip. 80486 processor is a 32/33-bit microprocessor, which introduced in 1988. 80486 can work at the speed of 16 to 40 MIPS at a clock speed of 25-66 MHz.

PENTIUM

Pentium microprocessor chip is the fastest among all the chips introduced by Intel. It was launched in May 1993. The performance of the Pentium chip is almost twice as that of fastest 80486. Pentium process 64-bit internally and has a 64-bit external data path. It has 16 K of internal memory cache (8K for data and 8 K for instruction) where as 80486 contains only 8 K internal cache for both data and instructions. It consists over 3.1 million transistors in it in comparison to the 80486's 1.2-1.3 million transistors. Pentium chip has a speed of 112 MIPS at the clock speed of 60-100 MHz.

MOTOROLA

Another major chipmaker company is the Motorola is the biggest competitor of Intel in the chip market. Motorola's microprocessor chips are generally used by Apple Computers. This range contains—MC6809, MC68000, MC68008, MC68010, MC68012, MC68020, MC68040, and the Power PC.

MC6809 was the first microprocessor chip released by Motorola Company. In 1997, the nest generation and much powerful processor chip MC68000 came in the market. In MC68000 a 16-bit external data bus is used between the chip and primary storage but processing is done internally 32-bit at a time. It is thus a 16/32 bit microprocessor and is much powerful than the Intel's 8080/86, This chip also consists a 24-lines address bus and permits to the access the storage locations up to 16 MB. After MC68000 Motorola introduced MC68008 in 1982. It works, at a clock speed of 8 MHz. In 1983, another released was MC68010, which consists a 32-bit internal bus and 32-bit external data path; hence it is a true 32/32-bit microprocessor. MC68020 is the next one in MC series chips. It is a full 32-bit microprocessor and workers at a clock speed of 12-20 MHz. One of the next popular processor MC68040 introduced in 1988. It consists dual cache (4K data/4K instructions) and dual memory management units, and works at the maximum clock speed up to 33 MHz, Power PC is the latest one in Motorola's is chips range. Motorola, IBM Corp. jointly develops power PC processor and Apple Computers. It contains about 2.8 million transistors and runs at a clock speed between 50-66 MHz. It uses a 32K unified instruction/data cache; Different models of power PC are available now such as Power PC-601, 603, 604 and 620.

EXERCISE QUESTIONS

Give the answer in your own words:

1. What is Microprocessor?
2. Explain the Math Co-processor, Clock Speed of Microprocessor and its registration.
3. Write about the types of Microprocessors:

   a. 4004 b. 8080

   c. 8086/88
4. What is chip in computer and write its utility?

Fill in the blanks:

1. Two operators which microprocessor does are................. and.............
2. Some special purpose storage areas inside microprocessor, called.............
3. .... acts as a salves to the main processor.
4. Maximum memory supported by any microprocessor, can be calculated by formula.............
5. In theory............. Registers are..........................and.............
6. Four segment registers are..........................and............
7. A stalemate of 8086 is.............
8. 80286 can work in two fundamental modes. These as.............and.............
9. ....and.............are two major chipmaker companies.
10. Power PC is product for.............

True/False:

1. Clock speed of microprocessor in measured is MHz.
2. Microprocessor consists ALU, CU registers and motherboard.
3. The number of registers various from processor to processor.
4. Maximum memory supported by any microprocessor depends on external data bus.
5. Higher the clock speed means higher the execution speed of microprocessor.
6. Motorola develops Pentium.
7. In general, a 16-bit processor is slower than 8-bit processor chip.
8. General-purpose registers can be used as whole 16-bit or in two parts, each one of 8-bits.
9. In real mode 80286 behave, just like 8088 and 8086.
10. 80386 don't permit to run several conventional DOS applications at the same time through an appropriate crafted OS.

Pick the correct one:

1. 601, 603, 604 and 620 are the different models of—

   a. Pentium b. Power PC

   C. 80486 d. None of the above

2. An 8-bit microprocessor can manipulate only..........at a time..........

   a. 8-bit of data b. 4-bit of data

   c. 16-bit of data d. none of the above

3. Intel's..........was a 4-bit chip.

   a. 8080 b. 8088

   c. 4004 d. None of the above

4. Chip used in first microprocessor kit Altair 8800 was—

   a. 8080 b. 8088

   c. 8086 d. None of the above

5. 8086 contains..............registers.
   a. 10 b. 11
   c. 14 d. None of the above
6. Which is general-purpose register?
   a. AX b. BX
   c. CX d. All of the above
7. CS is the—
   a. Segment register b. Flag register
   c. Instruction pointer register d. All of the above
8. In real mode, 80286 can access up to............memory.
   a. 16 MB b. 1 MB
   c. 640 KB d. None of the above
9. Power PC is developed by—
   a. IBM Corp. b. Apple Computers
   c. Motorola d. All of the above
10. Name of Motorola microprocessor chips starts with—
    a. PC b. TC
    c. MC d. None of the above

CHAPTER 8

OPERATING SOFTWARE IN COMPUTER

- Introduction
- Computer Software
- Function of Operating System
- DOS
- Unix
- Computer Language 'C'
- Exercise Questions

INTRODUCTION

Computer performs all types of operating such as arithmetic calculation and logical operations. CPU does these operations through a set of instructions. These instructions are written by computer users for solving their problem and by computer manufactures for managing the activities of the computer. Hence these instructions arranged in a systematic manner to perform a specific task are called 'Software'. In general we can define software as, all kind of instructions and programs that instruct the hardware to perform the desire operations. All the software can be classified into three categories as follows—

1. System softwares
2. Application software
3. Development software

Computer Softwares

These are the master control programs and are used to control the computer system. They enable the machine to accept and run other system or application programmes, eliminates the necessity of human intervention at each stage. Specialists in machine/assembly languages often develop these Operating Systems (OS) fall in this category, such as DOS, UNIX, and CP/M OS/2 etc.

FUNCTION OF OPERATING SYSTEM

- Operating system manages the memory i.e. keeps track of the state of each location of main memory and determine whether the main memory has to be shared by one or more programs/microprocessors. If shared then with microprocessor/program will use first.
- Operating system manages the peripherals i.e. keeps track of all the input/out devices. These devices include printers, plotters magnetic disks, magnetic tapes, and keyboard, VDU etc.
- Operating system controls the system resources, if a program crashes from any type of error, control returns to operating system, which then determines the type of error.
- Operating system acts as commands from the user, verifies their accuracy, loads what is needed from disk and initiates the execution of the user command.
- Operating system controls the execution of application programs. An operating system can be of either types.
- A single user operating system; allow all computer resources to use by a single user at a time. DOS falls in this category.
- A multi-user operating system allows all computer resources to use by many users at a time. UNIX and XENIX fall in this category.
- A multi-tasking operating system is one that supports several tasks at a time, but only by a single user. IBM's OS/2 falls in this category.

DOS

DOS stands for Disk Operating System. There are many companies, which develop the DOS, but two of them are most popular. One is MS-DOS developed by Microsoft Inc. other one is PC-DOS developed by IBM Corp.

Version	*Date of Release*	*Primary Reason For Release*
1.0	August, 1981	First release
2.0	March, 1983	Fixed disk drive supported, data redirection commands added
3.0	August, 1984	1.2 MB Floppy disk supported (5½")
3.2	December, 1985	3½" disk supported
3.3	March, 1987	Capable of creating disk partitions larger than 32 MB, MODE and RESTORE commands added.
4.0	April, 1989	Support for expended memory
6.0	January, 1993	Allow connecting more than one computer. A data compression command added.

In early eighties when 8080 based 8-bit microcomputers were in use, it was being run on an operating system called CP/M-80 at that time was one of the world's most popular operating system.

Tim Paterson of Seattle Computer Products had written a 16-bit operating system called 86-DOS for Intel's 8080 microprocessor based machines, Microsoft purchased 86-DOS from Seattle Computer Products and promptly christened it as MS-DOS version 1.0.

MS-DOS Versions

The DOS software is divided into three different files.

These are—

- IO.SYS
- MSDOS.SYS
- COMMAND.COM

The disk, which contains all the three files, is called bootable disk.

UNIX

Kan Thompson of AT & T Bell Laboratory U.S.A. developed UNIX operating system in 1969. This was initially written in Assemble language. After the development of 'C' language. This conversion made UNIX portable because software written in assembly language wants many changes to run on different platforms.

There are two popular UNIX versions. These are AT & T version of AT & T Bell Lab, U.S.A and BSD version of University of California, Berkeley, At & T version are concentrated on commercial applications, whereas BSD version are concentrated on improving system performance. UNIX operating system is divided into two parts:

1. Kernel
2. Shell

Kernel is the master programme that directly interacts with hardware and controls the computer's resources, allotting them to different users and to different tasks. However kernel does not deal directly with user. Instead, it starts up a software interactive programme 'Shell', for each user and the system. In its role as a command interpreter, the shell takes the commands from user and sets them for execution. After that Kernel decides exactly when each requested program runs. Since UNIX is a multi-user operating system, hence different shells are used by each user, which helps to separate one user's task another, while the Kernel maintains unified overall control.

UNIX operating system has two powerful features. One is, that, UNIX is highly programmable and contains its own programming language, which is called as 'shell script'. Second one is, that, UNIX has powerful file security feature. Any user can handle any file in the permitted mode only. This feature of UNIX prevents the unauthorized access of files.

Application Softwares

Application software is designed for specific applications. Applications soft wares are designed for different purposes. All these software are available either for common applications like word Processors or Data Base Management System (DBMS), or for user's specific need solve these own problems. This software may be written in any language. These days 'C' is the most popular language for writing application softwares. Some standard application software are—

DBMS

A data base management system helps to define a data structure and can organize, process and present selected data elements from the database. A simple database is organized on paper and frees the programmer from the need to money about the organization and location of data. Some popular DBMS are dBase and FOXPRO.

Word Processor

Word processor package gives the facility to create, view and manipulate text. Word processing gives facility the checking spelling of text, moving a block of text from one position to another find and replace a word string from another word/string automatically and let more. Some word processors Word Star, Word Perfect etc.

Spreadsheet

Spreadsheet packages are used for processing numeric figures. In a spreadsheet, file is divided into vertical columns and horizontal rows. Intersection of rows and columns forms the Cell. Each cell can hold one value of formula. Spreadsheet package automatically updates the resultant cell, if a change is made in any related Cell. These also allow seeing the values in various types of graphs. Some spreadsheet software is LOTUS 1-2-3, Super Calc, and Visual etc.

CAD/CAM

Computer Aided Designed/Manufacturing is one of the most popular application software for designing purpose. This software allows drawing computerized designed of different engineering products. Draftsmen, engineers, and other designers most frequently use this software.

Development Software

Development software are the translator software which are used to translate different programs written in different language, into machine language. These are necessary because computers under stand only machine language. Development software are—

- Assembler
- Interpreters
- Compiler

Assembler

Assembler is used to translate programming language. Assembler takes less space in computer memory hence it is faster the interpreters and compilers.

Interpreter

Interpreter is used to translate the programs written in high-level language. Interpreter is software, which is easy to write for system programmers than the compilers. Interpreters translate one line of source code at time and translate into object code, if the line is syntactically correct. In interpreter debugging is easy due to it's line is by line translation hence it saves time of programmer for removing the errors. Each language consists it's own interpreters is that it doesn't store the object code for future, use, so every time when program runs interprets translates of program. Interpreter takes more memory in computer than any assembler.

Compiler

Compiler is also used to translate the programs written in high-level languages. Like interpreter separate compilers are used for different languages. Compilers work differently from interpreters, compiler accept whole sources code and translate into machine code. Once the object code is created, it store this code into a file permanently for future use. So next time it directly runs the object code rather than translating again. Compiler also stores the error in a separate area/file if any and displays them on the screen as a whole. So debugging is difficult with compilers but the execution is faster than the interpreter.

Languages

Each nature language has a systematic method of using symbols of that language. These methods are given by some rules those tell us which words to use and how to use them. Computer operations are also completely controlled by the systematic set of instructions. These set of instructions are known as computer languages. All programs developed for any purpose are written in computer languages. There are different types of computer languages available. All these languages can be classified in the following four broad categories—

- First generation languages
- Second-generation languages
- Third generation languages
- Fourth generation languages.

First Generation Languages

We have already studies that computer can do a variety of jobs; it can process numeric as well as non-numeric data very efficiently. But computer doesn't understand directly this data. To process this data it has to be converted in the binary code. This set of instruction codes, which can be directly understood by the CPU of a computer without the help of a translating program is called 'Machine language'. Thus, machine language is the fundamental language of a computer. The instructions of machine language have two parts—

- Operation code or function code
- Operand

Operation code sometimes called 'Opode', tells the computer what the instruction will perform. The other part (i.e. operand) is the address of memory location where the data or instruction are to be found or where the results are to be put.

The execution of machine language is very fast. In fact it is the fastest in all the languages. Machine language has more disadvantages than its advantages. Machine language is hardware depended language and vary from hardware to hardware. That means each computer manufacturer has its own code in binary form. This drawback of machine language programming. These programmers should have an extensive knowledge of hardware before the programming. Also debugging in machine language is very difficult. In other words we can say that machine language is difficult to learn for programmers but easy to understand by computers.

Second Generation Languages

Second generation language is the assembly language. Both, first generation language and second generation language also called as 'low level language' due to its closeness with CPU. Assembly language is slightly higher than the machine language. This consists of two parts—

- Mnemonics
- Operands

Mnemonics are the replacement of operation code present in machine language, and suggest the meaning of functions to represent operations. Operand is similar to the operand of machine language and is the addresses of memory locations where the data or instructions are to be found or where the result is to be put. Due to use of the mnemonics programs written in assembly language are not directly understood by CPU, hence a translator program is needed to convert this language into machine language. This translator program is called 'Assembler' and supplied by the computer manufacturer.

Assembly language is relatively easy to learn than machine language because of the use of mnemonics. Debugging is also relatively easy than machine language. Similar to machine language, this language also suffers with non-portability.

Third Generation Languages

Third generation languages are frequently called as High Level Languages or HLL in short. These languages are English like languages and follow some rules called 'syntax'. HLL languages are first converted into machine code by some translator program by either interpreter or by complier, for execution due to the English problem rather than locations of memory. High-level languages are standardized to a large extent hence the programs written in one language for one computer can be used on a different computer with slight or no modification. Because of the portability of high-level languages programmers need not have to know more about hardware. Only drawback of these languages is that the execution of these languages is slow, because of the use of translator program. High-level languages are slow, because of the use of translator program. Programmers frequently use high-level language these days. Some major high-level languages are—

- BASIC
- COBOL
- PASCAL
- FORTRAN
- ADA
- ALGOL
- RPG
- SNOBOL

BASIC

BASIC stands for Beginners All purpose Symbolic Instruction Code. BASIC can be said as 'Mother language' for these days computers, because it is designed for beginners and non-specialists. BASE was developed by professor John Kemeny and Thomas Kurtz at Dartmouth College of United States, in 1960. As the name suggests this language can be easily learn by beginners and non-programmers. After the development of this language different versions were there in the market with different features. ANSI (American National Standard Institute) of USA standardizes the BASIC language in 1978, first time. Most versions of BASIC are interpreter based. Due to its simple English-like syntax, simple friendly statements and few keywords, BASIC is widely used in schools to develop programming skill in children. BASIC is also business and scientific applications. A simple program written in BASIC looks like as—

- 10 REM EXAMPLE PROGRAM OF BASIC
- 20 REM SUM OF TWO NUMBERS
- 25 PRINT "ENTER THE VALUES OF A & B"
- 30 INPUT "TWO VALUES;" A, B

- 40 LET S = A+B
- 50 PRINT "THE SUM OF"; A; "AND"; B; "IS;" ;S
- 60 END

This sample program calculates and prints the sum of two numbers which are entered by user through keyboard.

BASIC has got line numbers to direct the interpreter/compiler to executive the program in the number order. So a new line can be entered even after completing the entering of the program (line no. 25 in the above example), by simply assigning a new line number between the numbers of the line between which we want to enter the new line.

Expressions are formed by combining variables, constants and arithmetic operators like (+, –, *, /,). The words REM, PRINT, INPUT, END, are some keywords used in BASIC language which performs specific operations and are the part of language whereas the letters A, B, S, etc. are called 'variables' and may have other names, and defined by the programmer.

COBOL

COBOL stands for Common Business Oriented Language. COBOL were developed by an American committee name CODASYL (Conference of Data System Languages). The first version of COBOL was developed in 1960, but first standardized in 1996 by ANSI of United States. ANSI has introduced three standards of COBOL till now. These are called as COBOL-68 (Standardized in 1985). It is a compiler based language. There are many reasons of it's popularity. It is one of the most structure languages and is divided in to various divisions, sections and paragraphs COBOL is highly portable language and execution is also very fast. English is like statements of COBOL makes quite easy to program and debug for programmers. It is a file oriented programming language and provides a powerful framework for data management and processing, hence it is one of the most popular languages for business applications. The one drawback with this language is that programs written in COBOL tends to get too long.

- A SIMPLE COBOL PROGRAM LOOK LIKE AS—
- A SAMPLE COBOL PROGRAM:

- IDENTIFICATION DIVISION.
- PROGRAM-ID EXAMPLE.
- ENVIRONMENT DIVISION.
- CONFIGURATION SECTION.
- SOURCE COMPUTER. IBM-PC OR ÇOMPATIBLE.
- OBJECT COMPUTER. IBM-PC OR COMPUTER.
- DATA DIVISION
- WORKING-STORAGE SECTION.
- 01 NAME PIC X (25) VALUE SPACE.
- PROCEDURE DIVISION.
- CONTROL-PARA.
- DISPLAY "PLEASE ENTER YOUR NAME:".
- ACCEPT NAME.
- DISPLAY "YOUR NAME IS:" NAME.
- STOP RUN.

This is a simple program written in COBOL, which accepts name from user and display on the screen. IDENTIFICATION DIVISION, ENVIRONMENT DIVISION, DATA DIVISION and PROCEDURE DIVISION, are the four divisions and are necessary to define in each COBOL program. Each division is divided into one more than one sections. Each section is used for some particular purpose. All division names, section names, section names, and works like PROGRAM-ID, SOURCE COMPUTER, OBJECT-COMPUTER, PIC, VALUE, SPACE, ACCEPT, DISPLAY etc. are the few keywords used in COBOL and the words like NAME, EXAMPLE etc. are used-define word which the user define. COBOL compiler required that certain parts of every statement be placed in certain columns. There are 80 columns in each line out of which columns 1-6 are used for page numbers and line numbers. These are optional and can be left blank.* in column 7 indicates a comment line and not compiled to produce object code. These lines are used for documenting purpose. All division and section names start between 8-11 columns, and all the COBOL statements are placed in column 12-72. Columns 8-11 columns, and all the COBOL called 'area A' and columns 12-72 called 'area B' in COBOL terminology. Remaining columns (73-80) are ignored by COBOL compiler.

COMPUTER LANGUAGE 'C'

C is a relatively new language, which was developed by Dennis Ritchi of AT & T Bell Laboratory USA in 1972-73. This is very popular language for writing application softwares these days. Actually C is not a high language like COBOL, but lies in between HLL and low-level languages. The reason is that it allows the programmer to access the memory locations by the use of pointers. Pointers are special type of variable, which points the locations of variables and arrays. C is also a programmer to directly access the registers of microprocessor. This feature put C language near to assembly of microprocessor. These features put C language near to assembly language and make it a powerful language. The popularity of C language can be imagined with this fact 95% part of UNIX operating system is written in C. Most of the compilers are also written in C. A sample C program looks like as—

- /* A sample program written in C*/
- # include <stdio.h>
- main()
- {
- char ans, name [20];
- ans= 'Y'
- While (ans ! = 'n' !! 'N')
- {
- print ("This is a sample program:);
- print (Please Enter Your Name:");
- scanf ("% s", name);
- printf ("n Hello % s", name);
- printf ("n want to Contain (Y/N)?")
- ans=getch ();
- }
- }

This program accepts a name from keyboard and display on the screen. This is a repetitive program and continues until user enters a 'n' or 'N'. Main () is the function from which C always starts its execution. Curly braces indicate the code block, printf () function is a function in C, which is used to display strings/values on the screen. Similarly scanf () and getch () functions are used to take input from keyboard. C language is a case sensitive language and has distinction between upper case and lower case. For example main () function written as Maim () gives a syntax error. Hence care must be taken at the time of writing C programs.

PASCAL

PASCAL language was developed in another language named ALGOL, by professor Nicklans Wtirth of Federal institute of Technology Zurick, in 1970. This was named after great French mathematician sir Blaise Pascal. PASCAL is the first language, which used structured programming concept. PASCAL is a highly portable language and executive at very high speed. It is a compiler-based language and interpreter versions are not available. Programming and debugging in PASCAL is very easy due to its readability. There are two versions of PASCAL which are popular is a popular language on microcomputers for business and scientific applications.

FORTRAN

FORTRAN is an acronym of formula translation. John W. Bakus and IBM CORPORATION jointly developed it in 1954. First version of this language was known as FORTRAN-1. ANSI standardized this language in 1966; FORTRAN-IV was the first standardized version. FORTRAN-77 version was developed for minicomputers while the others were developed for large computers. Like COBOL language FORTRAN program also required certain parts of every statement be placed in certain columns. It is a compiler based language and is popular among the scientists and mathematicians to solve complex algebraic calculations.

ALGOL

ALGOL is an acronym of Algorithmic Language. This was developed to solve complex algebraic problems, in 1960. Some other versions of ALGOL were ALGOL-58 and ALGOL-60.

ADA

ADA language was developed by a group of scientists headed by Ichbiah at Honey well Computer Company in 1980.

This language was named in honour of lady ADA Augusta Lovelace, the first lady programmer. ADA is a complicated language and is used in the field of defence.

RPG

RPG Programme Generator (RPG) is a business oriented general-purpose language developed by IBM Corp, in 1961. This language is designed to generate the output reports resulting from the processing of common business applications.

SNOBOL

SNOBOL is an acronym of String Oriented symbolic Language developed in 1962. This language has very powerful string manipulation features that facilities version types of operations on string like string comparison, splitting of string, concatenation of and many other string oriented operations.

Fourth Generation Languages

In short fourth generation languages are called '4GLs'. These languages have more advanced feature than the third generation languages and are much closer to the nature language. Programmer has to make less programming efforts in 4GLs. Some 4GLs are—

- Structure Query Language (SQL)
- LOGISTIC

EXERCISE QUESTIONS

1. What are Computer Softwares?
2. Explain the Function of Operating Systems?
3. Explain the DOS in 200 words.
4. What do you understand by the Unix Softwares?
5. Explain the Computer Language 'C' and write its application in computer.

Fill in the blanks:

1. ....are used to control the computer system.
2. DOS stands for.............
3. .... is used to designed the product through computer.
4. Supernal is a.............

5. .... is used to translate programs written in assembly language.
6. Computer can understand only.............
7. Two parts of assembly language are......... and...........
8. Third parts of assembly language are............. and.............
9. ....language is used for beginners and non-programmers.
10. Three standards of COBOLS are...................

True/False:

1. Development softwares are the master control program.
2. CP/M is application software.
3. UNIX is a multi-user operating system.
4. Ken Thompson developed 'C' language.
5. Kernel part of UNIX directly interacts and compilers.
6. Word Perfect is a word processor.
7. Assembly is faster than interpreter and compilers.
8. Assembly language is relatively easy to learn than machine language.
9. COBOL programs are divided into four divisions.
10. FORTRAN-77 version was developed for microcomputers.

Pick the correct one:

1. OS/2 is a.............operating system.
   a. Single user, single task b. Multi-user
   c. Single user, multi-task d. None of the above
2. First version of MS-DOS was?
   a. Version 1.0 b. Version 1.1
   c. Version 0.1 d. None of the above
3. .... Percent part of UNIX written in 'C' language?
   a. About 40% b. About 60%
   c. About 95% d. 100%
4. DOS software is divided into—
   a. 9 files b. 3 files
   c. 16 files d. 2 files

5. dBase is a—
   a. System software b. Development software
   c. Application software d. none of the above
6. Which is translator program?
   a. Assembler b. Interpreter
   c. Compiler d. All of the above
7. In which language programming is most difficult?
   a. Assembly language b. C language
   c. PASCAL language d. Machine language
8. In COBOL which area is called as 'area' A'.?
   a. Column 1-6 b. Column 8-11
   c. COBOL d. C
9. Which language use pointers?
   a. ADA b. AAD
   c. COBOL d. None of the above
10. Which language is used in defense?
   a. C b. ADA
   c. ALGOL d. FORTRAN

CHAPTER 9

NUMBER SYSTEM IN COMPUTER

- Introduction
- Positional number system
- Binary numbers system
- Decimal number system
- Octal number system
- Hexadecimal number system
- Conversion of Numbers in different forms
- Exercise Questions

INTRODUCTION

Even the computer can do a variety of jobs efficiently these days, but first when it was invented it was basically used for numeric calculations. Now computer is able to process text and picture text and picture, but neither it understand nor process text and picture in its usual form. To do so, it is first converted into numbers. There are various types of number systems, which can be classified in to two categories—

- Non-positional number system different symbols are used for different numbers such as I for 1, II for 2, III for 3 and so on. Large numbers are formed by combining these symbols such as XXV for 25 (i.e. X for 10 and V FOR 5). Each symbol is simply added to find out the value of a particular number. This number system is not very efficient for computers, hence is not used in computers.
- Positional number systems are widely used by human and computers. In this system, only few symbols called digits are used and represent different values on the position,

they occupy in the number. The value of each digits in such a number, is determined by three considerations—

- The digits itself
- The position of the digit in the number
- The base of the number system

TYPES OF POSITIONAL NUMBER SYSTEM

These are four types and explained below:

1. Binary numbers system
2. Decimal number system
3. Octal number system
4. Hexadecimal number system

1. Binary Number System

Binary Number System is the most popular number system for computers. All digital computers use binary number system. This number system has base 2. It means all the numbers can be represented by only two symbols 0 and 1. The reason for using this number system by digital computers because computer circuits have to handle only two digits 0 or 1 which could easily be represented by ON or OFF states of the circuitry.

In binary number system place value of each digit doubles for each successive digit starting from right. For example in binary number 1101—

Place value of 1 = 2^0 or 1

Place value of 0 = 2^1 or 2

Place value of 1 = 2^2 or 4

Place value of 1 = 2^3 or 8

BINARY ARITHMETIC

Addition

Binary addition has four rules—

(1) 0 + 0 = 0

(2) 0 + 1 = 1

(3) 1 + 0 = 1

(4) 1 + 1 = 0 carry 1

This carry is then added to next left binary.

Ex. Addition of $(110)_2$ and $(100)_2$

Sol.

		1	1	0
+		1	0	0
	1	0	1	0

From the right side, in first column according to rule (1), 0 + 0 gives 0. In second column according the rule (3), 1 + 0 gives 1. In third column according the rule (4), 1+1 give 0 and 1 carry. Hence in the third column we put 0 and 1 carry in left most column. This gives the total $(1010)_2$ of the above two binary numbers,

Subtraction

Computers cannot subtract two binary numbers. But this is not a problem for computers. Compliment method is used in computers for binary subtraction. Computers use two's compliment method most frequently for subtractions. Two two's compliment can be found by adding 1 is one's compliment, i.e.

2's compliment + = 1's compliment +1

1's compliment can be finding by reversing each bit of binary number

(i.e. ever 0 is converted into 1 and every 1 is converted onto 0).

Step in binary subtraction using 2's compliment method—

(1) Find the binary equivalent of first number.

(2) Find the binary equivalent of second number.

(3) Find the 1's compliment of the number, which is to be subtracted.

(4) Add 1 in 1's compliment to get 2's compliment.

(5) Add this 2's compliment with original binary number from which the number is to be subtracted.

(6) If there is 1 carry forward leave this carry. This will be the result.

(7) If there is no carry forward again find the 2's compliment of this number.

(8) If there is no carry forward put a minus (–) sign this will be the result.

(9) If there is 1 carry forward again repeat steps 7 & 8.

Ex. $(91)_{10} - (46)_{10}$

Sol. (1) Binary equivalent of $(91)_{10}$ = 01011011

(2) Binary equivalent of $(46)_{10}$ = 00101110

(3) 1's compliment of $(00101110)_2$ = 11010001

(4) 2's compliment of $(00101110)_2$ = 110100011

\+ 1

11010010

Add this 2's compliment with binary equipment of $(91)_{10}$ i.e.

11010010

01101011

Leave → 100101101

Hence the result is =00101101

Ex. $(42)_{10}-(92)_{10}$

Sol. (1) Binary equivalent of $(42)_{10}$ = 00101010

(2) Binary equivalent of $(92)_{10}$ = 01011100

(3) 1's compliment of $(01011100)_2$ = 10100011

(4) 2's compliment of $(01011100)_2$ = 10100011

\+ 1

10100100

Add this 2's carry forward hence again find 2's complement according to step 7.

1's complement of $(11001110)_2$ = 00110001

2's complement of $(01001110)_2$ = 00110001

+1

–00110010

According to step 8 the result is = –00110010

Multiplication

Binary multiplication follows the same rules of decimal multiplication. These are–

(1) $0 \times 0 = 0$

(2) $0 \times 1 = 0$

(3) $1 \times 0 = 0$

(4) $1 \times 1 = 1$

Ex. Multiply $(111)_2$ with $(010)_2$

Sol.

```
      1 1 1
      0 1 0
    1 1 1 x     these should be added by binary addition
  0 0 0 x x     instead of decimal addition to get the result.
  ---------
    01110
  ---------
```

Division

Binary division also follows the same rules of decimal division. The rules are—

(1) $1 \div 1 = 1$

(2) $0 \div 1 = 0$

(3) $0 \div 0$ = meaningless

(4) $1 \div 0$ = meaningless

Ex. Divided $(110100)_2$ by $(100)_2$

Sol.

```
100) 110100 (1101
     100
     ---
     101
     100
     ---
     100
     100
     ---
     xxx
```

2. Decimal Number System

Human in manual calculations most commonly uses decimal number system. This number system has base 10. It means all numbers can be represented by 10 different symbols (digits). These are 0, 1, 2, 3, 4, 5, 6, 7, 8, 9.

In decimal number system place value of each digit becomes ten times for each successive digit starting from right.

For example in decimal numbers 18990—

Place value of 0 = 10^0 or 1

Place value of 9 = 10^1 or 10

Place value of 9 = 10^2 or 100

Place value of 8 = 10^3 = 1000

Place value of 1 = 10^4 = or 10,000

3. Octal Number System

Octal number system uses base 8. It means 8 different digits. The different digits used to represent numbers are 0, 1, 2, 3, 4, 5, 6, 7.

In this system place of value of each digit become eight times for each successive digit starting from right. For example in octal number 1732—

Place value of 2 = 8^0 or 1
Place value of 3 = 8^1 or 8
Place value of 7 = 8^2 or 64
Place value of 1 - 8^3 or 512

4. Hexadecimal Number System

Hexadecimal number system is sometime called 'Hex number system'. This number system has base 16 and consists 16 different symbols. These are 0, 1, 2, 3, 4, 5, 6, 7, 8, 9, A, B, C, D, E, F. In hexadecimal numbers system any number is represent in 4 digits.

Equivalent Number in Hex, Binary, Decimal and Octal

Hex	*Binary*	*Decimal*	*Octal*
0	0000	0	0
1	0001	1	1
2	0010	2	2
3	0011	3	3
4	0100	4	4
5	0101	5	5
6	01110	6	6
7	0111	7	7
8	1000	8	8
9	1001	9	9
A	1010	10	10
B	1911	11	11
C	1100	12	12
D	1101	13	13
E	1110	14	14
F	1111	15	15
			16
			17

Conversions

Any number expressed in one number system can be converted into its equivalent number system, according to some rules.

(i) Binary number into decimal number
(ii) Decimal number into binary number
(iii) Octal number into binary number
(iv) Binary number into Octal number
(v) Hexadecimal number into binary number
(vi) Binary number into hexadecimal number
(vii) Decimal number into octal number
(viii) Octal number into decimal number
(ix) Decimal number into hexadecimal number
(x) Hexadecimal number into decimal number
(xi) Hexadecimal number into octal number
(xii) Octal number into hexadecimal number

Binary Number into Decimal Number

Since in binary the place value of each digit doubles for each successive digit starting from right, so that convert any binary number into it's decimal equivalent we multiply each digit of binary number with it's place value and add it.

Ex. Convert $(1010101)_2$ into decimal number.

Sol. $(1010101)_2 = 1 \times 2^6 + 0 \times 2^5 + 1 \times 2^4 + 0 \times 2^3 + 1 \times 2^2 + 0 \times 2^1 + 1 \times 2^0$

$= 64 + 0 + 16 + 0 + 4 + 0 + 1$

$= 85$

Hence $(1010101)_2 = (85)_{10}$

Ex. Convert $(1100.101)_2$ into decimal number.

Sol. $(1100.101)_2 = 1 \times 2^3 + 1 \times 2^2 + 0 \times 2^1 + 0 \times 2^0 + (1 \times 2^{-1} + 0 \times 2^{-2} + 1 \times 2^{-3})$

$= 8 + 4 + 0 + 0 + (.5 + 0 + .125)$

$= 12.625$

Hence $(1100.101)_2 = (12.625)^{10}$

Decimal Number into Binary Number

To convert any decimal integer number into binary, divide the decimal by the base of binary number (i.e. 2.). After every division we take the remainder and this process continues till we remainder 0. Finally this remainder put in reverse order (i.e. take from bottom to top).

Ex. Convert $(29)_{10}$ into binary number

Sol.

```
2| 29
2| 14     → remainder 1
2| 7      → remainder 0
2| 3      → remainder 1
2| 1      → remainder 1
 | 0      → remainder 1
```

Hence $(29)_{10} = (11101)_2$

(1) Similarly to convert the fractional part of decimal number into binary number, we multiple the fractional parts by the base of binary number. (i.e. 2) and take integer to the left. This process continues till the product of fraction part and based of binary number becomes zero or as many times required. Finally we put integer portions of each product-taking top to bottom.

Ex. Convert $(.125)_{10}$ into binary number.

Sol.

```
        .125
         × 2
------------------
0    ← 0.250
         × 2
------------------
0    ←   0.500
           × 2
------------------
1    ←   1.000
```

$= (.001)_2$

Hence $(.125)_{10} = (.001)_2$

Octal Number into Binary Number

To convert any octal number into binary first we find the binary equivalent of each octal digit separately. Finally, we combine all these digits. In octal to binary conversion or vice versa three digits binary number is used for each octal digit.

Ex. Convert (743.12) 8 into binary number

Sol. 7 4 3 1 2

↓ ↓ ↓ ↓ ↓

111 100 011 001 010

$= (111100011.001010)_2$

Hence $(734.12)_8 = (111100011.0011010)_2$

Binary Number into Octal Number

To convent any binary number into octal number we reverse the conversion method of octal to binary number. In this method we group the binary digits into three groups. These groups are formed from right to left in case of integer portion, and from left to right in case of fraction part of binary number. If there is less digits to form the group we can include 0 to form the group.

Ex. Convert $(10101101.01110)_2$ into octal number.

Sol. *Include digit* *Included digit*

010 101 101. 011 100

↓ ↓ ↓ ↓ ↓

2 5 5 3 4

$= (255.34)_8$

Hence $(10101101.01110)_2 = (255.34)_8$

Hexadecimal Number into Binary Number

This conversion is similar to the conversion of octal number into binary number. In this conversion first we find binary equivalent of each hexadecimal digit separately and then combine them. In hexadecimal to binary conversion or vice versa for digit binary number is used instead of three, digits binary for each hexadecimal digit.

Ex. Convert $(8FF.FF)_{16}$ into binary number.

Sol. 8 E F F F

↓ ↓ ↓ ↓ ↓

1000 1110 1111 1111 1111

$= (100011101111.11111111)_2$

Hence $(8\ EF.FF)_{16} = (100011101111.11111111)_2$

Binary Number into Hexadecimal Number

This conversion is similar to the conversion of binary number into octal number. Only difference is, four digits binary is used instead of three digit binary number.

Ex. Convert $(11010100100101.1011101)_2$ into hexadecimal number.

Sol. Include digit included digit

0110	1010	0110	1101	1001	1010
↓	↓	↓	↓	↓	↓
6	A	6	D	B	A

= $(6A6D.BA)_{16}$

Hence $(1101010011010010 1.1011101)_2 = (6A6D.BA)_{16}$

Decimal Number into Octal Number

Conversion of decimal number into octal numbers is similar to the conversion of decimal number into binary number. Only difference is here we use base of octal number (i.e. 8) instead of base of binary (i.e. 2) to divide the decimal number.

Ex. Convert $(385)_{10}$ into octal number.

Sol. 8 "358"

8 "44" → remainder 6

8 "5" → remainder 4

0 → remainder 5

= $(546)_8$

Hence $(358)_{10} = (546)_8$

→ Similar to convert the fraction part of decimal number into octal number, we multiply the fraction part by 8 and take integer to the left. This process continues till the product of fractional part and 8 becomes zero or as many times required. Then we put integer portions of each product taking from top to bottom.

Ex. Convert $(.335)_{10}$ = into octal number.

Sol.

$$
\begin{array}{r}
.335 \\
\times\ 8 \\
\hline
2 \leftarrow 2.680 \\
\times\ 8 \\
\hline
5 \leftarrow 5.440 \\
\hline
\end{array}
$$

3 $\leftarrow$ 3.520

= $(.253)_8$

Hence $(.355)_{10}$ = $(.253)_8$

Octal Number into Decimal Number

Since in octal number system the place value of each digit increases it's eight times for each successive digit starting from rights hence to convert any octal number into it's decimal equivalent we multiple each digit of octal number with it's place value and add it.

Ex. Convert $(669)_8$ into decimal number.

Sol. $(669)_8$ $= 8 \times 8^2 + 6 \times 8^1 + 9 \times 8^0$

$= 6 \times 64 + 6 \times 8 + 9 \times 1$

$= 384 + 48 + 9$

$= (431)_{10}$

Hence $(669)_8 = (431)_{10}$

Ex. Convert $(.253)_8$ into decimal number.

Sol. $(.253)_8$ $= 2 \times 8^{-1} + 5 \times 8^{-2} + 3 \times 8^{-3}$

= x. 25 + .078125 + .0058592391

$= (.333984391)_{10}$

Hence $(.253)_8$ $= (.333984391)_{10}$

Decimal Number into Hexadecimal Number

To convert the decimal number into hexadecimal number divides the decimal number by base of hexadecimal number (i.e. 16). Rest procedure is similar to the conversion of decimal number into binary or octal number.

Ex. Convert $(3479)_{10}$

Sol. 16 "3479"

16 "217" $\rightarrow$ remainder 7

16 "15" $\rightarrow$ remainder 9 $\uparrow$

0 $\rightarrow$ remainder E

$= (E97)_{16}$

Hence $(3479)_{10}$ $= (E97)_{16}$

$\leftarrow$Fractional part of decimal number can be convert into its hexadecimal equivalent, multiplying the fraction part by 16.

Rest procedure is similar to conversion of fractional part of decimal number into binary or octal number.

Ex. Convert $(.3875)_{10}$ into hexadecimal number.

Sol. 3875
× 16
6 ← 6.200
× 16
3 ← 3.2000
× 16
3 ← 3.2000
× 16
3 ← 3.2000
$= (.6333)_{16}$

Hence $(.3875)_{10} = (.6333)_{16}$

Hexadecimal Number into Decimal Number

To convert the hexadecimal number we multiply each digit of hexadecimal number with its place value and then add it.

Ex. Convert $(315)_{16}$ into decimal number.

Sol. $(315)_{16} = 3 \times 16^2 + 1 \times 16^1 + 5 \times 16^0$
$= 3 \times 256 + 1 \times 16 + 5 \times 1$
$= 768+16 + 5$
$= (789)_{10}$

Hence $(315)_{16} = (789)_{10}$

Ex. Convert $(.15)_{16} = 1 \times 16^{-1} + 5 \times 16^{-2}$
$= .0625 + .0195$
$= (.0820)_{10}$

Hexadecimal Number into Octal Number

To convert hexadecimal number into octal number, first we find the equivalent octal number of each digit separately and then combine them.

Ex. Convert $(FEA.8)_{16}$ into octal number.

Sol.

F	E	A	8	
↓	↓	↓	↓	↓
17	16	12	10	

$= (171612,10)_8$

Hence $(FEA.8)_{16} = (171612,10)_8$

Octal Number Into Hexadecimal Number

To convert the octal number into hexadecimal number, first we find equivalent binary number of each octal digit separately and then reconvert this binary into hexadecimal number by (vi) method.

Ex. Convert $(16126)_8$ into hexadecimal number.

Sol. First convert 16126 into binary—

1	6	1	2	6
↓	↓	↓	↓	↓
001	110	001	110	010

Group these binaries— 001110001010110

Separate these numbers into the group of 4 bits using (vi) method.

Include bit

	0001	1100	0191	0110
Reconvert into hex no.	↓	↓	↓	↓

$= (1C56)_{16}$

EXERCISE QUESTIONS

Fill in the Blanks:

1. Positional number systems are..................,...................., and......................
2. In positional number system a number is determined by......................................., and................
3. Computers use............... method for subtracting binary numbers.
4. .... can be found by reversing each bit of binary number.
5. Decimal number system is most commonly used by........
6. Octal number system uses base.............
7. In short hexadecimal number system is called..........

True/False:

1. Roman number system is widely used by computers.
2. In positional number system few digits represents different values depending on the position they occupy in the number.
3. Adding 1 in the 1's compliment of binary number can find 2's compliment.
4. 29 is a valid octal number.
5. Different symbols used in hexadecimal number system are 1-9 and A-F.
6. Two binary numbers can be subtracted by 1's compliment method.
7. Binary multiplication and division follows the same rule of decimal multiplication and division.

Give the answer of these Questions:

1. What do you understand by the Positional number system?
2. Explain the Binary numbers system in your own words?
3. What is Decimal number system? Explain.
4. What is Octal number system? Write in 20 words.
5. How you can Conversion the Numbers in binary form?

Pick the Correct One:

1. In non-positional number system 30 is represented as—
   a. VVVVVV b. XXVV
   c. XXX d. None of the above
2. In binary addition 1 + 1 gives—
   a. 0 b. 1
   c. 0 with carry 1 d. None of the above
3. In octal number 1234667, place value of 1 is—
   a. 8^6 b. 1
   c. 8^1 d. None of the above
4. Binary Equivalent of $(F)_{16}$ is—
   a. 15 b. 1111
   c. 17 d. None of the above
5. In binary .01101, place value of right most digit is—
   a. 2^{-5} b. 2^5
   c. 2^{-4} d. None of the above

CHAPTER 10

DISK OPERATING SYSTEM (DOS)

- Introduction
- Working with Floppy
- Organizing Information in Files and Directories
- Wildcard Characters
- Naming Guidelines
- Types of DOS Commands
- Internal DOS Commands
- External DOS Commands
- Exercise Questions

INTRODUCTION

DOS is an operating system for the IBM PC and PC-compatible microcomputers. PC-DOS is the product of IBM Corp. While the MS-DOS is the product of Microsoft Corp. many versions of DOS has been introduced till now with various new features.

One of the first things the computer does when turned on is to check its main memory (RAM). Usually computers display the amount of memory that has been checked as a rapidly changing number on the computer copies DOS from the disk into memory and gives control to it. DOS then checks the keyboard for the commands and starts the requested program. When the program is finished DOS takes control once again.

Command Prompt

After switching the system DOS is loaded in the memory, after that computer shows the following:

A:\>

WORKING WITH FLOPPY

If the computer is showing the prompt like—

C:\>

and the user wants to change the drive and wants to read and write directly with floppy disk, this can be done by simply typing A: at the C prompt and press ENTER key.

i.e. C:>a:

Which will change the prompt like—

A:\>

Similarly user can change the prompt like B :\> if the computer has two floppy drives.

There should be a floppy disk in the specific drive that user wants to change to.

ORGANIZING INFORMATION IN FILES AND DIRECTORIES

DOS organizes all the information in files and directories. A file is the primary unit of storage on the computer. A file enables DOS to distinguish on collection of information from another. Every file has a name, which generally indicates what type of information the file contains. There can be hundreds or even thousand of files on the computers depending on the storage capacity.

Storing groups of files in different directories makes files easier to find. Hence a directory is a collection of same types of files. For example all the files created in WordStar can be stored in a WS directory, similarly all files that come with DOS are stored in a single directory usually named DOS.

Directory can contain other directories. A directory within another directory is called a sub-directory. By creating sub-directories, user can better categories the files. For example different letters creating in WordStar can be store in LTR subdirectory, and various notice created in WordStar can be stored in NTC subdirectory.

The complete organization of files and directory can be represent sent like following structure.

This structure is called "tree" is DOS. The starting point of the three is the root directory. The root directory is the starting point from which all other directors branches out. The root directory does not have any name. Instead, it is represent by a backslash (\).

F1: Enter the character from the command line buffer on the active command line. Processing F1 again, appears next character on the active command line. So user can enter the entire command, by repeatedly pressing F1 key.

F3: Enters all the remaining characters in the command buffer, starting from the current cursor position. If the cursor is in stating position, pressing F3 enters the entire command at a time.

Ins key: Switch to insert mode, whereupon characters you types from the keyboard will be added to the command line buffer at the cursor position rather than over-writing the character at the position.

Del key: Deletes the character in the current cursor position.

Esc key: Cancels changes user has made to the command line buffer and restores its original contents.

Backspace key: Moves cursor to the left one position on the active command line and erases its character at that position.

Some key combinations are also used for some special purpose.

These combinations are called control keys. Some of these are:

Ctrl-C or: Stops the execution of DOS command and returns

Ctrl-Break: the control at DOS prompts.

Shift-Parts: Sends the current contents of the screen to the printer, the printer must be one-line.

WILDCARD CHARACTERS

DOS support two wildcard characters– * (asterisk) and ? (Question mark). These characters allow user to specify whole group of file names. The characters continuing to the end of the file name or extension. For example command—

C:\DIR A*.*

Will display those files, which start with the character A and have any extension.

The command prompt

C:\>

or

A:\>

show that current directory is the root directory. Because of root directory is the basis for all other directories, no one can delete it. Either it is floppy disk or hard disk DOS uses similar tree concept to organize the information.

NAMING GUIDELINES

(a) Every files and directory, except for the root directory on any disk, must have a name. Files and directories names can be up to eight characters long. Extension is separated by a period from the name. For example, HELLO.DOC shows that file name is HELLO and the extension is DOS.

Usually the extensions what types of information the file contains. For example, EXE or COM extension indicates the executable files; extension BAT shows the batch file (file that contains DOS commands), extension SYS shows, the device drivers (files that enable the computer to communicate with hardware devices).

Most of the software's append extension automatically when user gives the file name. For example, C extension append with program files created in C language. PRO extension append with program files created in FOXPRO or dBASE.

(b) Any file or directory name should be unique. Also legal characters in files directory names include all letters of alphabets (upper and lower case letters are treated the same), numeric digits, and punctuation marks except for the following:

*? = + ! ; < > , '

Some Special Keys

DOS provides a handy set of special function key that assist you when entering repetitive commands or correcting typing mistakes. These keys affect whatever command at a time is stored in this buffer, unless using a special utility like DOSKEY.

The other wildcard characters represent only one character on the specified position within the file name or extension. For example command—

C:\DIR*.*?Om

Will display those files which have any name and the last two character of extension are On.

TYPES OF DOS COMMANDS

All the DOS commands can be divided in three categories-

- Internal Commands
- External Commands
- Batch File Commands

Internal commands are memory-resident commands that are part of the COMMAND.COM file. COMMAND.COM is a MS-DOS command interpreter that provides an interface between user and computer system. All commands that user enters on the DOS prompt are interpreted by COMMAND.COM, which finds the command to be executed. If no command is found, COMMAND.COM display the error message like—

Bad command or filename

on the screen and redisplays the DOS prompt. If the command into the computer's found, COMMAND.COM load the command into the computer's memory and passes control to the command to execute it, when the execution of command is completed, control is returned to COMMAND.COM which redisplays the DOS commands are DATE command and TIME command.

External commands are not part of COMMAND.COM instead these founds in separate files with .COM or EXE extension. To execute these commands DOS must be able to find the files. For example type—

c:\chkdsk c:

At DOS prompt. If DOS finds named CHKDSK.EXE it will read that files into memory and execute the program stored in the file. Some example of external DOS command is SORT.EXE and MODE.COM.

Batch file command is used in batch files. Batch files are text files that have the file name extension .BAT and contain DOS commands Batch file can be created with a text editor program. User can execute the batch file by typing its name on the DOS prompt like any external command. DOS then reads the file and executes each command in the batch file as if user had typed it on the command line individually. Batch files have their own set of command. By using these commands, user can build a batch file that uses command-line parameters and executes program like loops and jumps. Batch processing commands are also the part of COMMAND.COM, no such. COM. or EXE files are associated with these commands. Although batch-processing commands are intended for use in batch files, they may be executed directly from the DOS prompt. While it is possible to do so, none of the batch processing commands are of much use except when used in batch file. Some example of batch processing commands are ECHO,REW and GOTO.

Some DOS Commands

This section is discussing some DOS commands, which are used most of the time. Some important command and their proper functioning are given here:

INTERNAL COMMANDS

MD

To categories files in the sub-directory, user must create it. User can created sub-directory either on root or under any sub-directory. User can created sub-directory using MD command. MD is an abbreviated from of 'male directory'.

Syntax

MD <sub-directory path>

The <sub-directory path> parameter specifies the path consisting the name of sub-directories separated with backslash (\.)

Example

C:\>MD\WS\LTR\MAILED

Above command will create a sub-directory named Mailed under LTR sub-directory, which is also under the WS directory. This WS directory is under root directory. User can check the existence of sub-directory with DIR command.

Each sub-directory created by user contains two pseudo-directory entries automatically placed in it. One of these sub-directory called '..' and the other is called '..'. These pseudo-directories are some times called directories markers. These directory entries have some special significance.

The make is a pseudo-directory entry that always refers to the current directory. The Maker always refers to the parent directory, the directory from which the current directory branches. The maker server no useful purpose for most command whereas the maker is particularly useful when it comes to moving among sub-directories.

CD

CD commands is used to changes the directory. CD stands for 'change directory'.

Syntax

cd <drive> <sub-directory path>

The <sub-directory path> parameter specifies the path consisting the name of sub-directories separated with backslash (\), and <drive> is the name of the valid drive letter in which user want to operate.

Example

C:\>CD\WS\NTC

Above command will change the sub-directory to NTC. After this command user can access the files are in NTC sub-directory, without explicitly identifying the sub-directory, path for the files. Another way to change the sub-directory is a shortcut method using directory entry.

Example

C:\CD..

Above way to change the sub-directory just to the parent directory i.e. WS sub-directory. DOS command also allows to change back to the root directory from any sub-directory. Command for it this is

CD\

COPYCON

User can create file in DOS through COPYCON command.

Syntax

CopyCon<filename>

where <file name> is only valid DOS filename. After giving the above command user can enter any number of DOS Command, one command of each line. To complete the file Press Ctrl-Z of F6 function key followed by ENTER key. Pressing these keys gives the message.

- 1 file (s) copied
- Which indicates the successful completion of file.
- Batch files can also be created with this command.

Example

C:\Copyconrfl0.bat

Dir\p

Dir\w

^Z

1 file(s) copied

Above procedure will created the batch file named rf10.bat consisting two commands. DIR\P and DIR\W. ^Z appears after press the Ctrl-Z key combination OR f6 function key and the message appears after hitting the ENTER KEY.

dir

DIR command is a short form of 'directory'. DIR command displays a list of files and sub-directories in the special sub-directory.

Syntax

DIR <. drive > <path> <switches>

where <drive> specifies any valid letter on which user want to operate. <directory path> specifies the path consisting the name of sub-directories separated by backslash (\). <switches specifies the format in which files sub-directories display. Two most popular switches are—

Example

\P- displays list one page at a time.

\W- display list width wise in five columns wide

C:\>DIR\WS

This command will last all the files and sub-directories of the WS directory.

A list similar to the following appears on the screen :

Volume in drive C is GZB

Volume serial Number is AKG

Directory of C:\WS

```
<DIR>      10:10:73                 5:00p
<DIR>      10:10.73                 5:00p
..    109  15:10:73    10:20a
WF1        <DIR>       25:10:73     10:55a
WF2        655         01:11:73     01:45P
LTR        <DIR>       01:11:73     1:46P
WF3        49          03:10:73     04:30P
WF4        12          03:10:73     04:30P
NTC        <DIR>       02:12:73     02:45P
9 file(s) 1869 bytes
31456698 bytes free
```

Copy

Copying files means creating duplicates of the original file. COPY command is used to copy the files. To use copy command two parameters must be includes source file and destination file.

Syntax

Copy <drive> <source file>   <drive> <path> <destination file>

where <drive> and <path> are the drive and drive and path of source or destination where the files is stored or to be stored.

After completion of COPY command following message appears:

Example

1 file(s) copies

C:\COPY C:\WS\NTC\rf1 c:\dos\RF1

Above command will copy the file names 'rf1' stored in sub-directory NTC, which is under the WS sub-directory, in the DOS sub-directory, which is udder's floppy disk. User can check the existence of the file by giving the following command:

C:\DIR A:

This command will give the list of filenames stored in floppy disk.

C:\COPY*.* A:

Above command will copy all the files stored under root directory of hard disk.

C:\COPY rf8+RF9RF10

Above command can be used to combine several files into one file. This command will copy the contents of files "rf8' and 'rf9' into a new file 'rf10'. Wildcards can also be used to combine several files into the one file.

If one of the source files named in the list of source files does not exits, the COPY command combine all the files that do exit into one file.

REN

To change the name of any file REN command is used. REN is the shortened name of 'rename'.

Syntax

REN <old file name> <new file name>

Where <old file name> is the current name of the file whereas the <new file name> is the new name which is to be given. <Old file name> can include the path if the file is not present in current sub-directory. REN command has some limitations—first a sub-directory cannot rename and the second one is file cannot be move.

Example

C:\REN C:\WS\LTR\IF1 C:\WS\LTR\If3

Above command will change the name of file 'iF1' to 'IF3'

C:\REN A:\ABC. Doc A:\abc. dot

Above command will change the name of file 'abc.doc' to 'abc.dat' stored in floppy disk. A group of files can be rename using wildcard characters.

DEL

DEL command is used to delete the files from disk.

Syntax

DEL<drive> <path> <file name<switch>

Where <drive> and <path> are the drive and path where is the file is stored and <switch> is the parameter used to improve the DEL command.

Switch most commonly used with DEL command is \P, which allows confirming from the user before deleting files from disk.

Example

C:\DEL C:\WS\LTR\rf3

Above command will delete the file name 'rf3' stored in LTR direct from the hard disk. Above command will delete all the files stored in floppy having. DOC extension, one by one. Command will prompt to user whether he/she want to delete file before files. Only those files will be removing from disk for that user will press 'Y'.

RD

RD Command is used to remove sub-directory from the disk. RM stands for remove directory is, the sub-directory. But the rule to remove sub-directory should be empty. If there is any file in the sub-directory first delete files from it then remove sub-directory.

Syntax

C:\RDA:WS\LTR

Above command will be remove the sub-directory LTR stored under WS sub-directory on floppy disk.

PATH

DOS search path is just a list of the sub-directories through which DOS must travel to get to the file where name appears at the end of the path. Where user enters a command on DOS prompt (other than a built in command that doesn't required a. EXE, com OR. BAT file to run), DIOS searches for appropriate file to execute. It first looks for a setting for the PATH variable stored in the environment.

The sequence in which the sub-directories are assigned to the path variable determines the order in which the sub-directories are searched. The search begins with left most sub-directory and continues until the file is found or the path list exhausted. If DOS doesn't find the appropriate command file, it informs to user by displaying an error message like Bad command or filename.

Example

C:\\PATH=C:\WS\LTR;C:\WS\NTC

Above command will set the path between LTR sub-directory and NTC sub-directories are separated by a semi colon (;) PATH can be set between many sub-directories like the above command.

C:\PATH

Above command can be used any time to check the currently set path. This command displays the currently set path like:

PATH= C:\WS\LTR; C:\WS\NTC

PROMPT

PROMPT command is used to change the DOS prompt or to see the currently logged sub-directories all the time without having to ask for it.

Example

C>PROMPTPG

Above command will change the DOS prompt and will show the currently logged sub-directories.

Various characters that can be prefixed with dollar sign in PROMPT command to change the DOS prompt are:

$	character Substitution
$	$
-	(underscore) Carriage return, line feed
D	Date
E	ASCLL escapes character
G	>(greater than)
H	Backspace
L	<(less than)
N	Current drive
P	Current drive path
Q	=
T	Time
V	DOS version

Any combination of three characters can be used to make various types of prompts.

TYPE

TYPE command allows the user to display the contents of one or more files.

Syntax

TYPE <drive> <path><file name>

Example

C:\>TYPE A:\WS\1TR1

Above command will display the contents of file 'ltrl' in WS sub-directory of floppy disk.

C:\>TYPE A: *. doc

This command will display the content of all the files having.DOC extension stored in floppy disk. TYPE command has one drawback, if the contents of files are more than one screen. TYPE command does not pause the screen after displaying one-screen full continents.

CLS

CLS command is used to clear the screen. After using this command DOS prompt and cursor appears in upper left corner of the screen.

VER

VERSION command is used to display the DOS version.

DATE

DATE command is used to display the current system date. This command also allows changing the system date. This changes date remain effective till the computer system is on or not reset.

Example

C:\DATE
Above command will display like this:
Current date is 12-12-1993
Enter New Date (mm-dd-yy):

TIME

Very similar to DATE command. TIME command is used to display the current system time and allows changing the current time.

Example

C:-> TIME

This command displays

Current time is 3:14:25:70p

Enter new time:

EXTERNAL COMMANDS

Redirection

DOS support command, which allows the user the change the direction of either standard input or output.

By default DOS takes input and displays the result on standard output. Standard input and displays the result on standard output.

Standard input is keyboard and standard output is screen.

Various devices supported by DOS for redirection of I/O are:

CON	Input a keyboard, output is screen.
PRN	Default printer

LPT	:	Parallel Port1
LPT	:	Parallel Port 2
COM	:	Communication port 1
COM2	:	Communication port 2
NUL	:	Null device

The NUL device is special. Redirect the output to a NUL device doesn't display the output.

In addition to these devices, DOS also support the redirection to a file. If the file that user does not exist it is created. If it exits it will be overwritten. Instead of overwritten. Instead of overwriting more data can also be append to an exiting file. Various redirection operators are:

<

>

>>

Operator '<' is used to redirect the input, while the '>' operator is used to redirect the output. '>>' Operator is also used to redirect the output but has some meaning from the '>' operator. ">>" Operator is used to append the contents in a file.

Example

C:\>TYPE A: FIRST. do<>porn

Above command will redirect the contents of file 'first.doc.' to the printer connect with computer. Printer must be on-line.

C:\SORT>abc.doc

This command will sort the contents of file 'abc.doc'. Here SORT command is taking input from 'abc.doc' file using redirection '<' rather than standard input.

C:\TYPEabc.doc >>A:FIRST.doc

This command will add the contents of abc.doc at the end of the file 'first.doc' stored in floppy disk.

FIND

FIND command is used to read those lines which contains the given pattern. By default it displays the selected lines on the standard output but can be redirected.

Syntax

FIND <switches> <pattern> <file>

<pattern> is the actual that is to be find, <file> is the name of the file and <switches> are the various switches used to improve the performance of command.

Various switches are:

\I : Ignore the case
\N : Display the number in the file where the matches occur.
\C : Display a count of the number of lines that match the pattern.
\V : Display those line which do not contain pattern.

Example

C:\> FIND "gupta" <names.dat

Above command will display those lines from the file 'names.dat' which contains the pattern 'gupta'. Assuming that the contents of 'names.date' are :

- Arvind Gupta
- Deepak Goel
- Bhupesh Kaw
- Vikash Jain
- Manish Gupta

SORT

Sorts the lines of text alphabetically and the stored text on the standard output. Output can be redirect to other device, using DOS redirection.

Syntax

SORT <switches> <drive:\path\file>

Different switches are:

\R : Sort in reverse are:
\TN : Sorts the lines on the nth column.

Where is the column number?

Example

C:\SORT<names.dat>

Above command will sort the lines of the file 'names.dat' and will display them on the screen like:

- Ajay Gupta
- Arvind Gupta
- Bhupesh Kaw
- Deepak Goel
- Manish Gupta
- Vikash Jain

Piping

Many DOS commands produce output that can be re-processed by other DOS command. One way to do this to redirect the output to a disk file, and then send the contents of the file as input to the next DOS commands. Other way is the piping. Piping is a DOS mechanism the connects two commands. The output of one DOS command becomes the input to another command, which in turn sends the output to another DOS command or displays it on the screen. DOS commands are connected by the pipe (I) symbol.

Example

C:\DIR\FIND "<DIR>"dir.file

Above command is a combination of piping and redirection. First DIR command will produce a listing of all the files and sub-directories; output of this command will become the input for FIND command. FIND command will be redirect to file 'dir.fill'. User can see the contents of this file with the help of TYPE command.

MORE

MORE command display output one screen at a time instead of continuous scrolling.

Syntax

MORE <drive\path\file>(using direction)

Syntax

COMMAND\MORE (using piping)

Example

C:\MORE <abc.doc

Above command will display the contents of abc.doc file one screen at a time. After displaying one screen information. It pauses the screen and display a message in bottom most line like:

MORE

Pressing any key allows to display next screen of information. Same task can also be complete by the following command:

C:\TUPE abc.doc\MORE

FORMAT

FORMAT command prepares a bland disk for receiving data or creates a new disk from a used one. A new purchased floppy must be format before use. FORMAT command removes all the data from a used disk.

Syntax

FORMAT <drive> <switches>

This command requires a drive letter for the disk to format. When the formatting operation is complete it allows entering a volume for the disk. After it prompts to format another disk otherwise control returns to DOS prompt.

Various switched, which can be use with this command, are:

\1	Formats a double-side disk as a single-side disk.
\4	Formats a single-density (160K) or double density (360K) disk with default tracks in 1.2 MB drive.
\8	Formats 8 sector per track instead of the default (i.e. 9 sectors double disk and 15 sectors for high-density disk).
\B	Formats a disk so as to leave room for the system files.
\F:size	Formats low capacity disk in the high capacity drive.

Where size can be:
160K for 5.25" single-sides disk.
360K for 5.25" double-sided disk.
720K for 5.25" double-sided disk.
1.2M for 5.25" high-density disk.
1.44M for 3.5" high-density disk.

\Q Formats the disk without reinitialize tracks and sectors on previously formatted disk.

\S Transfers DOS system files to the formatted disk.

\V"lable" Add label as disk's volume label

\T: nn Indicates number of sectors per track, where nn is the number of sector user specifies.

Example

C:\FORMAT A:\F: 360

Above command will format the floppy disk of 360 in high capacity drive.

DISKCOPY

DISKCOPY command is used to make copies of floppy disks. If the target disk is not formatted, DISKCOPY command formats the disk first then copies the source disk.

Syntax

DISKCOPY command compares the contents of two floppy disks track-by-track. This command can compares only disks with same size and same density.

Syntax

DISKCOPY<source drive> <target drive>

Example

C:\DISKCOMP A:B:

This command will compare the disk in drive A with disk in drive B.

xCOPY

Xcopy command copies groups of files, including files in lower sub-directories if specified.

Syntax

XCOPY <drive><path><file>

<drive><path><switches>

various switches are:

\S : Copies file matching the source specification that are found in sub-directories rested below the source sub-directories.

\O:date : Copies only those files that were modified on or after the specified date.

\P Issues a prompt asking to confirm the copy of each file.

\W : Causes XCOPY to pause before making copies allowing user to change disks in the drive.

Example

C:\XCOPY C:/WS A:\S

Above command will create the sub-directories LTR and NIC on the A drive and will copy all the files from corresponding sub-directories.

TREE

TREE command is used to display the sub-directory structure of a drive.

Syntax

TREE <drive><path><switches>]

<path> allows this command to start the tree from the specified sub-directory. Various switches are:

IF : Displays tree including all files in each sub-directory.

Example

C:\TREE\F

This command will display the tree of hard including all files in each sub-directory.

SYS

SYS command allows to copies DOS system files to other disk. After transferring the system files, it gives message like:

Syntax

SYS <source drive> <target drive>

Example

C:\SYS C:A:

This command will transfer the DOS system files from hard disk to the floppy drive.

CHKDSK

CHKDSK command stands for 'check disk' and used to examine the disk. This command also reports about sectors occupied for files, sub-directories, lost clusters etc.

Syntax

CHKDSK <drive><switches>

where <drive> is the drive letter which is to be checked.

<switches> are:

\F Enables auto-correction mechanism.
\V Display the name of each file on disk as it checks.

Example

C:\CHKDSK A:/F

Above command will check the floppy disk and try to fix any error it finds.

DOSKEY

DOSKEY command is used to create macros. Before creating any doskey macro DOSKEY must be execute first. With DOSKEY user can create macros and store them buffer. These macros can be recall by using up arrow and down arrow key. This eliminates the necessity of retyping command. DOSKEY stores macro in buffer till the system on or not reboot.

Syntax

DOSKEY macro name=<commands>

where <macro name> is the name of macro and <commands> are one or more commands to be attached with macro name. To attach more than one command $T operator is used.

Example

C:\DOSKEY dirs=DIR\P $DIR\W

Above command will create the macro 'dirs' containing two commands DIR/W. This macro can be execute by typing macro name of DOS prompt, like:

C:\>dirs

This will first display the listing of files and sub-directories page wise and after that width wise.

Bath file Commands

ECHO

ECHO command performs four functions:

- Turns the echo feature on.
- Turns the echo feature off.
- Display a message that follows the ECHO command on the same line.
- Display whether echo is on or off.

Examples

C:\>ECHO

This command shows whether ECHO is on or off.

C:\ECHO ON

Allows turning echo feature on.

C:\>ECHO OFF

Allows turning the echo feature off.

C:V>ECHO HELLO SIR,

Allows displaying the message 'Hello Sir' on screen.

REM

REM command is used to put the comments in batch files.

Syntax

REM <comments>

Example

C:\>COPY CON example, bat

REM demo of ram command using batch file.

DIR/P

^Z

Above example is showing the comment using REM command. DOS does not consider statements followed by REM at the time of execution.

IF

IF command is used to check the existence of files.

IF command has two formats:

IF EXIT

IF NOT EXIT

Syntax 1

IF EXIT <file><command>

Example

C:\IFEXIT rf2 TYPE rf3

Above command will check the existence of file "rf2'. If the file exit then TYPE command will execute otherwise not.

Syntax 2

IF NOT EXIT rf 13 TYPE rf!3

This is the reverse of IF EXIT command. With this command, TYPE command will execute only if the file 'rf13' not present otherwise not.

FOR

FOR command is used to execute another command iteratively.

Syntax

FOR %% <letter>IN <files> DO <command>

Where <letter> can be any alphabet or digit and <command> can be any command %% is used if the FOR command is stored in batch file and % is used if the command is using at DOS prompt.

Example

C:\FOR % IN (RF*) DO TYPE %se

Above command will take all files starting with 'rf' one by one and display the contents one by one-using TYPE command. This example is a replacement of several TYPE command, like:

C:\TYPErf1

C:\TYPErf2

Some Special Files

CONFIG. SYS

This is an ASCII file that contains instructions to DOS for making best of system's resources.

Typically CONFIG.SYS file contains these three entries.

- FILES = 30
- BUFFERS = 30
- DEVICE = C:\DOS\ANSI.SYS

Where FILES entry shows the maximum number of files that can be open simultaneously. If this entry is not specified then default is 8. Maximum 255 files can be open simultaneously.

BUFFERS command is used to establish the number of disk buffers that are to be reserved for use by DOS and application programmes, A disk buffer is an area of memory reserved for the temporary storage of disk data during disk access operations. Many application programmes require a certain amount of disk buffer space in memory. Number of buffer can be 1 to 99. DEVICE entry shows the mane of the device driver program file followed by drive and indicating where the file is stored. DEVICE command installs the named device driver. Device drives is added to a system, such as extended memory card.

Since the modification of ROM BIOS is impractical of DOS command. This batch file can be create and contains DOS command like any other difference is, AUTOEXE.BAT file executes automatically when system starts. Usually PROMPT and PATH commands are used in this file.

EXERCISE QUESTIONS

Write the answer in your own words:

1. How we can work with Floppy? Explain.
2. You can save organizing Information in Files and Directories, how? Write in 100 words.
3. Explain the Wildcard Characters with suitable examples.
4. Explain the types of DOS Commands.
5. What are internal and external DOS Commands? Explain in your own words.

Fill in the Blanks:

1. .... is a collection of files and sub-directories.
2. .... directory doesn't have any name.
3. DOS has and wildcard characters.
4. Type of DOS commands are.............,............. and............
5. ....Commands are defines in COMMAND.COM file.
6. Batch file can be create by.............

True/False:

1. AUTOEXE.BAT batch file executes automatically.
2. IF command is used to check the existence of file.
3. DOSKEY macros store permanently in buffer.
4. DISCOPY command can be used to copy files from hard disk to floppy disk.
5. Piping connects two DOS commands.
6. Direction of input can be change in DOS.

Pick the Correct One:

1. .... operator is used to *append* the data in file.

   a. >> b. >
   c. < d. None of the above

2. Device which doesn't display the output:

   a. CON b. NUL
   c. AUX d. None of the above

3. ....Command deletes the sub-directory.

   a DEL b. ERASE
   c. RD d. None of the above

4. ECHO Command

   a. Turns echo on b. ERASE
   c. Used to display d. All of the above

5. .... is used to separate DOS command in macros.

   a. $G b. $P
   c. $T d. None of the above

CHAPTER 11

MULTI-MEDIA AND ITS APPLICATION

- Multimedia
- Application of Multimedia
- Hardware Used in Multimedia
- Software Used in Multimedia
- Use of Multimedia in Education
- Exercise Questions

INTRODUCTION

Multimedia has become a popular technology in the ever-changing world of computers. Since last few years, it seems to be sought after and talked about, not only in the field of information technology but also in various functional fields like advertisement, cooperate sector, cinema, fashion designing and education.

Multimedia is a combination of Text, Graphic Art, Sound, Animation and video delivered by computer and other electronic devices. It is a rich presented sensation. Multimedia is a woven combination of: Text, Graphic art, sound, and animation and video elements.

- When we allow an end user - The viewer of multimedia project to control what and when the elements are delivered, it is called interactive multimedia.
- When we provide a structure of linked elements through which the user can navigate, interactive multimedia becomes hypermedia.

- The people who weave multimedia into meaningful tapestries are called multimedia developer.
- The software vehicle, the message, and the content presented on a computer or TV screen - Together Constitute a Multimedia Project.
- If a multimedia project is not interactive, the project is called Linear, starting at a beginning and running through to an end.
- If user is given navigational control and can go through the content as well multimedia become non-linear or interactive.
- The tools, which are used to recon the multimedia element into a project are called Authority tool set.

Multimedia Computer

APPLICATION OF MULTIMEDIA

The ability of multimedia materials to convey by picture, sound, animation, or movies what is otherwise hard to express, to capture for reuse on any occasion remote lands and singular events, and with the use of the computer, to provide this information in a form that can be engagingly interactive and easily recast by and aspiring communicator is the explanation for the popularity and particularly long history of multimedia technology's role in education. For many years educational titles have been one of the dominant product areas for multimedia computing, surpassed only by entertainment. Multimedia is the woven combination of text, graphic art, sound, and animation and video elements.

APPLICATION OF MULTIMEDIA IN THE FIELD OF HUMAN LIFE

1. Multimedia in Business

Business Applications of multimedia include presentations, training, marketing, advertising, product demos, and database. Catalogues and Networked Communication. A multimedia presentation can make audience come alive. Most presentation, software packages let us add audio and video clip to the usual slide Show of graphic and Text material.

2. Multimedia at Home

From Gardening to cooking to home design, remodelling and repair genealogy software, multimedia has entered the home. Eventually, the most multimedia projects will reach home via TV sets or monitors with built-in-interactive user input.

3. Multimedia at the Public Places

In hotels, train, stations, shopping malls, Museums and Grocery Stores, Multimedia will become available at stand-alone terminals or kiosks to provide information and help. A hotel Kiosk list nearby restaurants, 1J1aps of city, airlines schedules and provide guest services such as automated check-out.

4. Multimedia in School

Multimedia in school is perhaps the most widely needy destination. Many schools are using this multimedia application in their school for the purpose of teaching the students. In school the computer is become essential part of education as teaching the basic of reading, writing and arithmetic. Multimedia for learning takes many forms through showing the cartoon on particular subject. Multimedia for reading skills grows through word recognition a mouse clicks on any word play in back. The computer read the story aloud, sometimes spelling words individually. An interesting uses of multimedia in schools involve the students themselves. Student put together interactive magazines and newsletter, they make original art using image-editing tool, they interview students and towns people and coaches and teachers and they make quick time movie. Many computer games with the focus on the education are available. A simple example in this reference is an educational game, which plays various rhymes for little kids. In addition to playing rhymes, the child can paint the pictures, increase and reduce the size of the objects etc. Similar many other educational packages, which provide a lot of detailed information to kids, are available. Microsoft has produce many such CD's based multimedia such as 'Sierra', 'Knowledge Adventure' etc. which in addition to play provide some sort of learning component. The latest in this series is a package, which teaches about the computer, using games playing.

HARDWARE USED IN MULTIMEDIA

To prepare a good project of multimedia at quality level we have need of some basic hardware and software for this purpose and these are:—

1. Hardware Requirement.
2. Software Requirement
3. Creative Mind
4. Organization

1. Hardware for Multimedia

Minimum Hardware requirement to setup a Multimedia Program are:

- 486DX2 + Graphics Card
- 8 MB RAM
- 512 MB Hard disk
- SVG Display
- CD-ROM Drive
- Sound Card, Speakers & Microphone
- Key Board, Mouse

Some cards are also very important for multimedia computer system without there a multimedia computer system cannot work properly. These are given below:

A. Graphics Card

Graphics card accelerate takes the responsibility of generating picture on the screen. This slows the moving picture that does not move smoothly.

B. Sound Card

A sound card is an electronic device that is inserted into any free expansion slot on the motherboard. The sound card can act like a tape recorder that play and record sound. Most sound card built in the motherboard with having amplifiers.

C. CD-ROM Drive

CD-ROM stands for Compact Disk Read Only Memory, It is used to read large amount of data from compact disk. It is a circular plastic made disk, which is used to store Pictures, Software in salvation file, Music etc.

2. Software Required for Multimedia

To produce a media element various types of software are available in the market, such as MS-word, Sound Recorder, Winamp, Media player, Xing player, Wave Studio, Corel draw, photoshop, 3-D studio, Jip Animator, Jet Audio etc.

3. Creativity

Before beginning a multimedia project, we must first develop a sense of its scope and content. Let the project take shape in our head, as we think through the various methods available to get our message across to our viewer. The evolution of multimedia is evident when we look at some of the first multimedia project done on computer and compares them to today's titles.

4. Organization

It is essential that we develop an organized outsize and a plant flat rationally detail the skill, time, budget, tools and resources we will need for a project. There should be in place before we start to render graphics, sounds and other components, and they should continue to be monitored through out the project.

USE OF HARDWARE AND SOFTWARE IN MULTIMEDIA

In multimedia mostly we used these hardware, and these are very comfortable to run multimedia. These are:—

1. CPU
2. Monitor
3. Graphic Acceleration Card

4. Sound Card
5. Video Capture Card
6. CD ROM Drive
7. Printer

1. CPU

The CPU, which is recommended for a multimedia computer, should be Pentium processor on a PC or the other advanced chips such as Power PC etc. Likewise Apple Macintosh and Silicon Graphics have their own set of powerful processor do multimedia. The CPU of a multimedia should be at least 486 with coprocessor attached otherwise the response time of the multimedia will be poor.

2. Monitor

The multimedia PC should be equipped with monitors having Super Video Graphics Arrays (SBGA) card. The basic advantage of having SVGA is that it has a better resolution, thus the display will be of better quality and picture. A typical representation which may be used in multimedia can be 720 × 40 or 1200 × 80 etc.

3. Graphic Acceleration Card

Generation graphics takes up considerable amount of system resources. The slows the moving pictures that do not move smoothly. The graphics a acceleration card takes the responsibility of generating picture on the screen without interaction of the CPU, generating excellent output of picture and movies.

4. Sound

A sound card is an electronic card that is inserted into any free expansion slot on the motherboard.

5. Video Capture Card

This capture movie or picture from external devices like TV, VCR, or Camcorder. Video Capture Cards come in two basic models, still Image Grabber and Frame Grabber. Both work like a film in a camera. To match the colours on television set, computer screen should also support 16 million colours.

6. CD ROM Drive

CD-ROM stands for Compact Disk Read Only Memory. CD-ROM drive is used to read data from Compact Disks. A CD is a circular light reflecting plate that can hold very large data. Commonly CD's are used to store picture, software installation files, music, movies etc.

SOFTWARE USED IN MULTIMEDIA

The computer has need of different types of application software for this purpose we used different platforms. The same is used in multimedia. The two most significant platforms for producing and delivering multimedia project are categories into two:—

1. The Machintosh Operating System from Apple.
2. Intel pared IBM PC or PC clone running Microsoft Windows.

There computer with GUI and huge installed bare of many million of users throughout the world are the most commonly used platform today for development of multimedia. Machintosh and PCs offer a compelling combination of a affordability, software availability and worldwide availability. Windows 95/ 98/ME/2000 are available for developing multimedia from Microsoft. Multimedia software tells the hardware what to do. Like, Play red colour, move the liger, 3 loap to the left sided the words, turn the volume on MP3 or etc. The software is divided into several part based on what the software is designed to do for us.

Tools Used in Multimedia

Some basic tools are used in the multimedia. These are as:—

1. To work with text, are work processor, spread sheets and database.
2. To work with sound, images and videos are win-amp, window media player, Jet Audio etc.

There is some authoring tool provided for multimedia like for video production, animation, games, interactive websites, demo disk and guided to presentation, kiosk application, interactive training, simulation, prototype, technical visualization and us. The hardware and software are the basic requirements for developing a multimedia project. As discussed above, in software part there are two specific platform as suitable for development of multimedia i.e. Macintosh & Windows.

Software for multimedia among various types also includes software for creation of graphics, animation. Designer, CorelDraw, Picture publisher, Photo magic, Animator pro etc. are most common used programs. In software we need all the software, which is provided by authoring tool set of multimedia. Software tool for text, painting, drawing, animation etc., are included the multimedia development. Without hardware and software, the multimedia cannot be developed. Some examples of the software used in multimedia are Corel, Photo paint. Jip Animator, Paintbrush and Photoshop.

Mackintosh Platform

The Macintosh has been defined as, "A multimedia computer at the famous roll-out of Machintosh in January 1984 from apple. The Macintosh has a good hold on built-in audio right from the star. In 1984 JBM personal computer could not process sound without every expensive add on computer."

The entire Macintosh can record and play sound. Many include hardware and software for digitalizing and editing video and producing DVD disc High quality graphics capability is available.

1. Apple introduces the first power Macintosh computer based on reduced instruction set computing (RISC) microprocessor during 1994.
2. In 1997, the G3 series was introduced with clock speed greatly than 233MHz and offering higher performance than existing Pentium based window.
3. In 2001, G4 complete offered 733MHz speeds.

The Windows platform

It is the collection of parts that are tied together by the requirement of the windows operating system. Power supplies, processors, hardies, cd-rom players, video and audio components, monitors, key-boards and mouse—do not matter where they come from or who make them, there component are assembled into computer that run windows.

Microsoft organized the major PC hardware manufacture into the multimedia PC marketing council to develop a set of specification that would allow develop a set of specification that would allow window to deliver a dependable multimedia experience, PCs can talk with your Macintosh and your network printers as well. This is many times more deficient than carrying removable media among your machines. Macintosh have Ethernet network built in your PC will require in expensive Ethernet card. Window PC allows it to connect to a network of Macintosh that uses apple talk. Both require Ethernet as the connection method Window & Macintosh both are the suitable platform for developing multimedia but now a day, the window PCs are mostly used because of advanced feature that the Macintosh platform:

STORAGE DEVICES USED IN MULTIMEDIA

To estimate the memory requirements of multimedia project. The space required on a floppy disk, hard disk, or CD-ROM or the RAM used while our computer is running. We must have sense of the project's content and scope. Colour images, text, sound bites, video clips, and the programming coded that guides it all together require memory: -

1. RAM (Random Access Memory)
2. ROM (Read Only Memory)
3. Floppy and Hard disk
4. Suquest Zip, Jazz, and Optical Storage Device
5. Digital Versatile Disc (DVD)
6. CD ROM Player

1. RAM (Random Access Memory)

If you are faced with budget constraints, you can certainly produce multimedia project on a slower or limited memory (RAM). Shortage time after time, when you are attempting to keep multiple applications and file open simultaneously. On Macintosh, the minimum RAM configuration for serious multimedia production is about 32MB, but even 64 MB and 256MB system are becoming common. A fast processor without enough RAM may waste processor.

2. ROM (Read Only Memory)

ROM is not volatile. Unlike RAM clip, when we turn off the power to a ROM chip, it will not forget or lose its data, ROM typically used in computer to hold the small BIOS program that initially boot up the computer and it used in printers to hold built in fonts. There are variety or PROM, ERROM allow changes to be made that are note forgotten. A new and expensive technology optical ROM (OROM), is provided in proprietary data card using parented holographic storage.

3. Floppy and Hard Disk

Adequate storage space for our production environment can be provided by large capacity hard disk, floppy disks and hard disk are mass-storage devices for binary data that can be easily read by a computer. Hard disk can contain much more information than floppy disk and can operate at for greater data transfer rates. Floppy disk is made of flexible plastic coated with a very thin layer of special magnetic material. A hard disk is actually a stack of hard metal platters coated with magnetically sensitive material with a series of recording heads or sensors that however a hair breadth above the fast spinning surface, magnetizing or demagnetizing sports along formatted tracks using technology similar to that used by floppy disks and audio and video tape recording hard disks are the most common mass storage devices used on computers and for making multimedia. We will need one or more large capacity.

4. Suquest Zip, Jazz, and Optical Storage Device

1. Suquest 44MB removable cartridge has been the most widely used portable medium among multimedia developer and professionals, but lomega's.
2. Inexpensive zip drives with their likewise inexpensive 100MB cartridges have significantly penetrated SyQuest's market share for removable media.
3. Lomega's Jazz cartridges provide a gigabyte of removable storage media and have fast enough rates for audio and video development.
4. Magneto optical (MO) drives use a high power laser to heating spots on the metal oxide coated of disk while the spot is hot, a magnet aligns the oxides to provide a 0 or

1 (on or off) orientation large format magneto optical drives with 5.25 inch cartridge offering 650MB to 1.3GB of storage are available.

5. Digital Versatile Disc (DVD)

To promote new optical disk technology for distributors of multimedia and feature length movie called DVD. With a new medium capable not only of Gigabyte storage capacity but also full motion video (MPEGZ) and high-quality audio in surround sound, the bar again risen for multimedia developer. Commercials multimedia projects will become more expensive to produce as consumer's performance expectation arises. There are two type of DVD:-

1. DVD video and
2. DVD ROM

DVD can provide 720 pixels per horizontal line, whereas current televisions (NTSC) provide 240 TV pictures will be sharper and more detailed. With do by AC-3 digital surround sound as part of the specifications, six discrete audio channels can be programmed for digital surround sound. DVD also supports dull by pro-logic surround sound, standard stereo, and mono audio.

6. CD ROM Player

Compact disc read only memory (CD-ROM) player have become an internal part of the multimedia development work-station and an important delivery vehicle for large, mass-produced projects. A wide variety of develop utilities, graphic backgrounds, applications, games, reference texts and educational software are available only on this medium. CD-ROM player have typically been very slow to access and transmit data but developments led to double-triple, quadruple speed, 24x, 48x and 52x drives designed specifically for computer use.

Sound and Video in Multimedia

Multimedia is combination of text, graphic art, sound, animation and video delivered in the multimedia project. In a multimedia application txt, images, animations can be greatly complemented by the use of sound. Sound is an intrigue part of various multimedia presentations. Sound can be used in a number of ways in multimedia application. Some of them are:—

(a) Sound of the surrounding a multimedia environment can be recorded for example while showing a photograph of jungle the associated sound track can make the image more impressive.

(b) Sound helps the users to receive and retain the multimedia message in a better way.

(c) Sound an also be used for catching attention in a boring graphic oriented presentation.

(d) Sound may also break the monotony of multimedia-based tutors.

Need of Sound in Multimedia

Sound is perhaps the most sensuous element of multimedia. It is meaning "Speech" in any language form a whisper to a screen. It can provide the listening pleasure of music, the starting accent of special effects, or the ambience of a mood-setting background. Some feel good music powerfully fills the heart, generating emotions of love, or otherwise elevating listens closer to heaven. Sound is energy, like the waves breaking on sandy beach, you feel sound more than hear it.

Multimedia System Sound

We can use sound night off the both the Macintosh and on a multimedia PC running windows because beeps and warring sounds are available as soon as operating system is installed. On the Macintosh you can choose one of several sound of alert, chute, glass, indigo, laugh, logion, pong 2003, purr, simple beep etc. In window, system sounds are way files and they reside in the window/media sub-directory.

Video System

Video in itself is multimedia as it combines visual and oral information the seamless integration of computers and video represent the most difficult aspect of multimedia from the technology point view and most rewarding from the communication point of view. No degree of integration anticipates the technology, tools or techniques that have changed the way we communicate from the communication point of view. Some of the basic consideration, which need to be addressed for integrating video in a multimedia application are:

1. Data transfer rate in capacity of storage device.
2. Size of the window to be used for display.
3. Frame rate and image resolution.

In multimedia systems one needs a high data transfer rate and capacity to sustain full motion video capabilities the size of displayed window can be controlled to lower sizes to reduce the transfer rate requirements, a low frame rate or resolution may reduce the data handing rate but will result in poor quality of video.

Need for Video in Multimedia

1. Video makes the multimedia presentation effective.
2. Video helps in understanding the things better.

Motion video is a element of multimedia that can draw gasps from a crowd at a trade show or firmly hold a student's interest in a computer based learning project. Digital video is the most engaging of multimedia Venus and it is a powerful tool for bringing computers user closer to the real world. It also is an effective method for delivering multimedia to an audience raised on T.V. with video elements in our project, we can effectively present our message and reinforce our story and viewers tend to retain more of what they role. Video that is not thought out or well reduced can degrade our presentation of all the multimedia elements. Video places the highest performance demand on our computer and its memory. Using video in multimedia gives wed the ability to presents information in a variety of ways we can add animation where it is needed video standard and formed are still being refined as transport, storage, compression and display technologies take shape in labs and in the market places. If our project will include video, consider whether we should shoot new footage or acquire pre-existing content of our video clips. There are many sources for film and video clips from 'Stack' footage house or a T.V. station or movie studio.

Digital Video

Full integrated of motion video on computer eliminates the analog T.V. form of video form the multimedia delivery platform. If a video clip is stored as data on a hard disk, CD-ROM or other mass storage devices, that clip can be played back on the computer's monitor without overlay boards, video disk player or second monitors. This playback of digital video is accomplished using software architecture such as quick time or AVI. AS a multimedia producer or developer, we may need to convert video source material from its still common analog from to digital form manageable by the end user's computer system.

Audio File Format

When we create multimedia, it is likely that you deal with file formats and translators for text, sounds, images, animations or digital video clips. A sound file's format is simple a recognized methodology for organizing the digital sounds data bits and byte into a data file. In machine, digitalized sound may be stored as data file like as, AIF or SDII. They may be stored as resources in the resources fork of the system or application as SNDS. In windows, a digital sound is most commonly stored as WAV files, for Internet, new format are emerging as companies develop solutions for streaming and playing sound on the web. Both window and Macintosh uses MIDI files. A Midi interface is built into many soundboards on PC. The various audio file formats are:—

Sl. No.	*File*	*Extension*	*Mime Type*
1	MIDT	MID	Audio/mid
2	MP3 Audio	.MP3	Audio/Mpeg
3	MPEG audio	.MPEG	Audio/Mpeg
4	VOC sound	VOC	
5	WAV sound	.WAN	Audio/WAN
6	AIFF audio	.aiff	Audio/aiff
7	Amiga 8-bit	.8ux	....
8	Amiga:FF sound	.Sux	....
9	Amiga MID sound	.Med	....
10	Av audio	.VLW	Audio/basic

Different Tools for Development of Graphic

Painting and drawing tools, as well as 3-D modellers, are perhaps the most important item in our toolkit because of all the multimedia elements: the graphical impact of our project will likely have the greatest influence on the end user. There are so many tools for development of graphics. Some are given below for information:—

Photoshop, fireworks and painter are dedicated to producing crafted bit mapped images. Example: Corel draw, freehand, illustrator, designer, and canvas are dedicated to producing vector base line art easily printed to paper at high resolution. Some software combines the feature of drawing and painting. But many authoring system can impart only bit mapped images. The bit mapped images provide the greatest choice and power to the artist for rendering fine detail and effects and today bit maps are used in multimedia more after than drawn objects. Some vector based packages such as macromedia's flash is aimed at reducing file download time on the web and many contain both bit maps and drawn art.

Features of Painting and Drawing Packages

1. An intuitive graphical user interface with pull-down menu, status bas, palette control and a dialog box, palette control etc.
2. Scalable dimensions, we can resize, stretch and distort both large and small bitmaps.
3 Paint tool to create geometric shapes from squares to circle and from curves to complex polygons.
4 Ability to pour a color, pattern or gradient into any area.
5. Ability to paint with patterns or gradient into any area.
6. Customize pen and brush shapes and size.
7. Zooming for magnified pixel editing.
8 All color depth; 1-4-8 and 16-24 or 32 bit color and gray scale.
9. Good color management and dithering capability among color depth using various color model such as RGB, HSB and CMYK.
10. Color palette management when in 8 bit mode.

11. Good file imparting and exporting capability for imager format such as PIC, GIF, TGA, TIP, WMF, JPG, PCX, EPS, PTN and BMP.

If we are new to multimedia and to these tools, we should take time to examine more than one graphics software packages.

Relationship between Text, Graphics and Background

Text is one of the most widely building block in multimedia application the intensity of the text depends on the purpose of the program. We can use and display text in different form for different purposes. These are:—

1. Titles
2. Buttons
3. Bullets
4. Paragraph
5. Scrolling Text

A graphics in a multimedia application can be more appealing and meaningful than a thousand of Characters. According to ancient Chinese saying a picture is worth a thousands words. From a planning and production management point of view the selection of graphics, sound, video and the text to be instigated in multimedia applications is critical for its success. The integration of graphics into multimedia application could include the following elements:—

1. Background
2. Photos
3. 3-D Pictures
4. Charts
5. Flowcharts
6. Organizational Charts
7. Drawings
8. Clips-Art
9. Buttons (Icons)

Background

The background is one of the most important graphic elements of a multimedia application. In a way, the background establishes one tone and the theme if our application. In some instances, the background also determines the complexity of the production especially when we are using 3-D graphics. The choice of background design, complexity, richness depend on a number of factors:

A. Theme of the Application.
B. Color display capacity of the projector.
C. Storage capacity of the medium to be used distribution purposes.
D. Amount of text to be placed over the background.

Text is related to other multimedia building blocks. When planning to place over a background, we must consider font colour, font size, and the contract against the background. If the characters are not legible against the background, we may have to place the text over a text box with a solid or translucent colour. On the other hand using clip arts graphics is considered amateurish in most other application. Graphics with text and also with a good background make together the best output in multimedia application.

Authoring Software

Authoring software is the main production tool for multimedia. An authoring system is a program, which has pre-programmed elements for the development of interactive multimedia software. Authoring software can package a multimedia project to play another computer type with appropriate planning. It provides with a great degree of control over each multimedia elements than presentation programs. The four basic functions provided by almost all the authoring software are:—

1. Importing
2. Creating
3. Integrating
4. Delivering

It should be able to import various media elements, which may have been developed using other software package. The creating is a basic feature for creating of text, graphics, and may be sound if not video. The integrating, should allow us to define sequences and provide linkages. The delivering allows developing self running application and encryption of application of data.

Icon Based Authoring Tools

Icon based event driven tools provides a visual programming media. First, we build a structure on flowchart of events, tasks and decisions by dragging appropriate icons from a library. These icons can include menu choices, graphic images, sounds and computations. The flow chart graphically decides the projects logic, when the structure is built, we can add our content that is the text, graphics, animation, sounds and video movies. Then to refine our project, we edit our logical structure by rearranging and tine-tuning the icons and their properties.

With icon based authoring tools, non technical multimedia authors can build sophisticated applications without scripting by placing icons on a flow line, we can quickly sequence events and activities including decisions and user interactions. These tools are useful fern story boarding as we can change sequences, add options, and restructure interactions by simple dragging and dropping icons. We can print out our navigation map or flowchart, an annotated project index with or without associated icons deciding and presentation windows and a cross-reference table of variables.

In these authoring systems multimedia elements and interactions cues (Events) are organized as object in a structural framework or process. Icon base, event driven tools simplify the organization of our project and typically display flow diagram of activities along breaching path.

Time Based Authoring Tools

Time based systems are popular multimedia authoring tools. Each uses its own distinctive approach and user interface for managing events over time many use a visual timeline for sequencing the events of a multimedia presentation often displaying layers of various media elements or events along side the scale in increments as precise as one second others arrange long sequences of graphic frames and add the time component by adjusting each frame's duration of play.

1. Director

Macromedia's director is a powerful and complex multimedia-authoring tool from macromedia with a broad set of features to create multimedia presentations, animations and interactive multimedia applications. It requires a significant learning curve, but once mastered, it is among the most powerful of multimedia development tools. In director, we assemble and sequence the elements of our project using a cast and score.

2. Cast

The cast is a multimedia elements for ours project and place them into our cast, we ties cast member together using the score facility. Score is a sequence for displaying, animating and playing cast member, and it is made up of frame that contains cast members, tempo, and palette, timing and sound information.

3. Lingo

Director utilizes lingo, a fun featured object-oriented scripting language to enable interactivity and programmed control. A build in script editor offer lingo-debugging facilities. Because we call attach scripts to individual element of CAST, we can copy and paste complete interactive sequences.

The functions of multimedia authoring software

A. In multimedia we does video product

B. Animation > games > interactive training > simulation, prototype and technical visualization.

Multimedia authoring tools provide the important framework we need for organization and editing the elements of our multimedia project, including graphics, sounds, animation and video clips. Authoring tool are used for designing interactivity and the use interface, for presenting our project on screen, and to assembling multimedia elements into a single, authoring software provides an integrated environment for binding together the content and function of our project.

TYPES OF TEXT NEED FOR MULTIMEDIA

1. Text

A single item of menu text accompanied by a single action requires little training and is clean and immediate. Use text for title and headlines, for navigation and for content, help to provide information about that particular thing. Computes screen provide a very small workspace for developing complex ideas. At some time or another; we will need to deliver high-impact or very concise text message on the computer screen in as condensed as possible. For designing perspective, our choice of font size and the number of headlines for, place on a particular screen must be related both to the complexity of our message and to its venue. The text should be given according to situation like: if we are providing public-speaking sport, the text will be keyed to a live presentation where text accents the main message. In this case we use the large fonts and few word with a lot of space.

2. Animating text

There is plenty of way to retain a viewer's attention when displaying text. We can animate bulleted text and have it "fly" onto the screen. We can "group" a headline a character at a time. For speaker, simply highlighting the most important point works well as a pointing device. When there are several points to be made, we can stack keywords and flash them past the viewer in a timed automated sequence. There are some powerful but inexpensive application are available like:- Xaos tools type Caster let us to create 3-D text using both true type and types adobe fonts. We can use illustrator and freehand EPS encapsulation postscript outline file to create still images in 3-D and then animate the result to create quick time movie with broad cast quality rendering.

3. Using text in Multimedia

In multimedia the text is uses for the title, headlines and for navigation and for contents.

4. Font and Faces for Text

A typeface is a family of graphic characters that usually includes many type sizes and style. A font is a collection of character of a single size and style belonging to a particular typeface family, typically font style are the bold face and Italic face. Our computer software may add other style attribute, such as underling and outlining of characters. Type size is usually expressed in points; .0138 inches or about of an inches. The font size doesn't exactly describe the height or width of its characters leading can be adjusted in most programs on both the Macintosh tool in window> leading is providing appropriate line spacing. Kerning is the spacing between character pair. For example we can adjust the body width of each character from regular to condensed to expanded in the suborn font.

Regular—a Condensed—a Expanded

5. Cases

These are basic all two cases for each word is available> lowercase held the small letter. Today a capital letter is called uppercase placing an uppercase letter in the middle of a Word called an intercept, is a trend that emerged from the computer programming communication. Most Common font for window & Macintosh windows: Arial, book antiquam, bookman old style, bookshelf symbol, century gothic, comic sans MS, Courier New, Lucida Console, Marlette, MS Sanssarig, MS Serif, Times New Roman.

6. Macintosh

Monaco, New York, Palatino, symbol, times, Chicago, Geneva, Helvetica, charcoal. Making pretty text: To make our text pretty, we need a toolbox full of font and special graphics applications that can stretch, shade shadow, colour, and anti-alias our words into real art network pretty text is typically found in bitmapped drawing where characters have been tweaked, manipulated with proper tools and a create mind, we can create. Endless variation on plain-old type and we not only choose but also customize the styles that fill with your design.

Hypermedia and Hypertext

Multimedia become interactive multimedia when we give the user some control over what information is viewed and when it is viewed. Interactive multimedia becomes hypermedia when its designers provide a structure of linked element through which a user can navigate and interact. When a hypermedia project includes large amount of text or symbolic content, this content can be indexed and its element than linked together to afford rapid electronic retrieval of the associated information. When word are keyed or indexed to other word, we have a hypertext system.

Analog and Digital Audio

In analog, physical sound presser waves are converted to corresponding electrical signals by an acoustic transducer such as microphone or phonograph cartridge. The electrical output of transducer is called an analog signal because electrical signal is analogous to (representative) of the pressure pattern of sound wave that created it. Sound signals are most often represented in the form of two-dimensional wave pattern whose y-axis is the intensity or amplitude of the signal and whose x-axis represents the passage of time. ADC are used to measure the analog signal and express in stannous values of signals amplitude in digital form. In digital audio, the sound is a repeated pattern of pressure in the air and a microphone converts a sound wave into an electric wave. The shape and frequency of the electric wave is identical to the shape and frequency of the sound wave and clarity of what we hear is entirely dependent on the shape of frequency of sound. Audio has to be converted into digital form to produce digital audio in order to use it in multimedia. And the digital audio system will then re convert the entire digitized audio into analog form, which can be herd on speaker. Storage space required for digital audio is huge then analog audio. In multimedia it is more advisable to keep all audient digital format then in audio format.

Digital Videos

Digital Videos one of the many technologies used in the development of interactive multimedia. It is one of the ways to play and record video in multimedia program. It offers a wide range of flexibility as compared to standard video signal' Unlike regular, quality of image would not degrade from copy to copy as digital video is made up of a digital code and not an electrical analog signal. Video places the highest performance demand on computer and its memory. Let us consider that a high-quality color still requires as much as a megabyte of memory. Carefully planned well-executed video clips can make a dramatic difference in multimedia project. Consider whether you should shoot new footage or acquire preexisting content for your video clips. These are many source for film and video clip:- a friend's home movies may suffice or you can go to "stock" footage house or a TV station or movie studio. In analog system, the video signal from the camera is delivered to the video in connector(s) of a VCR, where it is recorded on magnetic video tape. The video signals can write on tape by a spinning recording head that changes the local magnetic properties.

Use of Digital Videos

Digital video has supplanted analog video as the method of choice for making video for multimedia use. While broadcast station and professional production and post production houses remain greatly invested in analog video hardware, digital video gain produces excellent finish add products at a fraction of the cost of analog. Full integrated of motion video on computer eliminates the analog TV form of video from multimedia delivering platform. If video clip is stored on a hard disk, GO-Rom or other mass storage device that clip can be played back on the computer's monitor without overlay boards, video disc player or second monitor. This play back of digital video is accomplisher using software architectures like quick time or AVI. As multimedia producer or developer, you may need to convert video source material from its still common analog form to a digital form manageable by the end user's computers system.

Frame rate

TV video builds 30 entire frames or pictures every second. The movies on film are typically shot at ash utter rate of 24 frames per second, but using projection trick. The flicker rate is increased to 48 times per second. On some projects each frame is shown 3 times before the pull-down claw moves to the next frame for a total of 721 licker per second.

Frame Size

A minute of animation may require as mangos 1,440 separate frame, the term cell derives from the clear celluloid sheet that were used for drawing each frame, cell animation artwork begin with key frame (the first and last frame of an action). The services of frame between the key frames are drawn in a process called twining. Twining is a action which is required to calculate the number of frame between key frame.

Color Depth

Colour palettes are mathematical table that defines the colour of a pixel displayed on the screen on the Macintosh, these table are called colour look up table or GLUTs, Window the term palette is used the most common palette are 1, 4, 8, 16 and 24 bits deep:

Color Depth	*Color Auditable*
1 bit	Black & White
4 bit	16 Colour
8 bit	256 Colour (Good Enough)
16 bit	Thousands of Colours
24 bit	More than 16 Million Colors (Totally Photo Reediest)

For 256 colour, 8 bit VGA system your computer users a colour lookup table or palette to determine which 256 colour out of the millions possible are available to you at any time.

Design Consideration for the Multimedia Application

The designing part of a multimedia application development requires our knowledge, skills in graphic art, video, music etc. Designing is thinking, choosing and making a product. This is the phase where the idea conceived in the planning phase gets a shape or we can say this is the realization of idea in the planning phase. While designing certain consideration are to be kept in mind. Some of these are:

1. The multimedia application should be full of Text, Sound Clips, and Graphics.
2. It should be well equipped with latest technology,
3. It should be user friendly.
4 Multimedia application should focus its main objective.

Designing is thinking, choosing, making and doing, It is snapping, smoothing, reworking, polishing, testing and editing. When we design our project, our idea and concept are moved one step closes to reality complacence in the design phase is what separates amateurs from professionals in the making of multimedia. A multimedia project is no more than an arrangement of Text, graphic, Sound and video elements or objects. The way you compose these elements into interactive experiences is shaped by your purpose and message.

USE OF MULTIMEDIA IN EDUCATION

Multimedia in school is perhaps the most widely needy destination. Many schools are using this multimedia application in their school for the purpose of teaching the students. In school the computer is become essential part of education as teaching the basic of reading, writing and arithmetic. Multimedia for learning takes many forms through showing the cartoon on particular subject. Multlmedia for reading skills grow through word recognition, a mouse click on any word pays in back. The computer read the story aloud, sometimes spelling words individually.

An interesting use of multimedia in schools involves the students themselves. Student put together interactive magazines and newsletter, they make original art using image-editing tool, they interview students and towns people and coaches and teachers and they make quick time movies. Many computer games with the focus on the education are available. A simple example in this reference is an educational game, which plays various rhymes for little kids. In addition to playing rhymes, the child can paint the pictures, increase/reduce the size of the objects etc. Similar many other educational packages, which provide a lot of detailed information to kids, are available. Microsoft has produced many such CD's based multimedia such as 'Sierra', 'Knowledge Adventure' etc., which in addition to play provide some sort of learning component. The latest in this series is a package, which teaches about the computer using games playing.

EXERCISE QUESTIONS

1. Discuss the characteristics of multimedia to be developed for importing education to school children. Identify the hardware and software component of above system. Discuss each in brief.
2. Name various storage devices used for multimedia application. Write in Brief.
3. Why are sound and video important in multimedia presentation naming various audio file formats?
4. What is multimedia? Explain its use in the different aspects of human life.
5. What is the basic requirement for multimedia project?

CHAPTER 12

INTERNET AND SERVER-CLIENT TECHNOLOGY

- Introduction
- Web and Net
- http:URL
- Engines Search
- Configuration of E-Mail
- Configure Outlook Express, Netscape Messenger and Eudora
- Use of Brackets and Quotes
- Wildcard and Server-Client Technology
- Exercise Questions

INTRODUCTION

It's not a place, it's not a thing and it's not even an office. So, what is it? When you connect two or more computers together, it's called a network. When you connect all these networks in the world, it's called the Internet. These networks and computers use telephone cables to connect to each other. So just like you can call anywhere if you have their telephone number, you can connect to any network or site if you have their address.

WEB AND NET

As different as black and white, though everyone keeps confusing one with the other. While the Internet is the network of networks, the World Wide Web is a collection of linked pages on this network. You can look at it this way - the Internet is the cable TV system and the Web is like the programs and channels that go on this system.

Being online means being connected to at least one other computer through a modem and phone line. When you dial your Internet Service Provider (ISP), you're online. When you surf the Web, you're online. When you can send and, especially, when you can receive e-mail, you are online.

Can I be on the Internet forever and ever?

Not if you don't want to give thousands and thousands of rupees for the phone bill. Your PC uses your telephone line to connect to the Internet. So till the time you're on the Internet nobody will be able to call you up.

What if the Internet stops working?

It's hard to believe that life existed before the Internet, isn't it? If it stops working again, you won't get to all those lovely colourful Websites and get all the useful information and fun stuff they have on them, and you won't be able to get in touch with all your friends and relatives spread around the world so easily.

Who keeps the Net neat?

Well, no one, and that's why it's not neat. In fact, it's a mess. There are millions of Websites on it and new ones keep coming up every hour. This is why we need search engines to giving us all the information on the Net in some sort of neat way.

Does the Internet have an office?

Not at all, the Internet is actually millions and millions of computers connected together. These computers could be anywhere—USA, India, Japan, even Fiji islands. So it's not possible for any one office to keep track of all these computers.

What's http?

Stands for Hypertext Transfer Protocol. First part of the name of a Website—it tells computers it's a Web page they're trying to find. What's a link? Links are those underlined (usually in blue) words that connect hypertext pages. Every time you feel the urge to click on highlighted text, or pass your mouse cursor over an image and the arrow becomes a hand, you've got yourself a link. If you click on and follow that link, it may take you somewhere else on that page to another page on that site or to an entirely different site.

What's a URL

Uniform Resource Locator or URL is a string of characters that identifies the accurate location and type of an Internet resource. For instance, http://www.hclinfinet.com/matter/page .html indicates the domain narne of the computer on which this site is stored, describes the document's location within the folder structure and also has the document's name and extension.

How does Engines Search?

Some of them use robots! Not like the ones that have blinking lights and digital voices—they're actually very smart, little programs. Search engines have tiny robots in them that they send sniffing all over the Internet to search for the sites on which the keyword you're looking for appears again and again. The more times the word comes up on the site, the more the robots like it.

Configure Your E-Mail

There is a number of software, which let you send and receive e-mail. Outlook Express comes bundled with Windows, whereas Netscape Messenger is a part of Netscape Communicator. Eudora, Pegasus Mail, Fox Mail, etc., are several third-party e-mail clients. To configure these e-mail clients to send and receive e-mail, you will need to know before hand your e-mail address, the names of your incoming (POP3, IMAP or HTTP) and outgoing (SMTP) e-mail servers and your e-mail account password. Your e-mail service provider should have provided the incoming and outgoing server names to you.

CONFIGURE OUTLOOK EXPRESS, NETSCAPE MESSENGER AND EUDORA

Outlook Express

Open Outlook Express. Go to Tools > Accounts > Mail. Select the add button and go to Mail. This opens the Internet Connection Wizard, which will guide you through the steps required to set up your e-mail account.

After the wizard guides you through the process once, you can repeat it to add your other e-mail accounts. When you're finished, select one of the accounts to be your default account by highlighting it and clicking on the Set as Default button in the Internet Accounts window. The default account is the one used for sending mail. If you set up only one e-mail account, it will automatically become your default account. Close the Internet Accounts window to finish configuring Outlook Express 5.

That's all there is to it! The next time you're on the Net, just click on the Send/Revco button and watch Outlook Express collect all your mail from your account(s) and stash it in your Inbox. You can then read the mail at your leisure.

Eudora

Open Eudora and go to Tools > Options.

Select Getting Started.

- Enter your name in the Real Name box
- Enter a Return Address if it's different from the one you use to send mail
- Mail Server (Incoming) is the POP3 server
- Login name is the part before the @ sign in your e-mail address
- Enter the SMTP server name. And you are done.

Netscape Messenger

Launch Netscape Messenger. If it's the first, time you are running it, you will be displayed a wizard which will guide you through the process of setting up a mail account for the Messenger. To do it directly from the Messenger window, in the Edit menu, open Preferences. Select Mail & Newsgroups and go to Identity. Enter your name and e-mail address. Go to Mail Servers and then to Incoming Mail Servers. If there is already a server name there, click on Edit to make changes to it. Else click on Add. Type the incoming or POP3 server name in Server Name. In Server Type, choose POP3 from the drop-down list. Enter the login name for this account - this is the first part of your e-mail address before '@'. Click on OK.

In Outgoing Mail Server, enter your SMTP server name in Outgoing Mail (SMTP) server. Enter your login name in Outgoing Mail server user name. Click on OK and you are done. You are now set to send and receive mail with Netscape Messenger.

Add Power to Your Search

A search engine is a website that helps you find stuff on the Internet. It could be a website that's dedicated to finding information from all over the Net, or a part of a larger site that can find stuff on its own parent site. Just type in a word, or a phrase in the blank space provided for it at search engines, hit 'Search' or some such button, and the engine is off to search the Net.

Planning a search strategy

A good search begins with a clear understanding of what you want to search for. Suppose you want to find information about the Taj Mahal. Simply entering the words Taj Mahal at your favourite search engine will bombard you with hundreds of useless URLs about Donald Trump's Taj Mahal hotel in Vegas. Add a few words like India and Mughals and see the difference. Hence, the first step in effective searching is to include relevant words that you think may appear in your document in the search field.

Refining your search

To find some web site, we use some important technical words mostly which used by the user time to time. Some hints of words are given below:

Use Boolean operators

To do more accurate search and avoid getting too many unrelated documents or sites. Boolean operators can be used with some Internet search tools.

AND

Insert AND between keywords; for instance, automobiles AND airbags to search for documents with both the words in them.

OR

Wrestling OR Basketball will search for pages with either word in them.

NOT/AND NOT

Archie NOT comics (or Archie AND NOT comics on some search engines), will search for sites with the word Archie but not comics.

Use of Brackets and Quotes

Enclosing a word or group of words in double quotes searches for the exact string as you have typed it. A search string in brackets searches that first and then narrows the search down using the rest of the search string.

Wildcard symbols

Entering a keyword like teen* will search for all words like teenager, teenage, teen sand teeny.

Search by field

Suppose you want to search for a particular word only in the title of a Web page (the part that appears in the top coloured bar in Explorer), or you want to search for a particular image file or a URL. Saying image:comet.jpg will search for all pages with this image in them. Or title: welcome searches for welcome in the title of Web pages only.

However, these techniques may not work with all search engines, Also note that some sites use the '+'.and '–' symbols instead of AND OR respectively. Check out the list of popular search engines for an idea of their specialities. Some common search engines

- http://www.altavista.com
- http://www.hotbot.com
- http://www.yahoo.com
- http://www.google.com
- http://www.123india.com
- http://www.khoj.com
- http: //www.rediff.com

Bookmark Your Sites for Easy Reference

What was that site where you found those interesting tips on exotic recipes? You had scribbled down its address somewhere-now you can't find it. If only the Web were like your book where you put bookmarks to remember the pages! Well, it is like your book. You can put digital bookmarks to remember your favourite sites.

What are bookmarks?

Bookmarks—when you talk about the Net—are a feature of your browser that lets you store the address (URL) of any Web page that you might want to visit again. So the next time you want to visit that particular page, there is no need to try and recollect the long and tedious URL. A single click of the mouse will get you there.

Bookmark is a term that is used by the makers of the popular browser 'Netscape Communicator'. Although this is the way they are generally referred to, Internet Explorer calls them Favourites. The difference is only in the names, the function remains the same.

How do I use bookmarks?

Using bookmarks is extremely simple and convenient. Here's how.

In Netscape Communicator

Open the page that you wish to bookmark. Go to the Bookmarks menu and click on Add Bookmark. (If the Bookmarks button is not available, you can find it in the Communicator menu). The new bookmark is added and is ready for use in the future.

In Internet Explorer

Open the page that you want to bookmark. Click on Add to favourites... in the Favourites menu. The page has now been book marked. Whenever you want to go back to the book marked page, just go to the same menu (Bookmarks or Favourites) and locate the title of the page that you want to view. When the title is highlighted, click on it. The page will now load in your browser window.

Avoiding getting framed

In case of sites that use frames creating bookmarks can get a little tricky. This is because when frames are used, the new page amply loads up in the predetermined frame without changing the URL. Since the URL is what bookmarks store, you might end up not marking the page that you are really interested in.

But there is a way around this. When you want to bookmark something delayed in a frame, just right-click on that frame in the browser. Doing this brings up a menu that will have the Add Bookmark option in Netscape Communicator and the Add to Favourites option in Internet Explorer. Using these will automatically save the URL of the frame that you are interested in even if that URL is not displayed in the address bar, simple and effective.

Get organized

Once your list, of bookmarks starts expanding, it's important to organize them. This will help you locate the particular bookmark that you are looking for quickly and also maintain some semblance of order in the otherwise disorganised and long list of book marked pages.

The best way to organize bookmarks is to create separate folders for the bookmarks on various topics. For example, it would be a good idea to store all entertainment related bookmarks in a folder called 'Entertainment' while all job related bookmarks could go into the 'Jobs' folder.

All you have to do is to create new folders, give them relevant names, and drag and drop the bookmarks into the respective folders. Here's how to do them.

In Netscape Communicator

Go to Bookmarks > Edit Bookmarks. In the new window that displays the bookmarks, go to the File menu and click on New Folder. Enter an appropriate name for the folder created. Once this is done, simply drag and drop the relevant bookmarks from your list into the new folder.

In Internet Explorer

Use the Favourites > Organize Favourites path. In the new window that opens you can create a new folder and give it a proper name. To transfer bookmarks into this folder, select the bookmark and click on the Move to Folder button. A list of the existing folders comes up. Just click on the name of the new folder created and you are done.

Both the browsers let you organize your bookmarks very well. Creating new folders is not all that you can do. You can also create folders inside folders to achieve a high level of organization and create a logical file structure, rename folders and bookmarks, and also delete them to keep your list up to date.

Mobile bookmarks

If you use a computer from a public place like a cyber cafe, college or office then the bookmarks you save there won't be accessible to you elsewhere. Save them on a floppy and carry them around.

In Netscape, go to Bookmarks > Edit Bookmarks. Once the new window opens, use File > Save As. You can now save the bookmark file as an htm or text file at any desired location including a floppy. In Internet Explorer, use the File > Export route. In this case too, you can get an htm or text file. An htm file is more advisable because it retains all the hyperlinks and is therefore convenient to use on another computer. Since this file is basically just a list of shortcuts, the file size is small and can be earned on a floppy disk.

Once you get to another computer, just open the htm file and use it as it is. Or you can also use the 'Import' function of the browser to add these new bookmarks to your existing list.

Back them up

As your bookmark list gets longer, it also becomes that much more precious. Losing it can be a major blow to your work. Bookmarks are also infamous for getting corrupted. Imagine all those links being lost at one shot. You can use the method described above to back up your bookmarks from time to time. So even if your bookmarks do get corrupted, you can use the backup file to restore them immediately. The backup can be maintained in a different folder on the same machine or on a floppy disk.

Bookmarks on the Web

A lot of bookmark related sites are available on the Internet. Some of these help you organize and maintain your bookmarks online. For example, *www.coolsync.com* allows you to upload the bookmarks from your local machine to a cool sync account. This account is offered free. All you have to do is fill up a form, choose a username and password and your account is ready for use. This is particularly useful if you browse from a number of different places and still want all your bookmarks to be accessible all the time. It's also good for people who do not have computers of their own but would still like to maintain a list of their favourite sites. Another advantage is that if you have a computer crash and all the data is lost, your bookmarks will still be safe on the Website. Other sites offering similar services include *www.bookmarkbox.com* and *www.bookmarksplus.com.*

Bookmarks are convenient, simple and easy to use. They save you the tedium of noting down or remembering URLs and provide easy access to frequently visited sites. The next time you come across a site you want to bookmark, hit Ctrl + D on your keyboard—it's as simple as that!

Web bookmarks

- *http://www.coolsync.com*
- *http://www.bookmarkbox.com*
- *http:.//www.bookmarksplus.com*

A Guide to Instant Chat

Chat is cool, chat is in, has been for a long time, and it's here to stay. There are thousands and thousands of Web sites with cool chat rooms. But why chat when there's e-mail? Because chat is real time! Type out a message and you get the reply immediately. It's instantaneous. Well, not always, Chatting at Websites could take long. But then (here are other ways to chat too, which are truly instant. Like instant messengers and Internet Relay Chats.

Here are a few tips to become a pro chatter, including the language that goes around, do's and don'ts and step-by-step instructions.

- So what's your kind of chat?
- Cyber lingo
- Chatiquette

So what's your kind of chat?

Chat-room

Are you a newbie? Totally uninitiated into the world of chat? Then a site with a simple button, which says something like "click here to chat", would be the right place for you to start off. That's generally how people get to know about chatting. Also, if you come across a Website on a topic of interest to you, and the site happens to have a chat room, then you just might want to stroll in and put forth your opinions.

ICQ

Would you prefer to talk to only a select few friends? Then go for ICQ. You'll get to know whenever your buddies are online and can single them out for instant messaging or a private chat. Instant messaging is convenient since it lets you carry on working or browsing, while letting you communicate with your friends at the same time. Private chats are easier on ICQ because you and your friend don't have to spot each other amongst the countless people at a chat site and then make your way to a private or less crowded room for some tête-â-tête. Besides ICQ has now integrated a lot of elements of regular chat rooms along with add-ons such as voice messaging and greetings, so it is definitely a very versatile forum for fun.

IRC

The chronic chatters prefer to head towards IRC. Since IRC is totally dedicated to chat and has been around for a long time, if you're in the mood to talk to just about anybody, you know what will work for you.

ICQ or I Seek You

ICQ lets you have a one-to-one conversation or a conference with a group of people. You can send messages to the people you have included in your contact list. You can also send files, URLs (Website addresses), contacts of other persons in your list, an e-mail using ICQ itself, electronic greeting card, or even voice messages if you have a sound card and a microphone installed. You can also send phone call requests to that person if you want to call him up or want him to call you up.

Setting up ICQ (www.icq.com)

Installing ICQ is just as simple as installing any other software that you download from the Web. Run the executable (exe) file and follow the instructions.

Getting registered with ICQ

The work starts after the installation is done. Get connected to the Net. When you run ICQ for the first time, you will be asked to register at their site. Here's the bare minimum you have to give: A nickname, your full name and an e-mail address.

Give a password

The next step will ask you to give a password. This is needed to maintain the sanctity of your login. You can also opt to or not to publish your online presence in ICQ.

Get an ID number

Now you're registered with ICQ as a user and will be issued a unique ICQ ID number. This number is just like a pager number but you can use it on any system anywhere in the world. You can also install ICQ on multiple systems and use them simultaneously with the same ID number.

Chat's up

After you install ICQ, you will see a small icon in the system tray in the shape of a flower. The flower is green if you are connected to the server. If it goes red, it means that you aren't connected, and that you won't be able to send messages. When you receive a message, you'll see the icon in the system tray change from a flower to a small stick-it note that flashes on and off. Doubleclick on the stick-it note to read the message.

Looking for old friends?

ICQ lets you search for people on three different criteria: e-mail address, contact information (nickname, first name or last name) or by the ICQ ID. If you know the ID number of the person, the result will be accurate, as no two people will have the same ID number. But if you are searching for a nickname, you might end up with a long list of people. Pick the one you want. You can't just add him to your contact list, if he has chosen the authorization-required option when he installed

ICQ. You'll have to send him a message asking for authorization. If he authorizes you and adds you to his contact list you can start chatting.

Make new friends

What if you are searching for people to make friends with? People who share your interests? ICQ lets you do this in three ways: find an Active List, white pages and random chat.

Active List

It is a recent feature of ICQ. This lets you talk to a group of people that make up an Active List. Click on the ICQ button at the bottom of the main window and click on the Find a user option and then on the Find/Add an ICQ Active List option. If you know the name or ID number of the Active List, enter it in the window that appears. But if you don't you can search by a category. Pick the one you want. Once you find a list you want, register to become a member or just sign in as a guest. Click on the ICQ Active List button to see all your new buddies. You can send a new message to one of these buddies or broadcast a message to all the members in this group. You can also start your own Active List, but to do this you will need to install the server application to run on your system when you are online.

White Pages

Let you search for ICQers based on several criteria like name, e-mail, age, gender, language, interests, location, organization, etc. You can select one or more of the above criteria. ICQ will list all the matches and you can choose from them.

You can also opt for a **random chat** where you make yourself available for a chat or search for people available for a random chat, again based on your preferences. Random chat doesn't let you add the person to your buddy lists directly, but if the person wants, he can ask you for an authorization, and you can then add him to the list.

Start a group conference

Invite a person to start a chat. As soon as he replies positively, a chat window will open. You can have two types of windows: IRC style and Split window. In the IRC style, the window is divided into three parts - the main box where the transcript of the conversation appears, a side panel which lists the participants and a bottom strip where you type your part of the conversation. In a Split window, the whole window is split into boxes, and the comments of each member in the group appears in their respective boxes.

E-mail on ICQ

ICQ isn't just a messenger; it can also check your e-mail. ICQ has its own e-mail program, and will let you use your own e-mail programs like Outlook or Outlook Express. ICQ checks your mail servers and downloads the headers to your system. When you get new messages ICQ can alert you with sound or blinking icons. If you want to get to the full mail, ICQ can then launch your mail program to download the mail. But you do have to do a bit of tweaking before you can read your mail messages in ICQ. You'll have to specify your account details and password, the SMTP server name, the default e-mail client and so on. You can also specify more than one mail address.

ICQ is your personal organizer too

ICQ has a to-do list, a reminder and small notes. All these are stored locally on your computer and you don't have to go online to access them.

Maintain your privacy

One of the major concerns on the Net is to maintain your privacy. On might not be in a mood to chat but that friend of yours keeps bothering you with messages and chat requests. ICQ gives you some options to hold him off.

Available/Connect

In other words, you are online. This is the default setting and just notifies that you are available.

Free for chat

You are in a leisurely mood and would not grudge a small gossip.

Away

You are not present at your workstation, even if it is online. You can choose from the eight preset messages or write your own messages.

N/A (Extended away)

After an extended period of being on "Away", ICQ will automatically switch to N/A (Extended Away) mode.

Occupied (Urgent Mugs)

If you don't want to be distracted for any reason, use this status. Users will still be able to send you urgent messages, or leave a message on your Contact List (the message icon will not blink).

DND (Do Not Disturb)

Users will be able to send messages to only your Contact List.

Privacy (Invisible)

When you're in need of privacy, this is the best solution. You will be online but your friends won't know that.

Offline/Disconnect

Disconnect from the ICQ servers.

Connect Tips

1. If the server you're connected to is slow, try clicking online, offline and invisible in quick succession, this way you get ICQ to switch servers.
2. Add a few more to the ICQ servers' list. Here they are:

- icq2.mirabilis.com
- icq3.mirabilis.com
- icq4.mirabilis.com
- icq5.mirabilis.com
- 205.188.252.21
- 205.188.252.22
- 205.188.252.27
- 205.188.252.28
- 205.188.252.30
- 205.188.252.31
- 205.188.252.34

Use port number 4000 for all of them. You can get to these servers from the preference option in the ICQ main menu.

Cyber lingo

You might hear people in chat room's talk in a language that doesn't even remotely resemble any language you've heard before. Here's where you can find enough to stop your head from getting scratched out. We list down some of the common abbreviations and acronyms that you will frequently come across on chat.

- a/s/l = age/sex/location
- afk = away from the keyboard
- brb = be right back
- bbl = be back later
- lol = laughing out loud
- rofl = rolling on the floor laughing
- j/k = just kidding
- wb = welcome back
- imho = in my humble opinion
- np = no problem
- rtfm = read the freaking manual
- ttfn = ta ta for now
- cyl = see you later
- gr8 = great

Then there are emotions. These are symbols that convey emotions. Since nobody can actually see or hear the other person on chat, emotions are probably the best way to convey how you feel about something to the person you're chatting with.

Go ahead and make liberal use of the following:

- :-) a smiling face, for times when you're happy
- =) another variation of a smiling face
- (-: a lefty's smile
- :-(a frowning face, for times when you're unhappy
- :-0 a yawning face, when you are feeling bored or sleepy (or both)

- :-P sticking your tongue out, after you say something mischievous usually
- ;-) a wink

There are plenty more. But the ones listed here should be more than sufficient to allow you to get a feel of the conversation. Remember, if ever in doubt, ask them what they mean!

Chatiquette

There are a few do's and don'ts that, everyone expects you to be well versed with before you utter your first word on chat. These are the little things that separate the newbies from the regulars. Be sure to observe proper chat etiquette and you'll be assured a better response from everyone around you on chat.

1. Don't type your messages in ALL CAPITAL LETTERS in a channel. It is considered shouting and is rude. Occasional use of capital letters is OK if you want to emphasize certain words.
2. Don't go on typing nonsensical characters or repeating a message in a channel either. This is called scrolling or flooding and is highly disruptive. You can be kicked out of a channel for scrolling.
3. You will in all probability find people asking you your a/s/l (age/sex/location). This is okay when the question is popped in the middle of a conversation. But messaging someone for the first time with an ominous looking "a/s/l" alone is not only absurd but is downright rude. Go ahead and give the cold shoulder treatment to anyone who throws that line as a means to start, a conversation with you. And avoid doing the same.
4. Avoid disclosing any information about yourself to anyone on chat unless you are absolutely sure that the person on the other end won't not misuse it. This includes your passwords, your telephone number and your residential address. Remember that there are bad elements on chat, just like in real life. You must be on your guard constantly.
5. Being rude, racist, using abusive language or harassing someone isn't a good idea. Chat gives you freedom to express your thoughts but you must use the freedom responsibly. Otherwise you will end up making enemies

and being ignored by everyone. You may even be kicked out of channels or altogether banned from entering them if you don't behave. Likewise, if you notice someone misbehaving on a channel don't hesitate to bring it to the attention of the channel operator or the other chatters.

Be quick with your responses, Make sure you get your point across to the others you are chatting with. Use abbreviations, emotions and even resort to shortening long nicknames if it helps you respond quicker. Don't worry about errors while you type. Typographical errors or typos as they are fondly called can be a source of great amusement for all. If you proofread everything before pressing Enter, you'll be slow and by the time you send your reply it might be taken out of context by the other chatter(s).

Netiquettes

Today almost everyone you know is busy exchanging e-mail addresses rather than the good old postal ones. The best part of this new emerging community is that you can't see each other, so it doesn't, matter how you look. Mental wavelength is all you need to match. But it also means that all your impressions are formed on the basis of what you write. You can't rely on your facial expressions to convey your mood or intent. So it's a good idea to follow some basic social etiquette in order to be understood well.

Netizens

It has been putting together some guidelines that they fondly call Netiquette. For instance, try sending a seasoned Net user some e-mail typed in ALL CAPS. The response will be immediate a sharp online rap on the knuckles informing you that all caps amounts to shouting in the online world. And you thought it would make things more readable! Here are some suggestions that might help you avoid such faux pas and make your online correspondence better and more fun.

Keep in touch

Used effectively, e-mail can cut down on time and costs - so meet your friends halfway by staying in touch. If you're a technophobe, get over it. It isn't much fun ignoring mail just because you get it electronically. Reading e-mail is just, like answering your phone. Imagine if you call someone and they don't answer the phone. Isn't it frustrating? So check your mail sometimes and reply. You'll have a lot of friends if you give them time on the mail.

Just kidding

It's safe to say that 75 per cent of the traffic on the Net contains jokes. Yes, it's fun to get those, but don't you get mad when you get the same ones from ten different people? And not everyone has a sense of humour. So choose your joke mailing list carefully. It's also a good idea to delete the long list of e-mail addresses when you're forwarding mail. The joke loses its punch if you have to go through a mile-long list of IDs to reach it. It also fails to protect people's privacy. Almost every e-mail program lets you send e-mail via blind carbon copy. This is a very good tool if you are going to send e-mail to a lot of people.

Mail to the world

If you have a small business or home office, you may well think sending mass mail is a good tactic. In reality, it's one of the rudest things you can do online. And it's called Spam. Consider what you're doing sending mail to someone you're not sure wants it, giving the person no choice at all. If you think your one little message won't make a difference and it can always be deleted anyway, think again. Add up all similar messages and that's quite a lot of deleting to do each day. Spam may well get you some responses, but in the long run it'll mark you as an entirely unprofessional person. Sending unsolicited mail is also a violation of privacy. A better strategy is to make sure those who are looking for you fin d you.

Who are you any way?

An anonymous sender, a suppressed list of other recipients, no subject. Such mail only says: I don't care who you are and you don't need to know who I am, you have to go through my entire message to figure out why I'm sending this to you. Not a great way to win friends, don't you think?

With a lot of attachment

Remember the time your friend was sending you her Birthday pictures and they took forever to download? Bad connection? Or bad sender? Respect others' bandwidth, as you would have them reject yours. Next time you send out an attachment with your mail, stop to double check if a) the recipient really wants it and b) you can lighten the load for instance; reduce a fat.bmp to a jpg or gif. Or simply zip the files. Never send an unexplained attachment. A message that says, "Dear friend, please see attachment", with no further ado, should be hurled straight into infinity. It could be a virus! Politely explain what the attachment contains and why you're sending it, When sending attachments to colleagues, restrict this to those who are not on the same network. For co-workers on the same network, send a filename and path instead.

Look before you...oops!

The Internet abounds with horror stories of e-mail disasters (try cnet.com). All because people were a little bit too hasty with the reply, reply to all, or forward buttons. If you run a business from home, you have to be extra careful of what you are clicking. You wouldn't want your deals with one client reach their rival, would you?

What's this about?

Many people just don't bother with putting anything in the subject line of their e-mail. Or they'll put in something vague because it just seems too much effort to think of a subject. It may seem useless to think of a subject every time you write to a close friend, but if it's a serious business message, take some time to think of a smart subject line. Smart headers will also help people identify messages quickly later when they need to act up on them.

How R U? I m OK

Cute. But such messages take longer to figure out than you think. It's a misconception that you save on anything when you use abbreviations like BTW, B4, JLT, and so on. Our reading habits tune us to associate words with their shapes. Also the person you're writing to may be a newbie on the Net and would be totally lost if your message abounds with such words.

Other rules are :

- Use a short, polite auto-response if you're away and will not be able to check your mail for a certain time.
- Think before you give out someone else's e-mail address—would you be comfortable giving out his phone number? Apply the same logic to the address.
- If your mail is not being stored locally on your hard disk, make sure you delete periodically.
- Avoid gossip on newsgroups and mailing lists. This can be an area of potential and large-scale disaster.

Remember that the person you are mailing cannot see you, so whatever support you get from your facial expressions and voice modulations is not being conveyed. Be careful with your choice of words. They should convey your message in the manner that you intend it to be conveyed.

Five Ways to Prevent E-mail Viruses

While virus makers continue to propagate destruction, it is important for you to do your best to protect yourself from these vicious attacks. Though nothing can guarantee complete protection, here are a few things that you must do.

1. Keep in touch with virus news

There's nothing safer than being forewarned. Bookmark and regularly visit sites that keep you updated on virus-related news. Many general technology sites will do this job. If the problem is a really widespread, it's sure to make headlines on sites like CNN, Reuters, and BBC. Sites like news.com, cnet.com, wired.com or any tech news sites will fili you in on any new virus that have been unleashed into cyberspace. Makers of antivirus software also carry virus news and updates on their sites.

For instance, Symantec at http://www.symantec.com/avcenter/indexhtml and MeAfee at http://www.meafee.com/support/techdocs/vinfo/index.html. Portals and search engines such as Yahoo often have a prominent section on viruses with dozens of links.

2. Don't open attachments carelessly

You can't get a virus by just reading your mail. But you can set it from attachments. Dozens of attachments make their way into your Inbox everyday. People send electronic visiting cards, pictures, business documents, and a lot else. Before you do anything else...

- Never click-open an unexplained or inadequately explained attachment, no matter whom it comes from. Even if it's a trusted friend who sends you stuff everyday. Check back with the sender first.
- If there is an explanation, be alert and check if it seems to fit. a known sender's language. You may not expect your grandmother to send you a message that says, "Here is the important file you wanted." It may instead say, "I'm sending some lovely pictures.... So, if all does not seem to be as usual, stay on the safe side and don't open it.
- Set an example by explaining all attachments that you send in your own style-something that will immediately be recognized as yours by the recipient. And ask your friends and associates to do the same.

3. Scan your system regularly

Not all viruses go into action on entering your system. Some of them might remain dormant, for some time before they mess around. It's a good idea, therefore, to scan your system for viruses regularly, say every week. In addition, every single e-mail attachment that you receive must be scanned before opening.

4. Keep your antivirus programs updated

New viruses keep appearing every day, Makers of antivirus software are quick to develop an antidote to most of these. These antidotes are mostly available in the form of updates from them. Download these updates and any fixes offered for viruses doing the rounds and do this from reliable sites only. You will find these at the Websites of antivirus software manufacturers. Scanning your system with a program using age-old virus definitions that have not been updated for months together is probably as good as not using an antivirus program at all.

5. Back-up your data regularly

Troublesome though this may seem, backing up your data will stand you in good stead in case of a bad viral attack. If possible, try and maintain your back up on media other than your hard disk. Use floppies, CDs, Zip drives or something of the like for complete safety. This measure will be the one thing that will allow you to save all the files that contain your work, your mail, addresses, and other important things, if a virus should tamper with your hard disk. It is also important for you to have legal copies of your programs so that you can reinstall them easily if you need to format your hard disk.

Browse Offline and Save Browsing Time and Money

Surf the Web at your leisure without having to worry about the money you spends being online. Offline browsing is nothing more than using a browser to view Web pages without being connected to the Net while doing so. You can use any old browser even Internet Explorer 2 or Netscape Navigator 2 will do in a pinch, though you'll miss out on JavaScript and frames (IE2). Once you've downloaded a site, you can look up Web pages without the pressure of counting the rupees being spent for each additional minute online. Obviously this isn't going to work out unless the site you're downloading is full of useful information to you or if there are several people interested in viewing the same site. Just imagine a dozen people browsing, say, CNET.com and then the same dozen folks browsing it off-line, at their leisure, after a Web download which would take around half an hour on a 28.8 modem with a good line. The benefits are pretty obvious.

Who needs it?

Schools and offices can make good use of offline browsing to reduce time spent online. An application such as Web Downloaded will let you save the contents of a site to a local or network hard disk. From there everybody can access it at a much faster speed than they would on the Web. As most sites, with the notable exception of news sites, are updated weekly or monthly—a weekly download of the most wanted sites, say half a dozen, should suffice and take not more than a couple of hours. Of course, you'll have to turn off graphics on the larger sites to keep download times down. Once this is done, everybody in the class or the office can browse those pages to their heart's content. Imagine the amount of time spent by people reading stuff online, line-by-line. You'll be saving on all that by using an offline browser. Or if you want to make a presentation about your business you can use an offline-browsing tool to download your company's Web site. Then you can show your site to prospective clients or dealers without having to worry about your chances of getting a connection right at the time of the presentation.

How does an offline browser work?

An offline browser does its magic by downloading a particular Web page and all the pages linked to that page. Let's assume that we are about to download http://www.hclinfinet.com. Now if we decide to get the first level of links, then the offline browser will get the page computersathome.com and all the pages directly linked to it. Or if you want to go deeper into the site, you can set up your offline browser to get two levels of it. The app will now also get all the pages linked to the first-level pages. Other than this, offline browsers let you decide whether or not you want to download applets, images and other bandwidth-hungry elements.

Popular tools

There are lots of offline browsers out there. We've listed some of the best for you.

Web Down loader

This application is very small and very simple. Plus it's free. It's been written by a Russian programmer and does its job in a simple and efficient manner. To use Web Down loader you have to:

- Add your favorite URLs.
- Decide if you want to save images or not.
- Specify how many levels deep you wish to download the site.
- Optionally schedule a specific date and time for the download (if you have a LAN connection to the Net), ***Tip:*** Use the File-Defaults dialog to set the default settings for this application.
- Pick the Offline Browsing option.
- Deselect the Load Other Servers checkbox in order to avoid links to servers other than the site you are downloading.

For instance, the HCLInfinet site has links to other Websites. If you don't uncheck this box, Web Down loader will get pages from the other site(s) along with those from hclinfinet.com.

Once Web Down loader is through you can browse the downloaded sites offline from C:\temp\hclinfinet.com (or C:\temp\whatever-site-you-downloaded.com).

Download from

http://www.geocities.com/SiliconValley/Vista/2865/wd22eng.zip

Best for folks who want to download entire sites for sharing over a network. Schools could use this to make only particular sites accessible to their students.

OFFLINE BROWSING TIPS

Avoid images, applets and plugging

If you download images and applets you'll significantly slow down the Web download process. So stick to text (*.htm) for better results.

Stick to one level downloads

The more levels you download from a Web site the longer the process takes. You can often get by with a one level download of a particular section of a site (say, from the What's new page) in place of a two level download of the entire site.

Saving pages to disk

Using the File-Save As option in Navigator or IE is the fastest and easiest way to start offline browsing without a dedicated tool. This way, you get to speed up your browsing. With Navigator 3 Gold or Communicator you can use the File-Edit Page command and then File-Save to get a page with all the graphics.

Offline With IE5

There are two ways you can do offline browsing with IE5, Which one you use depends on your needs. If the recipe you are interested in, or the article you want to read, is only on one HTML page, you can just use the 'File - Save As' feature of IE5.

Here's how. When connected and visiting a site, just, load up the page you want to view offline on your browser, and click File - Save As. The File Type list gives you four options. Web Page Complete means all the content of that page including images, sounds etc. along with the text will be downloaded for viewing later. IE will create a directory for that page on your hard disk where it will store all the data. Choose Web Archive to compress all the data on the page into a single file. That's handy if you want to e-mail the site to someone or simply reduce the number of folders on your hard disk. Web Page HTML allows you to exclude everything but the HTML text; i.e. no images, sounds. That's useful if you are short on disk space. And finally, Text Only abandons all formatting and saves the page as plain text. Whichever option you choose, this feature only allows you to save a single page. What to do if the information you want is scattered across multiple pages? That's where the second way of doing offline browsing comes in - Favourites.

IE4 first introduced Favourites, and in IE5, this feature has been enhanced to make it easier for you to download your favourite Web sites for offline browsing. Favourites can make a single page or a group of pages 'offline browseable'. All you have to do to make a Web page available offline is click Favorites - Add To Favorites. Notice that you get a choice for making it available offline, list select the Make Available Offline check box and fill in a name for the offline site. Most often, the site will have its own name appear. When you click Ok, IE5 will automatically download the page, along with all the images. Onto your hard disk. Now any time you are offline and feel like revisiting the page, just start up IE and click File - Work Offline to tell IE that all your offline content be activated. Now select the name for the site (that you filled in earlier) from your Favorites menu and browse away.

But as mentioned earlier, not only can favorites make a page but also a group of interlinked pages offline browseable. But before doing that, it needs you to do a bit of spadework. You need to figure out where the information you need is sitting on the site. Click a few links of interest on the site and see where they take you. Only when you are familiar with the site structure, can you know about where your desired content is located.

For example, the stuff that you need may be a bunch of pages, all linked with one main page in the same directory. Once you have figured out the structure, move to the main page. Again click Favorites · Add to Favorites. But this time, click on the Customize button in the Add to Favorites dialog. The Offline Favorite Wizard comes along. Here is where you actually tell IE that in addition to the main page, you want it to download those interlinked pages as well. The wizard allows you to specify things like how many links deep into the main page to download, how often would you like to check this site for updates, and whether the site requires a password to access. Let's take up all of these concepts using a simple example.

As mentioned, the first thing to do when you are going to download a site is to decide what you want and where it is located. In our case, all the necessary pages lie in the root directly linked to the main page, which has the above URL. You can see this when you hold the cursor over a link and notice the text on the status line at the bottom of your screen. Now lets move on.

Load the URL above and click Favorites - Add to Favorites and check the Make Available Offline button. In Customize, the first option IE asks you are whether you want to download pages linked to this page and how many levels deep, i.e. one level deep would download only pages directly linked to this page. A word of caution - don't fill in more than two to three levels deep here unless you want the entire Web server to be sitting on your disk. You'll be surprised to know just how many pages are linked to each other on the Web. If all the pages of interest are one level away from the main page, fill in 1, and click next. Now it asks what schedule you want for the downloading. If it is a fast changing site like a news site, you can specify a daily schedule. IE will log on daily at the specified time and download the latest pages for you. But this option may only be practical if you are online very often. If the site is not likely to change often you can do away with the schedule altogether and tell IE to only download the pages when you tell it to, by selecting the first option in this dialog. Do that and press Next. The last option asks you to enter a password if required. No such thing here, so just leave it blank and click Finish. Your page will now be available offline.

When you visit the site again and want to update the information, you "synchronize" from the Make Available Offline menu. The Synchronize box comes up showing your site being downloaded and the download progress indicator at the bottom of your page. (If you asked for more than 3 levels deep, the effects will be perceptible now). Once the download is complete, you can disconnect.

Holy Grail?

So, is IE5 the last word in offline browsing? Not necessarily. The most obvious reason is that even the Customize button does not customize the content very much, All you can do is specify the number of levels deep to go. That's not good enough. Most sites have links to other sites, and the last thing you want when you want to see site An offline is for sites B, C and D to tag along with. In fact, when you have a long article running into several Web pages, you may have to synchronize each page to ensure that you have the entire article. Specialized offline browsing tools like Web Whacker allow you to download a certain number of levels deep, but only from that site. So you end up getting only what you want and not unnecessary links to Yahoo and AltaVista.

Not just that, Web Whacker et al, also allow much greater content filtering like excluding certain file types, allowing only below a certain file size to be downloaded, and excluding all images, and audio files if you choose to.

But the usefulness of IE5 as an efficient offline browsing tool cannot be denied. When you consider that you have to actually pay to use Web Whacker, the use of IE for the occasional offline browser makes sense.

The Web Programming FAQ

The Web is where all the action is. So no one bats an eyelid when you say you want to be a part of the Web too. Maybe a designer. Not everyone can be a good designer—you had to be a creative person who can visualize things well and understand color, form, composition, and so on. Most dotcoms today have Web designers who also have programming skills. Maybe that's why a lot of people who know HTML consider themselves to Web designers. That isn't enough anymore.

Web technologies change so much that it's difficult to know everything. New terms crop up rapidly and you'll struggle to keep up with them. But for those who are fairly new to this scene, we bring an FAQ on the languages you need to know.

So what's HTML?

HTML is a ample computer language used to make Web pages. HTML documents are nothing but text files that contain HTML instructions. These documents don't actually contain the images, video or sound you come across on Web pages—they have the code that lets you integrate these into your Web page. Browsers like Internet Explorer and Netscape Navigator can understand these instructions and display a Web page in its proper form at.

HTML stands for Hypertext Markup Language. Hypertext is a special kind of text that is a powerful feature of HTML documents. When you click on this text (called a link), your Web browser can take you to another place in the same document, to another page on the same Website or to a page on any other Website. It is this ability to link documents together so seamlessly that has made HTML ideal for the Internet where one needs to navigate through documents scattered across the world. Markup Language is the system of codes that governs the format of your Web page. These codes—or 'tags' as they are called—control things like character size, fonts, paragraph alignment, the color of the text and links on the page, backgrounds, images, sound and animations and much more. You can recognize HTML documents by their extenstons either **htm** or **html.** To view the HTML code of any Web page, select the View menu in your browser and then click on Source.

Does one need to know HTML?

You probably won't need to worry about learning HTML if all you want to do is make a home page for yourself. But if you're planning to spend some serious money into building a good Website, as is all the rage these days, it will serve you well to know at least the basics of HTML. Here's why. There are many programs like Microsoft Frontpage and Netscape Composer, which let you design Web pages without needing any knowledge of HTML. But these programs aren't perfect. They add unnecessary code and format your page according to their own rules. To achieve exactly what you have in mind for your page, you will have to know enough HTML to tweak the code for the page till you're satisfied with the result. But if all you're going to do are homepages then you can forego going into minor formatting troubles and work with a program.

What programs do I need to learn HTML?

A text editor like Notepad and a Web browser like Internet Explorer or Netscape Navigator are all you need to start writing HTML code. You type the code in Notepad and save it with the extension htm or html. You can then view the HTML page in your Web browser.

Is it easy to learn?

HTML is not difficult and almost anyone can get the hang of it in no time. There are a number of guides available on the Internet, which takes you through the basics all the way up to the advanced topics. Books on HTML are available too.

Is HTML enough?

Not anymore. HTML has a number of powerful features including the capability to present images and text on a page and the capability to link pages together, which made it the language of the Internet. A few years ago this was more than enough to keep everyone happy. But gradually it was realized that HTML lacked in a vital department-interactivity. True interactivity requires instant responses to user actions. Another reason why HTML alone isn't enough is because it isn't dynamic enough—it can only give 'pre-prepared' pages for access. Websites today need to interact, with databases and other programs to generate pages with varying content on the fly. For example, sites giving stock updates get their data from some other programs and display the changing information on their Web page every few seconds. HTML alone can't be used to connect with other programs. Nor can it generate information dynamically. So you need to work with some scripting language like JavaScript or VBScript or other languages like Java.

Let's look at each of them.

JavaScript

JavaScript is a scripting language, which can be considered to be an extension to HTML. It lets you create interactive pages quickly and easily. Using JavaScript you can design your pages to act and react, by modifying content on screen or interpreting actions from the user. For example, you can change an image on the page when a mouse passes over it (commonly called a 'roll-over' effect). Or you can have a pop-up box thank the user after they have correctly filled out a form online and submitted it. The possibilities are endless. JavaScript is one of the many 'client-side' scripting languages in use today. 'Client' here refers to your computer or more specifically your Web browser. So 'client side' scripting is code that runs on your browser. This code does it need to transfer information back and forth over the Internet when you interact with your page—all the information needed is downloaded to your computer in one go and the results of your actions are thus displayed on your browser almost immediately.

VBScript

This is a client-side scripting language, much like JavaScript, VB stands for Visual Basic, which is Microsoft's full-blown programming language. VBScript is a simplified version of VB, snipped down of most of its complexities and biased towards use in Web pages. Both JavaScript and VBScript offer more or less the same capabilities, but VBScript is considered the more evolved of the two. But the only browser to support VBScript is Internet Explorer. So you'll consider using VBScript if your pages are aimed primarily at Internet Explorer users.

DHTML

DHTML or Dynamic HTML, is just what it claims to be—a dynamic, more interactive version of HTML. The powerful scripting of Dynamic HTML, allows for handling interaction on your computer without sending and receiving information over the Internet every time. This speeds up things . One of the main features of DHTML is the ability to change the look and style of the Web page after it has loaded. For example, DHTML lets you change a piece of text from one size or color to another, or a graphic can move from one location on the document to another in response to some kind of user action like clicking a button. DHTML is still in its development stage. And Netscape Navigator and Internet Explorer both implement DHTML differently.

CSS

CSS or Cascading Style Sheets is a set of instructions used to provide a consistent, universal look and feel to your Web pages. You can have instructions to define the fonts to use in your paragraphs and the color of your links in some or all of the pages of your Web site. You can put these rules in each of your HTML pages or put all the style rules in a separate file and link it to all the pages on your Website. You can then make changes at one location and it will affect your entire site!

What is Java?

Java is a powerful and feature-rich programming language that's used to create programs that can run on any platform, be it a Windows PC or a Unix Workstation. It's a simple, secure and robust language that finds widespread uses on the Internet and elsewhere. In fact, Java applets were one of the earliest proponents of interactivity on the Internet. These applets are small programs written in Java that are downloaded from a Website and run on your computer. The important thing here is that these programs are not just video clips or sound files. They are intelligent programs capable of interacting with the user and changing dynamically.

What are ASP, PUP, Java Servlets, CGI/Perl and Cold Fusion?

All of these are 'server-side' scripting tools that are commonly classified under Web application development technologies. 'Server' here refers to the computer on which the Web pages are stored. With these technologies, you can create scripts that run on the Web server to access databases, interact with other applications and create dynamic pages.

ASP stands for Active Server Pages. It's a technology that allows you to choose from a number of scripting languages like VBScript, JavaScript, Perl and Python. An ASP page is a combination of HTML and script, which is run on the server to generate Web pages. It's fairly popular among Web developers who prefer working in Windows because it lets them interact with popular Windows-based applications.

PUP borrows its syntax and style from many sources like Perl, C and Java. It can connect to all the major databases on the server end and is rapidly gaining in popularity. This is because it's not only powerful, but it's free as well.

Java Servlets is currently one of the hottest Web development technologies available. Because of its association with Java, it benefits from being platform-independent and is fairly secure. Servlet performance has been found to be better than quite a few of the more traditional server side scripting technologies.

CGI or Common Gateway Interface is perhaps the oldest. Web application development technology. CGI programs can be written in a number of languages including Perl, TCL, C and C++. It was fairly popular in its heyday but with the growth of the Internet, it has been found to be lacking in a few departments. One of its major shortcomings is that it is resource intensive and is unsuitable for sites, which generate a lot of traffic.

Finally, **Cold Fusion** is a powerful tool for developing all sorts of database application. It is so easy to use that you can set up a database driven site in an hour or so even if you don't know SQL. It's loaded with features, and many Web developers just can't stop raving about all its features, but it's not free like many of the other tools.

What about multimedia effects?

Let's face it. Web pages these days need to have more than just text to hold your interest. Multimedia holds the key to making a jazzier, more colorful page that you can be proud of. There are many tools used to create multimedia effects that can grace a Web page. For manipulating and tweaking images. Adobe PhotoShop and Paint Shop Pro are probably the best programs around. There are many other popular image editors as well like Xara 3D and Ulead Cool 3D for creating 3D logos, buttons, banners and even animation. For creating animation, you can try using animated GIFs, which you can create with programs like Coffee Cup GIF animator and Ulead GIF animator. Java applets are commonly used to create multimedia effects. You can directly write the code if you know Java or use one of the many programs that make things easier for novices, like Anfy Java and Applet Factory, QuickTime is another technology you can use to create interactive animations and graphics. LiveStage is one program that makes use of

QuickTime effects for making interactive Web media. Macromedia Shockwave and Flash are other alternatives that support audio, animation, video and the capability to handle user interaction. To create Shockwave and Flash effects, you use Macromedia Director and Flash respectively.

What makes a good Web designer?

You need to be extremely creative and have an eye for layouts and design and color. That apart, to be a good Web designer, you need to have a solid understanding of HTML. Experienced designers usually complement their HTML knowledge with easy to use graphical HTML editors like FrontPage and Dreamweaver. This saves time and allows them to concentrate on more important aspects like scripting rather than getting stuck with trivial HTML, formatting details. Knowledge of a scripting language, both for the client and the server side is essential too. Usually JavaScript is the preferred choice for client-side scripting by most developers. Things aren't that simple on the server side however, where the technologies are many, each with its own strengths and weaknesses. Whatever server side scripting technology you choose, master it inside out. That's what good Web designers do. You must also fiddle around with image manipulation programs. Photoshop is what most developers work on to create great looking images for Web pages. Finally, any other multimedia technology that you're comfortable with can add a whole new dimension to your Website. Let your imagination run wild and don't shy away from experimenting with new ideas. Only then can your work stand out from the rest of the crowd.

Terminology Used for Networking

In networking we commonly used some terms to define network process and these may divide in four parts or categories:

1. Network Description
2. Network Topology
3. Network Protocol and
4. Networking Services

Now, we will start to learn from first, step of important aspect of network description.

Network Description Terminology

1. Network

A group of interconnected computers that share resources and information. For example, some hardware resources typically shared on a network are printers, fax-modem, and hard disks.

2. Transmission Media

The physical pathway on which the computers are connected. Cable and wireless media can connect the computers in a network.

3. Stand-Alone Computer

A computer that is not connected to a network called "Stand-Alone'" computer.

4. Local Area Network (LAN)

A group of computers interconnected within a building or campus, called Local Area Network (LAN). For example, a LAN may consist of computers located on a single floor of a building or it might link all computers in a small company.

5. Metropolitan Area Network (MAN)

A network of LANs that covers a city or large campus environment called Metropolitan Area Network (MAN).

6. Wide Area Network (WAN)

A network consisting of computers or LANs connected across a distance. WANs can cover small to large distances using different physical topologies, such as telephone lines, fiber optic cabling, satellite transmissions, and microwave transmissions.

Network Topology Terminology

Network topologies are the physical cable or transmitters on the network. The following are the different types of physical topologies:

1. Bus Network Topology
2. Star Network Topology
3. Ring Network Topology

1. Bus

All computers are connected with a single cable with a terminator on each end. An example is an Ethernet network connected with Thinner coaxial (10Base2) cable.

2. Star

All computers' are connected to a device, typically a hub or switch. An example is an Ethernet network connected with twisted-pair (10BaseT) cable.

3. Ring

All computers network devices are connected directly to each other in a ring fashion. An example is an FDDI (Fiber Distributed Data Interface) network, where all the hubs connected to each other in a ring.

Network Protocol Terminology

Computers use protocols to communicate with each other. A protocol is language, or a set of rules the computers in a network need to follow in order to understand each other.

A protocol suite is group of protocols that are loaded together. An example of protocol suite is TCP/IP. The following are some common network protocols:

1. TCP (Transmission Control Protocol)
2. IP (Internet Protocol)
3. IPX/SPX (Internetwork Packet Exchange/Sequenced Packet Protocol)
4. NetBEUI (Net BIOS Extended User Interface Protocol)
5. HTTP (Hypertext Transfer Protocol)

1. TCP (Transmission Control Protocol)

   The Internet Protocol suite's transport services protocol.
2. IP (Internet Protocol)

   The Internet protocol suite's protocol for defining and routing data grams.
3. IPX/SPX (Internetwork Packet Exchange/Sequenced Packet Protocol)

   Reutable protocols created by Novell for NetWare networks.

4. NetBEUI (Net BIOS Extended User Interface Protocol)

   A protocol created by IBM for small workgroups.

5. HTTP (Hypertext Transfer Protocol)

   The WWW (World Wide Web) protocol used to transfer Web pages across the Internet.

Networking Services Terminology

The following are three terms related to TCP/IP networking services:

1. WINS (Windows Internet Name Service)
2. DNS (Domain Name Service)
3. DHCP (Dynamic Host Configuration Protocol)

1. WINS (Windows Internet Name Service)

A TCP/IP network service for Microsoft networks that resolves Net BIOS aims and facilitates browsing across sub networks.

2. DNS (Domain Name Service)

A TCP/IP network service that translates host names to Internet. Protocol (IP) addresses.

3. DHCP (Dynamic Host Configuration Protocol)

A method for automatically assigning IP addresses to client on a network.

SERVER BASED NETWORKING

In any network server is very important part of the network because it has to play a great role in the networking, A server can work in any network as a dedicated server or a server can perform different type of role in the network. Here, we will study about the network in which a server plays a different role to provide the services to their clients.

1. Dedicated Server
2. Client-Server
3. Peer-to-Peer Network
4. Hybrid Network

1. Dedicated Server

A server on a network is dedicated to performing specific tasks in support of other computers on the network. In a server-based network, not all servers are alike:

1. File Servers
2. Print Servers
3. Application Servers

1. File Servers

It offers services that allow network users to share files. File services include storing, retrieving, and moving data. File and print servers do not do processing for the client computers.

2. Print Servers

It always manages and controls a single printer or a group of printers on a network.. 'The print server controls the queue or spooler. Clients send print jobs to the print server, and the print server uses the spooler to hold the jobs until the printer is ready.

3. Application Servers

The application servers allow client PCs to access and use extra computing power and expensive software applications that reside on a shared computer. Application servers offload work from the client by running programs for the client and sending the results back to the client. For example, when a client asks a Microsoft SQL Server to find a record, SQL Server does all the processing to find the answer, and then sends the results back to the client.

Running applications from an application server rather than from separate client machines can reduce your licensing costs. With this setup, you can purchase licenses for every connection to the application. For example, if you have 120 users if only 60 users use the application at a time, you would buy a 60-user license.

File, print, and application services are the main services that servers provide. Although you can dedicate a server to a particular service, such as having a computer those servers only as a print server, you do not need a different, server for each type of service. One server can function as a file, print, and application server.

1. Client-Server

In a client-server network, a dedicated server is used to provide services to clients. For example, the server might provide file, print, message, database, and application services to the clients in the network.

2. Peer to Peer Network

In a peer-to-peer network, each computer is equal (Peer) in the sharing of resources. A peer-to-peer network does not have a dedicated server, and there is not hierarchy among the computers. Each peer is responsible for its own security. Usually, the computer users determine what data on their computer will be shared on the network.

3. Hybrid Network

A hybrid network is a combination client-server/peer-to-peer network. Typically, hybrid networks are client-server networks that also include some peers.

ROLE OF COMPUTERS IN NETWORK

There are three roles for computers in a network:

1. A client is a workstation used only to request services from a network service provider, such as a dedicated server or another workstation.
2. A server provides services to service requestors. A dedicated server functions only as a server, it is not used as a client or workstation. The use of a dedicated server is recommended for networks with more than ten clients.
3. A peer both equips and provides network services.

USER LEVEL SECURITY WITH ACCESS PERMISSION

One large difference in the way peer-to-peer and server-based networks operate is in how they implement security:

Share Level Security (Password-Protected Security)

1. Peer-to-peer network

It is usually less secure than server-based networks because peer-to-peer networks commonly use Share-Level Security, also known as Password-Protected Security.

With share-level security, each network resource can be assigned a Pass Word. For example, on a Windows 95 system, you can assign a password to a certain directory. Then, before a user can gain access to that directory, he or she must enter the correct password.

Share-level security can be used with both FAT and NTFS partitions. This type of security works at the directory (Folder) level, which means that it applies to all the files within the specified directory.

2. Access Permissions

Server-based networks commonly use access permission security, also known as file-level or user-level security. With this type of security, an administrator assigns rights to a user or group so that the user or group can access a certain network resource.

Rather than entering a password for access it each shared resource, the user first enters a user name and password to gain access to the network itself. Then the user's access is controlled by the permissions he or she has been granted or denied. In a system using access permissions. All share access is evaluated on the basis of account information. For example, a user must log on to Windows NT domain before being able to request to use a network printer, and that user will have access to that printer if that user's account has permissions for that network resource. Access permission security works only with NITFS partitions and can apply to individual files.

EXERCISE QUESTIONS

1. What do you understand by the website? Explain in your own words.
2. Explain the http and the term mostly used URL? Write its full form.
3. How you will configure the outlook Express and Netscape Messenger for E-mail?
4. Explain and write the use of Brackets and Quoted? What is its use in e-mail service?
5. What do you understand by the word Server and Client? What is the use of server in networking?

GLOSSARY

The purpose of this glossary is to present definitions of some of the terms that the often used in the field of computers and data processing.

A

Access control: Deals with the policies and mechanisms to prohibit a user/process from accessing those resources/ information, which he/she/it is not authorized to access.

Access time: The time interval between the instant at which data is called for from a storage device and the instant delivery begins.

Accumulator Register (A): A register, which holds the initial data to be operated upon, the intermediate results, and also the final results of processing operations.

Activity ratio: The ratio of the total number of records in transaction file and the total number of records in master file.

Adder: A logic circuit capable of forming the sum of two or more quantities.

Address: An identification, represented in the form of a name. Label, or number, for designating a particular location in storage arc.

Address register: A local storage register, which contains the address of the next instruction to be executed.

Algorithm: A sequence of precise and unambiguous instruction for solving a problem in a finite number of operations.

Alphabetic: Pertaining to a character set, which contains the letters A to Z and the blank character.

Alphanumeric: Pertaining to a character set, which contains letters, digits, and usually other special characters, such as comma, dollar sign, plus sign, etc.

American National Standards Institute (ANSI): A U.S. based national organization, which establishes uniform standards in several fields.

American Standard Code for Information Interchange (ASCII): A standard coding system for computers. ASCII-7 is a 7-bit code, and its extended version, ASCII-8, is an 8-bit code.

Analog computer: A computer, which operates on data, which is in the form of continuously variable physical quantities, such as electrical current.

Anonymous type site: On the internet, a computer, which allows a user to log in with a username of anonymous and then a password, which is the user's e-mail address.

Antiquaries' utility: A program used to cure a computer from virus infection.

Application programmer: A programmer who prepares application software.

Application software: A set of one or more programs designed to solve a specific problem or do a specific task, such as pay calculation, processing of examination results, stores accounting and inventory control, etc.

Architecture: The organization and interconnection of the various components of computer system.

Archiving: The process of storing old data files on separate disks or tapes to make room for new files on the hard disk of a computer.

Arithmetic Logic Unit (ALU): The unit of a computing system, which performs all mathematical and logical operations. It is one of the components of the central processing unit (CPU) of the computer.

Artificial intelligence: A branch of computer science, which deals with computers, which possess reasoning, learning, and thinking capabilities that resemble those of humans.

Assembler: A computer program, which translates on assembly language program to its machine language equivalent.

Assembly language: A programming language, which allows instructions and storage location to be represented by letters and symbols instead of numbers. Also know as symbolic language.

Assembly program: A program written in an assembly language. Also as symbolic program.

Asynchronous communication: A mass storage device, which uses a set of magnetic tapes and tape drives with a controller mounted in a single unit. All the tapes of an automated tape library form a single large storage unit. They are typically used for data archiving and as an online data backup device for automated backup.

Automatic Teller Machine: A storage, which supplements the main memory of a computer. Often referred to as secondary storage, this section of the computer's memory is non-volatile and has low cost per bit stored, but it generally has an operating speed far slower than that of the primary storage.

B

Backbone: The main trunk lines of a computer network, which facilitates the interconnection of other computers and computer network on the same network.

Background processing: The automatic execution of lower-priority (background) computer programs, when higher-priority (foreground) programs are not using the system resources.

Backup : Alternate facilities of programs, data files, hardware equipment etc., which are used in case the original one is destroyed, lost, or fails of operate.

Backup file: A copy of a file, created as a safety precaution against lose of data caused due to corruption, or inadvertent deletion of the original file.

Band printers: See chain printers.

Bandwidth: The range of frequencies available for data transmission. The wider the bandwidth of a communications system, the more data it can transmit in a given period of time.

Bar Codes: Representation of alphanumeric data by a combination of adjacent vertical lines (called bars) by varying their width and the spacing between them. A *bar-code reader* is a scanner, which is used for reading (decoding) bar-code data

Base: The total number of digits (symbols) available to represent numbers in a positional numbers system.

Batch processing: The running of several computer program one after another without the need of a human operator to run each program individually.

Baud: A unit for measuring data transmission speed. It is used to decibel the capacity of a carrier. In general usage, a baud in identical to bits per second.

Beginners All-Purpose Symbolic Instruction Code (Basic): An easy-to-learn, high-level, interactive programming language, which is frequently used with personal computers, and in timesharing environments.

Beta testing: The use of beta version of software by a selected set of users for identifying errors, which might have been overlooked during the regular testing phase.

Beta version: The version of software, which is released to a selected set of users for testing, before its actual release.

Binary: A characteristic or property involving a selection. Choice, condition, in which there are two possibilities.

Binary Coded Decimal (BCD): One of the early coding systems, which is based on the idea of converting each digit of a decimal number into its binary equivalent, rather than converting the entire decimal value into a pure binary form. For example, the decimal number 42 is represented by 01000010 in 8-4-2-1 BCD notation.

Binary number system: A number system with a base of two. It consists of two digits: 0 and 1.

Biometric device: A device used for user authentication, which verifies some characteristic of a user, such as the person's appearance, fingerprints, hand geometry voice, or signature.

Bit: Acronym for binary digit, which stands for one binary piece of information. This can be either 0 or 1.

Bitmap: A method of displaying graphic images on a monitor by altering the color (or turning on or off) of individual dots (pixels) on the coordinate system.

Block: A group of related items (records, characters, etc.) handled as a unit during input and output. A section of program code treated as a unit.

Blocking factor: The process of grouping two or more records together to form a block, and the number of records put together in each block is called a blocking factor.

Boolean algebra: An algebra, which deals with logical propositions, which are either true or false. This algebra is suitable for use with binary number system, and is very useful in designing logic circuits, which are used by the processors of computer systems.

Boolean function: A mathematical function in Boolean algebra For example, w = x + Y–Z.

Boolean variable: A variable used in Boolean algebra. It can assume a value true or tales.

Booting: The process of automatic loading of the operating system of primary storage, and readying a computer system for use.

Branch instruction: An instruction, which transfers program control to a non-consecutive instruction.

Bridge: An internet working tool, which is used to connect networks that use the same communication protocols above the data-link layer, but may not use the same protocols at the physical and data-link layers.

Broadband channel: Communication channels, which are capable of data transfer rates of I million baud (bit-second) or more. They are used to handle high volumes of data, and for gigs-speed computer-to-computer communication, or for simultaneous transmission of data to several devices.

Browser: A software tool, which provides several navigation facilities to help users do Internet surfing easily and effectively.

Buffer: A small storage area used to store information on a temporary basis for compensating the difference in rates of flow of data between various computer devices. For example, when data flows from an I/O device to the CPU, it passes through a buffer.

Bug: A error in a computer program.

Built-in-functions: Subprograms, which are provided with the language so that the programmer need only call them in a program to have them automatically invoked. Also known as intrinsic subprograms.

Bundled: The inclusion of software with the hardware of a computer system as part of the system's total price.

Byte: A fixed number of adjacent bits, which represent a particular character or symbol. Normally a byte consists of eighth hits.

C

C: A programming language, which was designed to have the virtues of gigs-level programming languages (mainly machine independence) with the efficiency of an assembly language.

C++: A programming language, which contains all the elements of the basic C language, but has been expanded to include numerous object-oriented programming features.

Cache memory: A small high speed memory, which is used to increase the speed of processing by making current programs and data available to the CPU at a rapid rate.

Call statement: A program statement, which transfers program control to a subroutine.

Canonical form: A Boolean function whose terms contain all variables (or their complements). This is the unreduced form of the Boolean function in midterm or maxterm form.

Carrier: Any device, which is used to transmit data from one location to another.

Cathode Ray Tube (CRT): An electronic tube with a TV like screen upon which information may be displayed.

C-band transmission: The use of 4 GHz of frequencies for transmission and retransmission of microwave signals in a satellite communication system.

CD-ROM jukebox: A mass storage device, which uses a set of CD-ROM disk, disk drives, and a controller CD-ROM jukebox form a single large storage unit. They are typically used for archiving read-only data.

Cell: The intersection of a row and column in a spreadsheet. A user enters text, number, or formula in a cell.

Central Processing Unit (CPU): The control unit and the arithmetic logic unit of a computer system are jointly known as the CPU. It is the brain of any computer system in which all calculations and comparisons performed by a computer are carried out. The CPU is also responsible for activating, and controlling operations of other units of a computer system.

Chain printers: Line printers, which print characters by striking a set of hammers on an inked ribbon and paper placed against a metallic chain on which all the characters of the character set supported by the printer are embossed.

Cjammel: (1) path for carrying signals between a source and a destination. (2) A track on a magnetic tape, or a band on a magnetic drum.

Character addressable storage: A storage device, in which each character addressable storage is variable-word-length storage.

Character printer: A printer with a print mechanism, which prints one character at a time.

Charge-Coupled Device (CCD): A completely electronic storage device fabricated on semiconductor chips. It stores data as pockets of charge in a semiconductor.

Chip: A thin wafer of silicon on which integrated electronic components are deposited.

Circuit switching: The simplest method of data communication in which a dedicated physical path is established between the sending and the receiving stations through the nodes of the network for the complete duration of information exchange.

Client computer: In a client-server computing environment, a computer, which does an end user to interact with the server computer use. It runs client processes, which send requests to the server.

Client-Server Computing: A network of computers, which consists of a server computer (such as, file server, database server, print server, name server), and multiple client computers, which share programs and data from the server.

Clip art library: A collection of graphic images stored on disk, which can be readily used in word processing or desktop publishing documents, or in presentation graphics, or for other purposes.

Clock Speed: The number of times the built-in electronic clock of a computer system pulses in one second.

Coaxial cable: A cable made up of a single wire in the centre of an insulator wrapped in mesh. It is often use as a medium to transmit data between computers, and between computers and peripheral devices.

Code: (1) The statements of a computer program. (2) A set of rules outlining the way in which data may be represented (like BCD, EBCDIC, ASCII).

Code generator: A very high-level programming language in which programmers specify through an interactive dialog with the system, the design specifications of a system (which tasks are to be performed), and it automatically generates (produces) the program source code for the system.

Coding: The process of writing computer instructions in a programming language.

Collate: To combine items from two or more sequenced files into a single one.

Collating sequence: An ordering assigned to the characters of a character set to be used for sequencing purposes. A commonly encountered collating sequence involves the special characters, letters, and digits, in that order.

Combinational circuit: A group of logic gates interconnected to form a logic circuit.

Command interpreter: The part of an operating system, which server as an interface for the user to communicate with the computer via its operating system.

Command-line interface: A textual user interface in which the user gives instructions to the computer by typing commands using the keyboard.

Comment: An entry in a computer program for the purpose of documentation or explanation. Comments are used within a program to assist anyone reading the source program listing. They do not contain any programs logic, and are ignored (not translated) by the language processor.

Common Business Oriented Language (COBOL): A high-level programming language developed for business data processing applications.

Common carriers: Data transmission service providers.

Communication protocol: A set of rules and procedures established to interconnect and communicate between computers. It provides a method for orderly and efficient exchange of data by establishing rule for the proper interpretation of controls and data transmitted as raw bits and bytes.

Communication processor: A processing unit, which coordinates networks and data communications. Within a computer network, it ensures that data flows to and from different computer systems correctly and deficiently.

Communications satellite: A microwave relay station precisely positioned 36000 kms above the equator with an orbit speed that exactly matches the earth's rotation speed. It is used for data transmission between any two randomly chosen points in a very large area.

Communications software: that enables transfer of data and programs form one computer system to another in a network of computers.

Compact Disk-Read-only Memory: (CD-ROM) A shiny, silver color metal disk of 5½-inch (12 cm) diameter having a storage capacity of about 650 Megabytes. It is so called, because of its enormous storage capacity on a compact-size disk, and because it is a read-only storage medium.

Compiler: A translator program (software package), which translates a high-level language program into its equivalent machine instruction.

Complement: For a number, which has in digits in it, a complement is defined as the difference between the number and the base raised to the *n*th power minus one. For example, complement of $37_{10}=10^2-1-37=62_{10.}$ In Boolean algebra, the complement of a variable is the reverse (NOT) of its value. For example, complement of A is A.

Completely connected network: A network in which there is a separate physical link for connecting each node to any other node in the network.

Complex Instruction Set Computer (CISC) Architecture: An architecture of CPUs with large instruction set, variable-length instructions, and a variety of addressing works.

Computer: An electronic device, which can automatically accept and store input data, process them, and produce output result by interpreting and executing programmed instructions.

Computer Aided Design (CAD): Use of computers to automatic design and drafting operations.

Computer Aided Manufacturing (CAM): Use of computers to automate manufacturing operations.

Computer animation: The area of computer science, which deals with the generation, sequencing, and display (at a specified rate) of a set of images (called frames) to create an effect of visual change or motion, similar to a movie film (video). Animation is commonly used in those instances where viewgraph is not possible, or animation can better illustrate the concept than video.

Computer audio: The area of computer science, which desalts with synthesizing, recording, and playback of audio or sound with the aid of a computer.

Computer graphics: The area of computer science, which deals with the generation, representation, manipulation and display of pictures (line drawings and images) with the aid of a computer.

Computer literacy: Having sufficient computer knowledge, so that an individual can work and live in a computerized society.

Computer network: A distributed data processing system in which multiple computers are linked together for the purpose of data communication and resource sharing.

Computer system: The various components (input and output devices, storage, CPU) of a computer integrated together to perform the steps called for in the program being executed.

Computer video: The area of computer science, which deals with the recording and display of a sequence of images at a reasonable speed to crate an impression of movement.

Computer-Based Training (CBT): Using computer technologies for training and education. The use of computers helps in making tutoring programs, which are tailored to the student's level of subject mastery, and can provide immediate feedback.

Conference on Data Systems Languages (CODASYL): A committee of computer users, manufacturers, and the United States government, which helps to establish programming standards for various programming language.

Constant: A value, written into a program instruction, which does not change during the execution of the program.

Control program: An operating system program, which controls the operations and management of resources of a computer system. The control program's major functions are job scheduling, input/output scheduling, and program monitoring.

Control unit: The unit of a computer system, which manages and coordinates the operations of all the other components of the computer system. It is one of the components of the central processing unit (CPU) of the computer.

Counter: A device, register or storage location for storing integers, which is suitably incremented or decremented to represent the number of occurrences of event.

CPU-scheduler: The part of an operating system, which is concerned with deciding which of the ready jobs should be allotted the CPU for execution.

CPU-bound jobs: Jobs which heavily utilize the CPU operations during the course of their processing.

Cryptography: A means of protecting private information against unauthorized access in those situations where it is difficult to ensure access control. The basic idea behind this security technique is that, if it is not possible to ensure access control, it *is* better to prevent comprehension of information.

Cursor: A highlight on the screen of a monitor, which indicates the location of the next keyed-in character on the display screen. It can appear as a small rectangular object, line, arrow, or I-beam pointer, or in a spreadsheet, as a large block covering an entire cell.

Cybernetics: The use of computers coupled with automatic machinery to carry out complex operations.

Cyberspace: The worldwide network of computers.

Cycle time: The time interval between the instant at which a read/write command is given to memory, and the instant when the next such instruction can be issued to the memory (also know as memory cycle time).

D

Daisy wheel printer: A letter-quality printer, which uses a printing head with the appearance of daisy and/or a wheel. Each petal of the daisy wheel has a character embossed on it.

Data: A collection of facts in raw form, which become information after proper organization or processing.

Data Base Management System (DBMS): A set of program provided to facilitate the users in organizing, creating, deleting, updating, and manipulating their data in a database.

Data Definition Language (DDL): A language used to define the structure of a database.

Data Dependence: Dependency of data on the application.

Data dictionary: A document, which maintains the data definitions of a database. It is automatically created/updated by the DDL as the database schema is defined or changed.

Data element: A meaningful collection of related characters. Also called a field or data item.

Data entry: The conversion of human readable data into a form, which a computer system can interpret. This is also called data preparation.

Data integrity: Consistency of data all files.

Data Manipulation Language (DML): A language used to enter and manipulate the data in a database.

Data processing: See processing.

Data processing system: A system that accomplishes data processing. It includes the necessary resources, which are people, procedures and devices needed to process the data.

Data redundancy: Repetition of the same data items in more than one file.

Data Storage Hierarchy: In data processing, organization of data into growing hierarchy for easy manageability. A typical data storage hierarchy consists of bits, characters, fields, records, files and database.

Data transfer rate: The speed at which data is transferred from main memory to another medium on which data are recorded. For magnetic tape, the data transfer rate in equal to the product of the tape speed and recording density. In a network environment, it refers to the speed of transfer of data from computer to another on the network.

Database: A collection data files integrated and organized into a single comprehensive file system, which is arranged to minimize access to information within that system to satisfy a wide variety of user needs.

Database administrator: One who is responsible for defining, updating, and controlling access to a database.

Database model: The manner in which the various files of a database are linked together. The four commonly used database models are hierarchical, network, relational and object-oriented.

Database schema: The database structure definition.

Database software: A set of program of which enables uses to create a database, maintain it (add, delete and update its records), organize its data in desired fashion, and to selectively retrieve useful information form it.

De Morgan's theorem: A theorem in Boolean algebra, which states how to complement a Boolean expression.

Debugger: A software tool, which helps the programmer in debugging the logic of a program by allowing him/her to follow the program's execution step-by-step, and to display intermediate calculation results and field values whenever desired.

Debugging: The process of finding and correcting program errors (bugs).

Decimal number system: A number system with a base of 10. The ten allowable digits are 0, 1, 2, 3, 4, 5, 6, 7, 8 and 9. It is used in our day-to-day life.

Decision logic: A selection logic.

Decoder: The part of CPU, which has the necessary circuitry to decode and interpret the meaning of every instruction supported by the CPU.

Dedicate line: A phase in the life-cycle of software system during which the detailed design of the system selected in the study phase occurs.

Desktop Publishing (DTP): An application software package, which allows a user to perform design, typesetting, and paste-up functions, and to produce high quality, camera-ready printed pages of the documents so prepared on a high-quality printer.

Development phase: A phase in the life-cycle of a software system during which a system is constructed to meet the requirements specified in the design phase.

Diagnostic routines: Programs used to print error messages by a computer to indicate system problems, and improper program instruction.

Dial-up line: A data transmission service, which operates in a manner similar to a telephone call. Also known as switched line.

Digital Computer: A computer, which works with discrete quantities. It uses numbers to simulate real time processes. Compare with analog computer.

Digitizer: An input device used for converting (digitizing) pictures, maps and drawings into digital form for storage in computers. This enables recreation of the drawing from the stored information whenever required, and easy incorporation of changes in the drawing as and when required.

Direct file: A file organization in which the desired record (piece of information) can be directly located by its key field value without having to search through a sequence of other records. Also known as random file.

Direct/leased-line connection: A method of connecting a computer to the Internet by using a dedicated (leased) telephone.

Directory: A mapping table, which is used by operating systems to map file names to their corresponding file attributes and file data, and also to provide greater flexibility to users in file naming.

Disk: A flat, circular plate coated with a magnetic material on which data can be stored by stored by magnetization of protons of the flat surface.

Disk array: A mass storage device, which uses a set of hard disks, hard disk drives, and a controller mounted in a single box. All the disks of a disk array form a single large storage unit. Also known as Redundant Array of Inexpensive Disks (RAID).

Disk drive: A removable direct-access storage medium containing multiple magnetic disks mounted vertically on a single shaft.

Disk pack: A removable direct-access storage medium containing multiple magnetic disks mounted vertically on a single shaft.

Diskette: A low-cost, thin, flexible magnetic disk storage device used on small computer system. Also called a floppy disk.

Distributed computing system: A computer system consisting of interconnected, multiple computers.

Distributed database: Seamless integration of multiple database located on different computers. A distributed database management system factions in a manner that the multiple distributed database managed by it appear as a single, centralized to the end users.

Documentation: Documentation of a software system involves collecting, organizing, storing, and other documents used or prepared during the different phases of the system.

Dot-matrix printers: Character printers, which form characters and all kinds of images as a pattern of dots.

Dots Per Inch (DPI): A measurement of the quality for printed output. It refers to the number of the dots, which can be printed per linear inch, horizontally or vertically.

Downloading: Moving a file during which a computer to ones own computer in a network environment.

Drum printers: Line printers, which print characters by striking a set of hammers on an inked ribbon and paper placed against a solid cylindrical drum with characters embossed on its surface in the form of circular bands.

Dumb terminal: A terminal, which has no local processing capability.

Dynamic Data Exchange (DDE): A technique for linking application, which allows a user to move data from one application into another, such as from a spreadsheet into a word-processor. Changes made in one application are automatically reflected in linked applications.

E

Edit: To modify the form or format of the data by inserting or deleting characters where needed.

Editor: Software used to interactively review and modify text materials and other program instructions.

Education software: Software, which allows computer systems to be used as a teaching and learning tool.

Electrically EPROM (EEPROM): An EPROM chip in which the stored information is erased by using high voltage electric pulses. Also known as flash memory.

Electronic card: A small plastic card having encoded data appropriate for the application for which it is used. An electronic-card reader, which is normally connected to a computer, is used to read the data encoded on an electronic card, and transfer it to the computer for further processing.

Electronic Data Interchange (EDI): The use of computers and data communications to transmit data electronically between digital computer.

Electronic Funds Transfer (EFT): A general term referring to a cashless approach used to pay for goods and services. Electronic signals between computers are often used to adjust the accounts of the parties involved in a transaction.

Electronic mail: A service on the Internet, which allows an Internet user to send a mail (message) to another Internet user in any part of the world in a near-real time manner.

Electronic pen: An input device, which serves as an effective point and erase device.

Electrostatic printer: A high-speed printer, which uses heated elements to create characters as matrices of small dots on heat-sensitive paper.

Elementary data item: A data item, which is not broken down into smaller units.

E-mail: See electronic mail.

Emulator: A program, which permits one computer to execute the machine-language instructions of another computer of different make.

Encryption: The process of transforming an intelligible information into an unintelligible form.

End user: Any individual who uses the information generated by a computer based system.

End-to-tape (EOT): A reflective marker, which indicates the responsibility of supplying all the hardware and software components of the solution.

Entertainment software: which allows computer system to be used as an entertainment tool.

Erasable Programmable Real Only Memory (EPROM): A memory chip in case of which it is possible to erase information stored in it, and the chip can be reprogrammed to store new information.

Ethernet: The most widely used LAN technology.

Explicitly Parallel Instruction (EPIC): A technology, which is fast emerging as the technology for next-generation processors. The three key features used in this technology for improved processor performance are explicit parallelism, predication and speculation.

Extended Binary Coded Decimal Interchange Code (EBCDIC): An 8-bit coding system, developed by IBM, which is used to represent characters in many computers.

F

Facsimile (FAX): Transmission of pictures, texts, maps, graphs, etc., over transmission lines, phone lines, and other carriers between geographically separated points. An image is sinned at a transmitting point, and duplicated at a receiving point.

Feasibility study: A study to determine whether the proposes solution is technically and economically feasible in all respect.

Field: In record, an meaningful collection of one of more related characters treated as a unit.

Fifth-generation computers: built since 1989 till now. They use ultra large-scale integrated circuits, very fast and large main memory and disk storage, and very powerful programming languages and operating systems.

File: A collection of related information.

File Management: A set of program provided to facilitate the users in organizing, creating, deleting, updating, and manipulating their files.

File Transfer Protocol (FTP): An application level protocol, which allows a users to move a file from one computer to another in a network environment.

File utilities: A set of routines, which perform a variety of generalized and controls the flow of incoming and outgoing, searching, merging, copying, printing and maintenance on data files.

Firewall: A software, which usually, runs on the proxy server of an organization, and controls the flow of incoming, and outgoing messages from within an organization for providing better security to the organization.

Firmware: A sequence of instruction (software), which is substituted for hardware, and stored in read-only memory (ROM).

First-generation computers: First generation computers built between 1942 and 1955, which used vacuum tubes, and were programmed in assembly language. Few examples are ENIAC, EDVAC and EDSAC.

Fixed-wireless system: A wireless computing system, which supports little or no mobility of the computing equipment, associated with the wireless network.

Fixed-head magnetic disk: A magnetic disk system, which that eliminates the use of an access mechanism by distributing all the read/write heads over the disk surfaces.

Flash memory: See Electrically EPROM (EEPROM).

Floating-point numbers: Signed numbers held in a fraction-exponent format. For example, 3216 would be represented as 0.3216×10^4 in floating point notation.

Flowchart: A pictorial representation, which uses predefined symbols to describe either the logic of a computer program (program flowchart), or the data flow and processing steps of a system (system flowchart).

Flowcharting: The process of drawing a flowchart for an algorithm.

Font: A complete set of characters with the same style and size.

Foreground processing: Automatic execution of high-priority (foreground) jobs by pre-empting held by low-priority (background) jobs. Contrast with background processing.

Formula Translation (FORTRAN): A high-level, programming language used for scientific and engineering application.

Fourth-generation computers: Fourth-generation computers built between 1975 and 1987. They used large-scale integrated circuits, semi-conductor memories, and powerful high-level languages and operating systems.

Frequency Division Multiplexing: A method used to concurrently transmit data between several transmitters and receivers over a single transmission medium. The available bandwidth of a physical medium is divided into smaller, disjoint, logical bandwidths, and each of the component bandwidths is used as a separate communications line (Channel).

Front-aid processor: A Processor designed specifically to handle the communications processing task. Its main purpose is to off-load communications processing task from the host computer, thereby the host computer can be dedicated for application and data processing jobs.

Full adder: An adder, which adds three binary digits and outputs a result bit and a carry bit.

Full duplex: A data transmission mode in which data signals can be transmitted between a source and a destination in both direction simultaneously.

Function: A subprogram, which returns a single value.

G

Garbage-in-Garbage-Out (GIGO): Refers to computer errors caused due to incorrect input data, or unreliable program.

Gateway: (1) A computer, which is connected to the Internet by using a dedicated (leased) telephone line, and is used to provide Internet connectivity to other computers via it. (2) An Internet work tool, which is used to interconnect dissimilar network that use different communication protocols.

Generation: In computer talk, it is a step in technology. It provides a framework for the growth of the computer industry.

Gigabytes (GB): Memory storage equal to 1,073,741,824 (2^{30}) bytes in computer.

Gig flop: 10^9 floating-point arithmetic operations per second.

Graphical User Interface (GUI): An interface for computer user, which provides icons (pictures) and menus (list of choices), which users can select with a mouse for telling the computer what they want it to do for them.

Graphics software: Software, which enables users to use a computer system for creating, dieting, viewing, storing, retrieving, and printing, designs, drawing, pictures, graphs, and anything else, which can be drawn in a traditional manner.

Gray scales: The number of a color that can be presented on a monochrome (black and white) monitor's screen, or on a monochrome printer's output.

GroupWare: See computer supported co-operative working (CSCW).

H

Hacker: A computer enthusiast who uses the computer as a source of recreation by pushing its capabilities to its limits (performance, security, storage, etc.).

Hacker: An adder, which adds two binary digits, and output a result bit and a carry bit (it any).

Half duplex: A communication system in which data can be transmitted between a source and a destination in both directions, but only in one direction at a time.

Hard disk: A magnetic disk storage device, which uses disk made of rigid metal (frequently aluminium). The hard disk platters come in many sizes ranging from 1 to 14-inch diameter.

Hard copy: A computer output, which is permanent in nature and can be kept in paper files, or can be looked at a later time, when the person is not using the computer. For example, output produced by printers or plotters on paper.

Hardware: The physical components of a computer system, such a electronic, magnetic, and mechanical devices.

Hashing: The process of using an address generating function (called hashing algorithm) to map a record's key field value to its storage address.

Hexadecimal number system: A number system with a base of 16. Its digits range from 0 to F. It is commonly used as a short-cut notation for groups of four binary digits.

Hierarchical database: A database model in which the data elements are linked in the form of an inverted tree structure with the root at the top and the branches formed below.

Hierarchical network: A communications network in which computer or processors are connected in a tree like structure.

High-level language: A programming language whose structure is application oriented, and is independent of the structure of the computer. Each statement of such a language is translated into many machine language statement.

Hotlist: A personal list of favourite URL addresses, which an Internet user is likely to frequently visit in future. A user's hot list is automatically created and stored on his/her local web client computer by a browser.

Hybrid network: A network, which is a combination of two or more different network topologies.

Hydra printer's: Multifunctional devices, which perform the functions of two or more of the following office equipment-printer, fax machine, copy machine and scanner.

Hypertext: Documents that are prepared by using special linking facility for easier electronic access and manipulation.

Hyper Text Markup Language (HTML): A powerful language used for creating hypertext documents.

Hyper Text Transport (HTTP): An Internet Protocol for interaction between computers on the Internet.

I

I/O ports: Sockets used to plug-in I/O devices to a computer system.

I/O bound bobs: Jobs whose CPU utilization is very low. They mostly perform I/O operations during the course of their processing.

Icon: A graphical object displayed on a visual display screen, which is used in place of words or phrases to allow users to select program options, when selected with a mouse or other pointing device.

Impact printer: A printer, which prints characters by causing hammers to strike against the paper and which information is to be printed.

Indexed Sequential Access Method (ISAM): See indexed sequential file.

Indexed sequential file: A file organization in which an index (directory) file is used to have both sequential and random access to the records of the file. Also known as the Indexed Sequential Access Method (ISAM).

Information: An processed data obtained as the output of data processing. People to enhance understanding and to achieve specific purposes use it.

Inkjet printers: Character printers, which form characters and all kinds of images by spraying small drops of ink on to the paper.

Input: Data and instructions entered into a computer for processing purposes.

Input device: A device used to enter data and instruction into a computer. Examples are keyboard, mouse trackball, joystick, scanner, digitizer, voice recognition system, and vision input system.

Input/Output (I/O): Pertaining to the techniques, media, and devices used for man-machine interaction.

Input/Output Register: A register, which is used to communicate with the input/output devices.

Instruction: A command or order given to a computer. It normally consists of a code to indicate the operation to be performed, and address in memory where the operand(s) would be found.

Instruction Register: A register, which holds the current instruction that is being executed.

Instruction Set: A set of machine instructions that the CPU has built-in ability to execute.

Integrated Circuits (ICs): Circuits consisting of several electronic components like transistors, resistors, and capacitors grown on a single chip of silicon, eliminating wired interconnection between components.

Integrated Services Digital Network (ISDN): A telephonic system, which provides digital (not analog) telephone and data services.

Intelligent Terminal: A terminal having extensive local processing capability. It has a built-in microcomputer, which can be programmed by users.

Inter Block Gap (IBG): When several records are in one block, these gaps separate the blocks of records on magnetic taps.

Inter Record Gap (IRG): A Blank apace between two consecutive records on a tape.

Interface: Electronic circuit used to interconnect I/O devices to a computer's UPS or memory.

Internet: A networks of networks of computers, which links many different types of computers all over the world.

Internet search engine: An application available on the WWW, which helps locate the web sites containing useful information and references to such information.

Internet Service Provider (ISP): An organization, which maintains one or more gateway computers, and provides Internet access facility to its own gateway computer(s) by using a modem.

Internet working: Internet working of two or more to search for useful information.

Interpreter: A language processor, which translates a statement of a high-level language, and immediately executes in before translating the next source language statement. It is the most common language processor for BASIC.

Iteration logic: A program construct, which is used to produce loops in program logic, when one or more instruction may be, executed several times depending on some condition. Also known as looping logic.

J

Java: A programming language, which was designed to have machine-independent compiled code. It is primarily used for Internet-based application.

Job: See process.

Job Control Language (JCL): A special purpose language, which is used to describe to a computer's operating system the resource requirements of a job fed to the computer for processing.

Joystick: All input device, which serves as an effective pointing device for application, such as video games, flight, simulators, training simulators, and for controlling industrial robots.

Jump instruction: An instruction or signal, which, conditionally or unconditionally, specifies the location of the next instruction, and directs the computer to that instruction. A jump instruction is used to alter the normal sequence of control of the computer.

Justification: The alignment of text at the left margin, the right margin, or both margins.

K

Kernel: The central controlling part of an operating system, which implements the most primitive of the system's functions. It is only part of an operating system, which a user cannot replace or modify.

Key field: A unique field in a record, which is used to distinguish one record from another.

Keyboard: An input device, which enables data entry into a computer by pressing a set of keys (labelled buttons), which are neatly mounted on a keyboard connected to the computer system.

Key-to-tape: A device used to enter data onto a magnetic bytes in a computer.

Kilobytes (KB): Memory storage equal to 1024 (2^{10}) bytes in a computer.

Kiosk: An unattended system, which is used to store information of public interest, and allows common people to access the stored information as per their requirement.

Ku-band transmission: The use of GHz to 14 GHz bands of frequencies for transmission and retransmission of microwave signals in a satellite communication system.

Label: One or more characters used to identify a statement, an instruction, or a data field in a computer program.

Label record: A machine-readable record, which is used to identify a data file, It is the first record of the file.

Landscape mode: A mode of printing in which the printed lines are parallel to the longer edge of the paper.

Language processor: Software used to convert source program instruction to object or machine language instructions. Few examples are assembler, compiler and interpreter.

Large Scale of Integration (LSI): Integration of over 30,000 electronic components on a single chip.

Laser disk: See optical disk.

Laser printers: Page printers, which produce very high quality output by forming characters and all kinds of images with very tiny ink particles. They use a combination of laser-beam and electro-photographic techniques to create printed outputs.

Leased line: A data transmission service in which a special conditioned telephone line directly and permanently connects two computers. A leased line can be used for both voice and data transmission. Also known as private line or dedicated line.

Library routine: A tested routine maintained in a library of programs.

Light pen: A pen shaped device, which is used as an input data into computers by writing or sketching on the screen of a cathode ray tube.

Linker: A program, which is used to properly combine all the object program files (modules) of software, and to convert them into the software's final executable form.

Linux: An open- source operating system enhanced and backed by thousands of programmer's worldwide. It is a multitasking operating system, which was originally designed to be used on personal computers.

List Processing (LISP) A programming language suitable for manipulating non-numeric data, such as symbols and strings of text. It is used in the areas of pattern recognition, artificial intelligence, and for simulation of games.

Load module: The final executable form of a software produced by a linker.

Local Area Network (LAN): A computer network, which interconnects computers and other peripheral devices within a limited geographical area of a new kilometres.

Logical circuit: See combination circuit.

Logical error An error, which occurs when the actual logic of a program is different from the desire logic. Such errors cause the program to produce incorrect output.

Logic gate: An electronic circuit, which operates on one or more input signals to produce standard output signals. For example, AND, OR and NOT gates. Logic gates are the building blocks of all the circuits in a computer.

Logical operators: Symbols used to show a logical relationship between two data items. Examples in FORTRAN are. EQ. For greater than.

Logo: An easy to earn programming language, which is commonly used to teach problem- solving skills to children.

Loop: A sequence of instructions, which is executed repeatedly, until a terminals condition occurs.

Low-level languages: Programming languages, which normally translate from the one source instruction to one object instruction. These languages are machine dependent.

M

Machine language: A low- level language, which is directly understandable by the computer system. Each model of a computer has a unique machine language.

Macro: A sequence of frequently used operations, or keystrokes bundled together as a single command, or keystrokes by software, so that the invocation of the single command or keystrokes leads to the invocation of all the operations/ keystrokes in the specified sequence. This helps speed user interaction with the system.

Macro flowchart: A flowchart, which outlines the main segment of a program, or shows less detail.

Macro-instruction: An instruction in a source language, which is equivalent to a specified sequence of machine instructions.

Magnetic core: Tiny rings made of magnetic material, which can be polarized to represent a binary 1 or 0.

Magnetic disk: See disk.

Magnetic Ink Character Recognition (MICR): A technology used by the banking industry for faster processing if the large volume of house. This technology also ensure accuracy of data entry, because most of the information is pre-printed on the Cheque and is directly fed to computer.

Magnetic storage: Magnetic storage devices such as disks, drums, tapes, cores, etc. which utilize the magnetic properties of materials to store data

Magnetic tape: A secondary storage device, which uses a long plastic strip coated with a magnetic as a recording medium.

Magneto- optical disk: A storage disk, which integrates optical and magnetic disk technology to enable regrettable storage with laser-beam technology.

Main memory: See primary storage.

Main system: A computer system, which is mainly used for handing the bulk of data and information processing of such organizations as banks, insurance companies, hospitals, railways etc. they are also used in such environment where a large number of users need to share a common computing facility, such as in research groups, educational institutions, engineering firms, etc.

Management Information System (MIS): An organized collection of people, procedures, and devices used to provide the right information to the right person at the right time for proper decision -making.

Manufacturer-programmed ROM: A ROM in which data is burnt in by the manufacture of the electronic equipment in which it is used.

Mass storage: Mass storage systems, which provide access to several terabytes of stored data. They use multi units of storage media (such as multi disks, multiple tapes, multi CD-ROMs) as a single secondary storage device.

Massively Parallel Processing (MPP): An approach to designing super computers in which thousands of processors are nitrated within a single computer, so that the super computer can perform thousands of tasks simultaneously.

Master file: A file containing relatively permanent data. Records in a transaction file often update this file.

Maxterm: A Boolean quantity consists of all terms (in its normal form or complete form) pared together. Any combination is permissible, provide all are include in the term.

Medium Scale Integration (MSI): A circuit with about 100 transistors fabricated on a single chip.

Megabytes (MB): Memory storage equal to 1,048,576 (2^{20}) bytes in a computer.

Memory Address Register (MAR): A device or medium, which can accept data, hold them, on demand at a later time.

Memory Buffer Register (MBR): A register, which holds the contents of the memory word read from, or written in, memory.

Memory dump: Contents of memory duplicated on another storage device or printed on a printer.

Memory partition: In a multiprogramming system, the area occupied by each job residing simultaneously in the main memory.

Menu: A list of processing choice displayed on the screen from which a user may select.

Menu bar: A menu in which the options are displayed on a horizontal bar (usually at the top of the display screen) display across the screen.

Merging switching: A data communications method in which the data (message) to be sent is first appended with the destination address, and then sent across the network to its destination.

Metropolitan Area Network (MAN): Networks, which share some of the characteristics of both LANs and WANs. They usually interconnect computers spread over a geographical area of about 50 kilometres.

Micro flowchart: A flowchart with more details. It is also called a detailed flowchart.

Macrocode: The very basic directions, which tell the CPU how to execute an instruction; located in the control unit.

Microcomputer: The smallest category of computer fabricate using a microprocessor, and other integrated circuits, namely a ROM, and RAM, and I/O interface chips.

Micro kernel: Technology, which allows operating systems to be modelled and designed in a modular fashion.

Microprocessor: An IC chip, which contains all the circuits needed to perform arithmetic logic and control functions, the core activities of all computers, on a single chip.

Micro program: Firmware programs residing in read-only memory (ROM). They deal with low-level machine functions, and are essentially substitute for additional hardware.

Microsecond: One-million of a second.

Millisecond: One-thousandth of a second.

Minter: A Boolean quantity consisting of all terms (in its normal from or complete form) Ended together. Any combination (2n for n variables) of terms and complements is permissible, provided all are included in the term.

MIPS: Any kind of mental trick we use to help us remember. For example, a computer may be designed to interpret the machine code of 11 11 (binary) as the subtract operation, but it is easier for a hum an being to remember it as SUB.

Mobile computing: A wireless computing system, which support mobility of the computing equipment, which the users use to access the resources associated with the wireless network. It allows mobile users to access information from anywhere and at any time. Also known as nomadic computing.

Modulation: The technique by which a digital signal is converted to its analog facility.

Modulator-Demodulate (Modem): Devices used to convert digital signals (to be communicated over an analog channel, such as telephone line) to analog form at the sending end, and back to digital form at the receiving end.

Monitor: A popular output devices used for producing soft-copy output. It displays the output on a television like screen.

Motherboard: The main circuit board of a computer system. It has the CPU chip, RAM chips, ROM chips, I/O handing chips, etc., mounted on it. Also known as system board.

Mouse: A small, hand-held input device, which serves as an effective point - and - draw device in today's computers.

MS-DOS: Stand for Microsoft Disk Operating System. A single - user operating system, which was popularly used for personal computers in the 1980s.

Multi-access bus network: A network in which a single transmission medium is shared by all nodes.

Multimedia computer system: A computer system, (such as text; graphics, animation, audio, and video) for the purpose of generation, storage, representation, manipulation and access of multimedia information.

Multiplexing: The method of dividing a physical channel into many logical channels, so that a number of independent signals may be simultaneously transmitted on it.

Multiprocessing: A term used to describe interconnected computer configurations, or computers with two or more independent CPUs, which have the ability to simultaneously execute several programs.

Multiprocessor: A computer system consisting of two or more CPUs under a common control.

Multiprogramming: Interleaved execution of two or more different and independent programs by the same computer.

Multitasking: Concurrent execution of multiple jobs (often referred to as *task* of same user) in a single-user system.

N

Nanosecond: one-billionth (10^{-9}) of a second.

Narrowband channel: Communication channels, which handle low volume of data, typically from 45 to 300 baud. They are used mainly for telegraph lines and low speed terminals.

Netiquette: Deals with the rules of framing messages while interacting with other Internet users.

Network database: A database model in which the data elements are organized in the form of parent - child relationships.

Network Interface Card (NIC): A hardware device, which allows a computer network.

Network topology: The structure of interconnection of nodes of a computer network.

Newsgroup: A group of Internet/ Intranet users, who use the Usenet facility of the Internet to exchange their views/ ideas/information on some common topic, which is of interest to all the group members.

Node: An end point of a branch in a network, or a common junction of two or more network branches.

Nomadic computing: See mobile computing.

Non-impact printer: A printer, which performs some type of operation to the paper, instead of physically striking it (as in the case of an impact printer). To print characters with no impact printers, the paper can be sprayed with ink, magnetized, electrically charged, heated, placed under pressure, or struck by laser beams.

Non-position number system: A number system in which each symbol represents the same value, regardless of its position in the number, and the symbols are simply added to find out the value of a particular number. It is very difficult to perform arithmetical with such a number system.

Non-volatile storage: A storage medium, which retains it contents when the power is turned off or interrupted.

Notebook computer: A small, portable computer mainly for use by people who need computing power wherever they go.

Numeric: Pertaining to a character set, which contains the numbers 0 to 9.

O

Object Linking and Embedding (OLE): A feature found in application software packages. Which allows joining of documents in different applications to that changes in either document are reflected in the other document.

Object program: A fully complied or assembled program, which is ready to be located into the computer. It results from the translation of a source program by a language processor.

Object -oriented database: A database model, which captures object, oriented concepts, such as class hierarchy, language processor.

Object-Oriented Programming: (OOP) A programming methodology, which deals with solving problems by identifying the real-world objects, and then creating stimulations of those objects, their process, and the required communications between the objects.

Object-oriented programming languages: Programming languages, which encapsulate data and sequence data and objects, providing a stronger encapsulation mechanism than procedure. Hence, object- oriented programming provides a more powerful modelling tool than procedure-oriented programming.

Octal number system: A number system with a base of 8. The octal digits range from 0 to 7, it is commonly used as a short-cut notation for groups of three binary digits.

Offline: A device or system not directly under the control of a computer system,

Offline data entry devices: Input devices through which data is recorded on some media, such as floppies or tapes, and then entered later into the computer from the media for processing.

Onlines: All devices, which are connected directly to the computer on which the entered data is processed.

Operand: The part of a machine level instruction, which tells the central processor the location of the data to be manipulated.

Operating system: An integrated set of programs, which controls the resources of a computer system, and provides its user with an interface or virtual machine, which is more convenient to use than the bare machine.

Operation code (op code): The part of a machine level instruction which tells the central processor what has to be done.

Operation phase: The life-cycle phase during which the system constructed in the development phase is used.

Optical bar Character Recognition (OCR) device: An input device (a scanner) equipped with a character recognition software. It is used for inputting text documents, and store them in a form suitable for doing word processing of the documents.

Optical disk: A storage medium, which consists of a rotating disk, which is coated with a thin metal or some other material that is highly reflective. Laser beam technology is used for recording/reading of data on the disk. Also known as laser disks.

Optical fiber: Hair thin threads of glass or plastic used as a data transmission is medium. They use light signals for data transmission.

Optical Marl Reader (OMR): An input device (a scanner), which is capable of recognizing a pre-specified type of mark made by pencil or pen. Any input data, which is of a choice or selection nature, can be recorded for OMR input.

OSI protocol: A communication protocol to interconnect geographically dispersed heterogeneous computers. The International Standards Organization (ISO) has standardized this protocol.

Output: The information generation as a result of processing by a system.

Output device: A device used in a computer system to supply information and result of computation to the outside world. Example is monitor, printer, plotter, screen image projector, and voice response system.

P

Packed decimal format: A modified form of zoned decimal number which places two decimal digits into each byte of the field with the exception of the rightmost byte, which contains one digit and the sign of the field.

Packed switching: A data communication method in which the data (message) to be sent it is first split up into packets of fixed size; each packet is then appended with source and destination addresses, and some control information; and then the packed are sent across the network to their destination. At the receiver end, the packed are reassembled to recreate the message.

Page: A program segment, which is loaded into the main memory only when it is needed for execution.

Page printer: A high speed printer with a mechanism, which appears to print an entire page at one time.

Palm top computer: A battery-operated computer assistance tools. It is small-enough to fit it once pocket, and operated by keeping it on ones palm.

Parallel binary adder: An adder in which all the bits of the two binary numbers are added simultaneously.

Parallel processing: A technology in which a multiprocessor system is used to solve complex problems, and allowing different sub-problems to be processed simultaneously by different processor of the multiprocessor system.

Parity bit: An extra bit added to a string of bits, which enables the computer to detect internal errors on the transmission of binary data.

Pascal: A high-level programming language named after Blaise Pascal, which facilities the use of structured programming techniques.

Password: A code by which a user gains access to a computer system. It is used for security purpose.

Patch: A modification of a software carried out between its two released versions. A patch (modification) is created to fix a newly discovered bug. All the patches are incorporated in a new release version of the software.

Peripherals: The various input/output device and auxiliary storage unit of a computer system.

Personal assistance software: Which enables users to use personal computers for storing and retrieving personal information, and planning and managing personal schedules, contacts, finances, and inventory of important item.

Personal Computer (PC): A small and inexpensive computer used by individuals for crying out personal jobs, or for applications, such as entertainment, home management, and hobbies.

Personal Digital Assistant (PDA): A pocket-sized computer having facilities, such as calendar, calculator, notepad etc.

Phase modulation: A form of modulation in which two binary values of digital data are represented by the shift in phase of the carrier signal. That is, a sine wave with phase-0° represents a digital 1, and a sine wave with Phase-180° represents a digital 0.

Pico second: One trillionth of a second.

Pixel: A picture element. It is used to represented one point in a raster scan display device.

Plotter: An ideal output device, which is often used by architects, engineers, city planners, and others who need to routinely generate high-precision, hard-copy, graphic output of widely varying sizes.

Point and draw devices: Input devices, which can be used to rapidly point to, and select a particular graphic icon, or menu item from the multiple options displayed on screen. Many of these devices can also be very effectively used to create graphic elements on the screen, such as line, curves and freehand shapes. Some of the commonly used point- and draw devices are mouse, trackball, joystick, and electronic pen and touch screen.

Point of Sale (POS) device: An I/O device capable of immediately updating sales and inventory records at a central CPU, and producing a printed sales transaction receipt.

Portrait mode: A mode of printing in which the printed lines are parallel to the shorter edge of the paper.

Positional number system: A number system in which there are only a few symbols called digits, and these symbols represent different values, depending on the position they occupy in the number. The value of each digit in such a number is determined by the digits itself, the position of the digit in the number, and the base of the number system.

Preview: A feature of a world-processing package, which permits the users to see what the document will took like (almost, if not executed) when it is printed.

Primary storage: A temporary storage area, which is built into the computer hardware, and in which instructions and data of a program reside mainly when the program is being executed by the CPU.

Printer: An output device used to produce hard copy output.

Private line: See leased line.

Procedure: A subprogram, which performs an action but returns no value.

Processing: Performing a series of actions, or operations on data to convert them into useful information.

Processor: A unit of a computer system, which interprets instructions and executes them.

Program: A set of sequenced instructions (written in a language that can be a computer) used to direct and control the operations of the computer to solve a problem, or to perform a particular task.

Program Control (PC) Register: A register, which holds the address of the next instruction to be executed.

Program Design Language (PDL): See pseudopodia.

Programs library: A collection of complete program modules, which have already been developed, tested, and document, usually as a result of other programming projects.

Programmable Read-Only Memory (PROM): Similar to read only memory with the exception that using special external equipment can reprogram these chips.

Programmer: One who designs, writes, tests, and maintains computers programmes.

Programming language: A language used to express algorithms in computer understandable form.

Prototyping: The processing of developing a small working model of a final operating system to demonstrate the concepts, look, and feel of the final system.

Pseudopodia: A programming analysis tool, which is used for planning logic. It is an imitation of actual computer instructions written in a nature language, such as English. Also known as Program Design Language (PDL).

Public-domain software: A software, which is available free, or for a charge from the bulletin boards, or user-group libraries on the internet. Also known as shareware or user-support software.

Q

Quantum: See time slice.

Query by example (QBE): A software tool, which enables database users to specify search criteria by providing a front end for the query from the user, and composes query statements internally.

Query language: A language, which enables users to define their requirement for extracting the desired information from the database in the form of queries.

R

Radix: Same as base. See base.

Random Access Memory (RAM): A memory in which the time to retrieve stored information is independent of the address where it is stored.

Random file: See direct file.

Random/direct-access storage device: A storage device in which access to any stored information is direct, and approximately equals access time is required for accessing any information irrespective of its location. Magnetic, optical and magneto-optical disks are typical example of such a storage device.

Raster-Only Memory (ROM): A non-volatile memory chips in which data are stored permanently, and cannot be altered by the programmer.

Record: A collection of related items of data treated as a unit.

Record length: A measure of the size of a record, usually specified in units, such as characters.

Reduced Instruction Set Computer (RISC) Architecture: An architecture of CPUs with a small instruction set, fixed length instructions, and reduced references to memory to retrieve operands.

Redundant Array of Inexpensive Disks (RAID): See disk array.

Registers: Small, high -speed storage units, which are used to hold the information on a temporary basis when there is an interpretation and execution of instructions by the CPU. Date stored in a specific register have a special meaning to the CPU.

Relation database: A database model in which the data elements are organized in the form of multiple tables, and the data in one table is related to data in another table through the use of a common field.

Remote access: Accessing a computer from a distant station using communication facilities.

Report file: A file, which holds a copy of a report generated by a data processing application in computer accessible form, until it is convenient to print it.

Report generator: A software, which enables the users of a database to design the layout of a report, so that it can be presented in the desire format.

Report Program Generator (RPG): A business oriented, general purpose programming language designed to generate the output report, resulting from the processing of common business applications.

Response time: The elapsed time between submission of a job to the system for processing, and the first response produced by the system for the job.

Ring network: A network in which there is no host computer for controlling other computers, and each computer in the network has communication subordinates.

Router: An internet working tool, which is used to interconnect those networks, which use the same high-level protocols about the network layer.

Routing: The selection of actual path to be used to transmit a message in a wide-area network environment.

RS-232-C interface: A standard interface used for interconnecting user terminals to computers. It was defined by the Electronics Industrial Association (USA).

Run time: The time required to complete a single, continuous, execution of an object program.

S

Scanner: An input device used for direct data entry into the computer system from source documents.

Schema builder: A software tool, which enables a user to define a database schema interactively by prompting the user to enter the field name, field type, field size, and so on for each field.

Screen image projector: An output device, which is used to project information from a computer on to a large screen (such as a cloth screen or a wall), so that it can be simultaneously viewed by a large group of people.

Scrolling: Using program-specified ways (by the use of keys or mouse) to move the items displayed in a window up or down, or left or right to see parts of the file that extend past the bottom or top or sides of the window.

Second-generation computers: Second-generation computers built during the period 1955 and 1964. They used transistors in CPU, and magnetic cores for main memory. On software front, they used high-level languages like FORTRAN and COBOL for programming, and batch operating systems.

Secondary storage: See auxiliary memory.

Sector: The smallest unit with which any disk can work. Disk drives are designed to access only whole sectors at a time.

Security: Policies and mechanisms, which deal with protecting the various resources and information of a computer system against destruction and unauthorized access.

Seek time: In a disk system, the time required for a read/write to move to the track where that data to be read or written in stored. Maximum seek time equals the time taken for the head to move from the outermost track to the innermost track.

Selection logic: A program construct, which is used for selecting the proper path out of two or more alternative paths in the program logic. Also known as decision logic.

Self-documenting language: Programming language, which do not require much explanation to be understood by someone reading the program instruction. For example, COBOL language.

Semiconductor storage: A storage device whose storage elements are formed as solid-state electronic components on an integrated chip.

Sequential logic: A program construct, which is used for performing instructions one after another in ascending or descending order determined by the value of the key field of the records.

Sequential processing: A technique in which a number of similar items or transactions to be processed are grouped together and processed in a designated sequence.

Sequential-access storage device: A storage device in which information can only be retrieved in the same sequence in which it is stored. Magnetic tape is a typical example of such storage device.

Server computer: In a client-server computing environment a provides a set of shared user services to the clients. It run the server process, which services client requests for use of the resource managed by the server.

Shareware: See public-domain software.

Simplex: A data transmission mode in winch data can flow only in one direction.

Single In-line Memory Module (SIMM): A memory board with memory chips on it. Memory chips can be added on the board to increase the computer's main memory capacity.

Small Scale Integration (SSI): Integration of only about ten to twenty electronic components on a single chip.

Smart card: An electronic card having a built-in microprocessors chip. Data to be encoded on the card is permanently soared in the memory of the chip.

Smart terminal: A terminal having local data editing capability, and the ability to consolidate input data, before sending then to the main computer. It has a microprocessor some internal storage, and I/O capabilities.

Soft-copy output: A computer output, which is temporary in nature, and vanishes after use. For example, output displayed on a terminal screen, or spoken out by a voice response system.

Software: A set of computer programs, procedures, and associated document (flowcharts, manuals, etc.) related to the effective operation of a computer system.

Software package: A group of program, which suave a specific problem, or perform a specific type of job. For example, a word-processing package.

Software piracy: The illegal copying or use of software.

Solid-state: Electronic components, whose operation depends on the control of electric or magnetic phenomena in solids, such as transistors and diodes.

Sort: The process of arranging data into a desired sequence.

Source program: A program written in a symbolic or high-level language, such as assembly language, COBOL, BASIC, etc.

Special character: A graphic character, which in neither a letter, a digit, nor a space character. For example, the dollar sign, comma, period, etc.

Special purpose computer: A computer, which is meant for doing only a particular type of jobs.

Speech synthesizer: A voice response system, which converts text information into spoken sentences.

Spreadsheet: A numeric data analysis toot (software package), which allows users to create a kind of computerized ledger.

SQL: A standard query language for relational database.

Stack: A memory in which information, which is stored last is on top, and is retrieved first. Also known as LIFO (List-in-first-out) storage.

Stand-alone: In a distributed data processing system, it refers to a computer system, which has an independent (from a central-site computer) processing and storage capability.

Star network: A network in which multiple computers are connected to a central host computer. These computers are not linked directly to each other, and can communicate only via the host computer.

Statement: In programming, an expression or generalized instruction in a source language.

Storage: See memory.

Storage hierarchy: A hierarchy of storage technologies (such as cache memory, main memory, secondary storage and mass storage) used in a computer system. The is usually done because a single type of storage is not superior in speed of access, capacity, and cost.

Stored program computer: A computer where the program to solve a problem, and the necessary data are stored in its memory.

Structured design: A system design approach in which is small enough to manage, but independent enough to solve separately.

Structured programming: An organized approach to programming involving the use of the three basic control structures-sequence, selection, and iteration, and the use of top-down concepts to decompose main functions into fewer-level components for modular coding purposes.

Study phase: A system life-cycle phase during which a problem is identified, alternative solution is studied, and the most feasible solution is selected.

Sub procedure: See subroutine.

Subroutine: A standardized program written in a manner that it can be used as part of another program whenever necessary. A subroutine is normally invoked through other program by the use of CALL statements. Also known as subprogram and sub procedure.

Swapping: Storing program on disk, and then transferring these programs into main storage as and when they are needed. The technique is used to process large programs, or several programs with limited memory.

Symbolic language: A See assembly language.

Symbolic program: See assembly program.

Synchronous communication: Data transmission mode in which the sender and receiver must synchronize with each other to get ready for data transmission, before it takes place.

Syntax: A set of rules of a programming language, which define the pattern or structure of the word order and punctuation of an instruction. It is analogous to rules of grammar in English language.

Syntax, errors: In computer programs, which typically involve incorrect punctuation, incorrect word sequence, undefined terms, or misuse of terms. These errors are automatically detected, and pointed out by language processors.

System: A group of integrated parts (people, methods, machines, and materials), which have a common purpose of achieving some objective(s).

System analysis: A detailed step-by-step investigation of related procedures to see what must be done, and the best way of doing it.

System analyst: The individual responsible for planning a computer data processing system. He/she utilizes tool, such as flowcharts, decision tables, and program design language, etc. These plans are then passed to the computer programmer.

System commands: System command used to communicate with the operating system of the computer.

System programmer: A programmer who prepares system software.

System software: A set of one or more programs designed to control the operating, and extend the processing capability of a computer system.

T

Tape density: The amount of data, which can be place over a given length of taps. The density is usually expressed in bytes or characters pre inch.

Tape drive: A device used for storage and retrieval of data stored on magnetic tape medium.

Telecommunications: Transmission of data between computer system and/or terminals at deferent locations through telephone facilities.

Telnet: A application level protocol, which allows a user to log in to another computer in a network environment.

Template: A standard format used to quickly create new documents in the same format.

Terabytes (TB): Memory storage equal to about one trillion (10^{12}) bytes.

Tetra-flop: 10^{12} floating point arithmetic operations per second.

Terminal: See Video Display Terminal (VCT).

Testing: The process of making sure that the program performs the intended task.

Thermal printer: A printing device, which utilizes paper that is sensitive to heat.

Third-generation computer: Computers built between 1964 and 1975, which used integrated circuits in CPU, high speed magnetic core main memories, powerful high-level languages, and time operating system.

Throughput: The total amount of useful processing carried out by a computer system within a given time period. It is measured as the number of processes, which are completed by the system per unit time.

Time division multiplexing: A method of sharing a communication channel in which the total time available in the channel is divided between several users and each user of the channel is allotted a time slice during which he/she may transmit a message. The channel capacity is fully utilized by interleaving a number of data streams belonging to different users into one data stream.

Time log: A log documentation automatically maintained by many computer systems, which describes in detail how the compute system was used during the day.

Time slice: The short period of time during which a user process gets the attention of the CPU in a time-sharing system. Also known as time slot or quantum.

Time slot: See time slice.

time-sharing: A mechanism to provide simultaneous, interactive use of a computer system by many users in a manner that each user is given the impression that he/she has his/her own computer. It multiprogramming with a special CPU scheduling algorithm achieve this.

Too-down approach: A disciplined approach to system design or program design in which top-level functions are decomposed into a hierarchy of understandable lower-level modules for better management and easy handling.

Touch screen: A simple, intuitive, and easy to learn input device, which enables the users to choose from available options by simply touching with their finger the desired icon or menu item displayed on the computer's screen.

Track: In case of magnetic disk, one of many circular concentric rings used for storing data. In case of magnetic tape, a horizontal strip, or channel, running the full length of the tape, and used for recording data.

Trackball: An input device, which serves as an effective pointing device.

Transaction file: A file in which current data are stored for subsequent processing usually in combination with a master file.

Transducer: A device capable of changing signals from analog form to digital form, or vice-versa.

Transistor: A controlled electronic switch fabricated using a semiconductor. It is extensively used in the design of various electronic equipment.

Transponder: A device mounted on a communication satellite, which receives, amplifies and retransmits signals from earth stations.

Truth table: A table, which gives the output values for the varies input combinations in case of a logical expression.

Topple: A group of related fields (a row of a table) in a relational databases.

Turnaround time: The elapsed time between the submission of a job to a computer system for processing, and the completion of the job.

Twisted-pair cable: A simple, inexpensive and slow-wired transmission medium. Ultra Large Scale Integration (ULSI) Integration of about ten million electronic components on to a single chip.

U

Ultra Violate EPROM (UVEROM): An EPROM chip in which the stored information is erased by exposing the chip for some time to ultraviolet light.

Unbundled: A term, which means that the application, software is priced separately from the computer hardware.

Unconditional transfer: A program instruction, which causes the program control to flow out of normal sequence unconditionally.

Uniform Resources Locator (URL): An addressing scheme used by WWW browsers to located sites on the Internet.

Uninterrupted Power Supply (UPS): A battery supported power unit between an external power source and a computer system. Which supplies clean and continuous power even during power failures.

Universal gate: A logical gate, which is alone sufficient to implement any Boolean function. For example, NAND and NOR gates.

Universal Product Code (UPC): A universal or standardized optical bar code, which normally appears on retail packages, and which is read by a laser beam scanner.

Unix: A multi user, time-sharing operating system. It is a very popular operating system, and can be used on a wide variety of computers, ranging from notebook computers to super computers.

Uploading: Moving a file from ones own computer to a remote computer in a network environment.

Uptime: The time duration when the computer system is in operation.

Upward compatible: The ability of hardware or software to function with all of the same equipment and software with which are predecessors could function.

Usenet: A service on the Internet, which allows a group of Internet users to exchange their views/ideas/ information on some common topic, which is of interest to all the members belonging to the group.

User authentication: Deals with the problem of verifying the identity of a user (personal or program), before permitting access to the requested resource.

User-friendly: A program or computer system designed in a manner that even individuals who lack computer experience can easily use the system without much training.

User-programmed ROM: A PROM in which the user can load and store "read only" programs and data

User-supported software: See public-domain software.

Utilities: A set of programs, which help users in performing system maintenance and other tasks of routine nature.

V

Value Added Network (VAN): Enhanced data transmission service provided by doing value addition to the standard services of the common carriers. Added value may include features, such as electronic mail, data encryption/ decryption, access to commercial databases, and code conversion for communication between incompatible computers.

Variable name: In a program, thc name assigned to a data field, which can assume any of a given set of values.

Vector graphics: Graphic objects composed of patterns of lines, points, circles, arcs, and other geometric shares (vectors), which can be easily represented by few geometric parameters.

Very Large Scale Integration (VLSI): An electronic circuit with about 10,000 transistors fabricated in a single silicon chip.

Very Small Aperture Terminals (VSATs): Small disk antennas having lower transmitters and receivers, which can be install at users' sites. It enables a large number of users to benefit from satellite communication.

Video conferencing: A system in which persons sitting at CTE screen see and talk to each other via a computer communications network. It saves travelling cost and the valuable time of executives.

Video Display Terminals (VDT) A monitor and a keyboard used together as both an input and an output device. Also known as terminal.

Virtual machine: The concept of adding the operating system layer on top of the bare hardware to manage all parts of the system, and present the users with an interface, which is easier to program and use.

Virtual memory: A memory management scheme, which allows the execution of process, which might not be complete, loaded in the main memory. The three basic concepts used for the realization of virtual memory are online secondary storage, swapping and demand paging.

Virus: A computer virus is a piece of code attached to a legitimate program, which, when executed, infects other programs in the system by replicating and attaching itself to them. In addition to this replicating effect, a virus normally does some other damage to the system, such as corrupting/erasing files.

Vision input system: An input device, which allows a computer to accept input by seeing and object. The input data in this case is normally an object's shape and features in the form of an image.

Visualization: Deals with exploring data and information graphically for better compression.

Voice recognition device: An input device, which allows a person to input data to a computer by speaking to it.

Voice reproduction system: A voice response system, which produces audio output by selecting appropriate audio output from a set of pre-recorded audio responses.

Voice response system: An output device, which enable a compute to talk to its users.

Voice band: Data communication system, which handles moderate volumes of data, typically from 300 to 9600 bauds. Phone lines, which we use to talk to other people is an example.

Volatile storage: A storage medium, which loses its contents when power fails or when power is switched off.

W

Web client: Any computer on the Internet, which can access web servers.

Web page: A hypertext document on the Internet.

Web server: Any computer on the Internet, which uses the HTTP protocol.

Web Area Network (WAN): A computer network, which interconnects computers spread over a large geographical area. It may also enable LANs to communicate with each other. This type of network may be developed to operate nationwide or worldwide, and the transmission medium used are normally public systems, such as telephone lines, microwave and satellite links.

Wildcard (character): A special character, usually a? or an*, which is used in software commands as a generic reference to any character, or any combination of characters, respectively.

Winchester disk: Medium-sized, non-interchangeable metal disks permanently housed in sealed, contamination-free containers, with built in read/write heads.

Window: A rectangular portion of a computer screen, which is dedicated to specific activity or application. The display screen can be separated into several widows to simultaneously show the status of the different application at any instance of time.

Windows NT: A multi-user, timesharing operating system developed by Microsoft, which has Unix-like features. It is designed to be used for powerful workstations, and network and database servers.

Wireless computing system: A computer network, which uses wireless communication technologies. It enhances the functionality of computing equipment by freeing communication from the location constraints of the wired commuting system.

Word: A group of bits or characters considered as an entity, and capable of being stored in one storage location. Also fixed-size storage areas, which form the primary memory of a computer system.

Word length: A measure of the size of a word, usually specified in unit, such as characters or bits, Each location of a computers system can store a fixed number of characters of bits, called its word length.

Word processing: The use of computers to create, view, edit, format, store, retrieve, and print text materials.

Word wrap: A word processing feature, which automatically moves words down to the beginning of the next line, if they extend beyond the right margin.

Word-addressable storage designed to store a fixed number of characters (equal to its word-length in bytes). For such a storage device, storage space is always allocated in multiples of word-length. Its another name is fixed-word-length storage.

Workstation: A powerful desktop computer designed to meet the computing needs of engineers architects, and other professionals, who need greater processing power, larger storage, and better graphics display facility than what PCs provide.

Word Wide Web (WWW or W3): Network of computers across the world interconnected together on the Internet, and using the concept of hypertext to link Internet sites and information on the Internet.

Worm: A computer virus designed to erase/alter the data/ program from a computer system's memory/disk.

Write-Once, Read-Many (WORM) disk: An optical disk, which looks like a standard CD-ROM disk, but allows the user to record his/her own information on it by using a CD/ Recoradable (CD-R) drive.

WYSIWYG: Stands for What You See Is What You Get. This feature of a word-processing package allows the users to display a document on the screen in a form, which closely resembles what the printed document will look like.

Z

Zip disk: See Bernoulli disk.